Justice and Society in the Highlands of Scotland

Legal History Library

VOLUME 53

The titles published in this series are listed at *brill.com/lhl*

Justice and Society in the Highlands of Scotland

Strathspey and the Regality of Grant (c. 1690–1748)

By

Charles Fletcher

BRILL
NIJHOFF

LEIDEN | BOSTON

A version of chapter 4.4.2 has appeared in 'Meddle in any manner of way with the rents and you will repent it': The Collection of Rents in the Regality of Grant, *Scottish Archives* 24(2018), pp. 53–65.

Cover illustration: A traditional township. Those in the regality of Grant would have been similar in appearance, and it was in buildings such as these that courts were usually held. (Photo: Author).

Library of Congress Cataloging-in-Publication Data

Names: Fletcher, Charles Jefferson, author.
Title: Justice and society in the highlands of Scotland : Strathspey and the Regality of Grant (c. 1690-1748) / by Charles Fletcher.
Description: Leiden ; Boston : Brill Nijhoff, [2022] | Series: Legal history library, 1874-1793 ; volume 53 | Based on author's thesis (doctoral - University of Edinburgh, 2020) issued under title: Justice and society in Strathspey: the Regality Court of Grant, c. 1690-1748. | Includes bibliographical references and index.
Identifiers: LCCN 2021036417 (print) | LCCN 2021036418 (ebook) | ISBN 9789004472518 (hardback) | ISBN 9789004472549 (ebook)
Subjects: LCSH: Manorial courts–Scotland–Spey River Valley–History–17th century. | Manorial courts–Scotland–Spey River Valley–History–18th century. | Justice, Administration of–Scotland–Highlands–17th century. | Justice, Administration of–Scotland–Highlands–18th century.
Classification: LCC KDC866.G73 F54 2022 (print) | LCC KDC866.G73 (ebook) | DDC 347.4115–dc23
LC record available at https://lccn.loc.gov/2021036417
LC ebook record available at https://lccn.loc.gov/2021036418

Typeface for the Latin, Greek, and Cyrillic scripts: "Brill". See and download: brill.com/brill-typeface.

ISSN 1874-1793
ISBN 978-90-04-47251-8 (hardback)
ISBN 978-90-04-47254-9 (e-book)

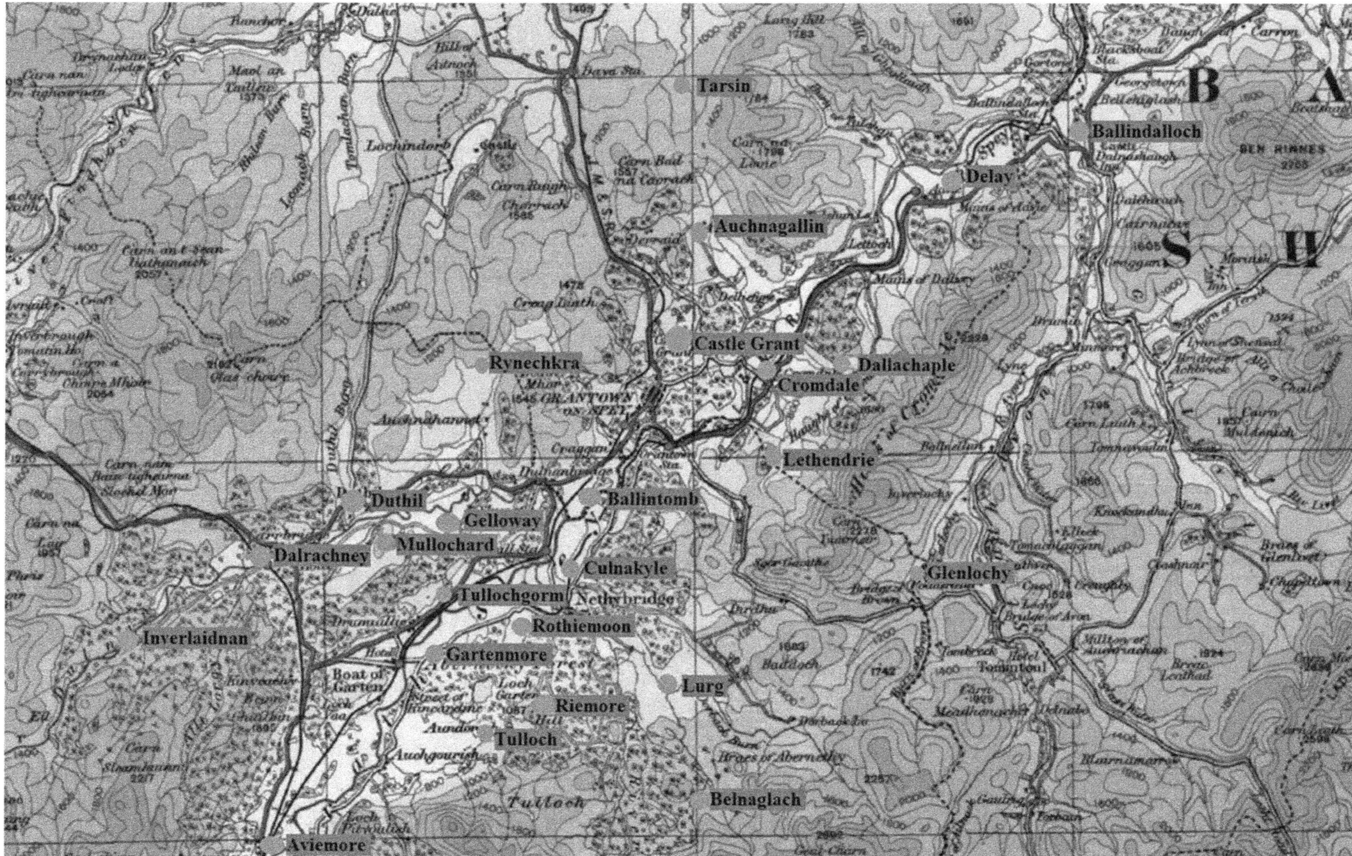

MAP 1 Map of Strathspey

SOURCE: NATIONAL LIBRARIES OF SCOTLAND

Contents

Preface

The rationale of this book is to provide a systematic overview of the functions of a seigneurial jurisdiction in the Scottish Highlands prior to the Heritable Jurisdictions Act 1747. In doing so, a detailed picture of life in the Highlands during this period emerges from the sources. These sources are the five surviving court books left by the regality court of Grant. These begin in the year 1690 and end in 1729. The Grant court records are amongst the most complete surviving eighteenth century regality court records and are supported by the copious Seafield muniments which record many aspects of life in Strathspey. By happy coincidence, the author grew up within the bounds of the old regality of Grant. It was thus a natural choice to employ his local knowledge of places and history in this evaluation of justice and society in the Highlands of Scotland.

Acknowledgements

Without the archives of the Seafield family this work would not have been possible. Material from the Seafield Muniments was made available by kind permission of The Right Honourable The Earl of Seafield.

I also owe a debt of gratitude to the University of Edinburgh where I studied for my PhD upon which this book is based. My ability to undertake this research was only thanks to the generous financial support of the University of Edinburgh Law School, who kindly saw fit to support this project through the award of a scholarship in 2016.

Particular thanks must go to my supervisors, Professor John Cairns and Dr Alasdair Raffe, who have been invaluable with their advice and expertise on Scottish history. Both have been a constant source of support and encouragement throughout my research.

Figures, Maps, Illustrations, and Tables

Figure

Maps

Illustrations

Tables

Conventions and Abbreviations

All values are given in pounds Scots unless otherwise stated. Quotations from original sources have been left with their original spelling and punctuation.Grant Court Book. 1-5. Regality of Grant Court Books, NRS, RH11/34/1-5.

HA	Highland Archives (Inverness)
JR	Juridical Review
NRS	National Records of Scotland
OSA	The Statistical Account of Scotland
SHR	Scottish Historical Review
SHS	Scottish History Society
RPCS	Register of the Privy Council of Scotland
RPS	Records of the Parliament of Scotland

Glossary

Absolvitor	A decision by a court in favour of the defender.
Assoilzie	To find in favour of a defender.
Auchtenpart	An eighth part of a davoch.
Bailie/bailzie	Presiding official in regality and baron courts.
Bear/bere	Primitive four or six row barley.
Boll	Unit of capacity for grain containing eighteen pecks or four firlots.
Brieve	Writ issued from a chancery.
Caber	Small roof beam extending from ridge to eaves.
Calp	Duty payable by tenants to landlords such as herezald.
Caput	The head place in the jurisdiction.
Casualties	A payment due from a tenant or vassal.
Chamberlain	Estate official in charge of estate finances and collecting rent.
Chancellor	Member of an assize nominated to deliver the verdict of the assize.
Cottar	Sub-tenant, with little stake in the land, reliant on labour or a trade to subsist.
Couple	Pair of curved timbers which support the roof and form the frame of a house.
Coyack	Heifer.
Cruck	Half of a couple.
Currach	A small wicker boat, also a form of net fishing.
Customs	Tributes.
Dacker	Judicially authorised search to find stolen goods.
Darrack	Feudal service owed to the bailie, chamberlain or laird. Exacted in labour or cash.
Davoch	Unit of land evaluation used as the basis of estate management.
Decreet	Court order.
Decreet Arbitral	Order issued after arbitration.
Dirk	A knife.
Dittay	A statement of the charges against an accused person.
Divot	Thin turf used in building.
Duthcas	The ancestral dwelling place of a family.
Dyke	Wall, usually built from turf.
Easter	Place name, usually referring to down-stream.
Fee	Wage paid to a servant/labourer.
Fine	The gentry of a clan.
Firlot	Unit of capacity equal to a quarter of a boll.
Flitting	Removal, sometimes seasonal.

Grassum	Sum of money paid or promised by a tenant to his landlord at the grant or renewal of his lease.
Hamesucken	An assault upon someone in their own dwelling house.
Haugh	Flat, meadow land.
Herd	Person responsible for preventing livestock from straying.
Herezald	The bailie's right to claim the best article of a deceased tenant's livestock.
Hog	Young unshorn sheep.
Infang	Within the lands of the jurisdiction.
Infeftment	The act giving a person title to heritable property.
Infield	Township arable.
Kist	Chest or coffin.
Liferent	Personal right to use or enjoy the profits from another's property for life.
Malander	Day labourer similar to a cottar.
Meikle	Big.
Merk	2/3 of £1 Scots.
Multure	Tax payable to miller for grain ground.
Mutchkin	Scottish measure equivalent to an English pint.
Outfang	Beyond the lands of the jurisdiction.
Oxgate	Land measure equal to 1/8 of a plough gate, or 1/32 of a davoch, notionally thirteen acres.
Peck	Unit of capacity equal to 7 ¾ pints.
Poind	A diligence, whereby certain goods or money are seized by legal authority for a fine or debt due.
Porteous roll	The official list of accused persons to be tried before the circuit courts of justiciary.
Quern	Hand mill for grinding grain.
Repledge	The right of a lord of regality to recall defenders in actions before other courts to his own court to undergo the law.
Runrig	System of communal landholding where the land was divided into strips known as rigs.
Sederunt	Session of a court.
Scots Pound	Worth 20 shillings, equivalent to 1/12 £1 sterling.
Sten part	A division of land in a runrig farm.
Stewartry	A regality reverting to the Crown.
Tack	Lease.
Tacksman	Principal tenant holding a lease directly from the laird and usually implying some managerial role in the clan system.
Teind	The tenth part of the produce of land levied as an ecclesiastical tax.

Thirlage	Obligation upon a tenant to grind their grain at a certain mill.
Vic	Son of.
Wadset	Mortgage of heritable property by conveying the property to the creditor until such time as the original sum was repaid, known as redemption.
Wadsetter	The holder of the wadset or heritable security. In practical terms this meant they were in possession of the wadset land.
Wedder	Castrated ram.
Wester	Place name usually up-stream of Easter.

CHAPTER 1

Introduction

1.1 Heritable Justice in Scotland

In 1773, twenty-five years after the abolition of heritable jurisdictions, Samuel Johnson travelled through the Western isles of Scotland. There he heard first-hand about the effects of the abolition of the region's seigneurial jurisdictions. He came to the following conclusion: 'The abolition of the local jurisdictions, which had for so many ages been exercised by the chiefs, has [...] had its evil and its good'.[1] Heritable jurisdictions were an important feature of the feudal system across medieval Europe.[2] Scotland in this respect was no different, with the judicial powers of local landowners surviving, theoretically unchecked, until their abolition in 1748. The consolidation and centralisation of power came late to Scotland. Lack of money and poor communications precluded the spread of central power beyond sheriff courts along the eastern seaboard, and the justice ayres, circuit courts irregularly held by the King's justiciar that visited the heads of the sheriffdoms. Thus, in the centuries preceding this process, government was dependent upon the delegation of political and judicial power by the Scottish crown to tenants in chief in the localities. The infeftment of these men with both land and judicial powers created a political and judicial network answerable to, and supportive of, the Scottish crown. The small number of royal representatives in the localities, especially in the interior, meant that the burden of administering local justice fell largely to the barons and lords of regality in these areas.[3]

Baronies were ubiquitous in Scotland. Grant has shown that of the 925 parishes extant in the first decade of the fifteenth century, some 94% were held either entirely or partially *in liberam baroniam*.[4] Thus, the baronies were the basic unit of the system of feudal justice in Scotland.[5] Grants of land in free barony first appeared during the reign of David I. Such baronies were created

1 R Black (ed.), *To the Hebrides; Samuel Johnson's Journey to the Western Islands of Scotland and James Boswell's Journal of a Tour of the Hebrides* (Edinburgh, 2007), p. 190.

2 A Grant, 'Franchises North of the Border: Baronies and Regalities in Medieval Scotland', M Prestwich (ed.), *Liberties and Identities in the Medieval British Isles* (Woodbridge, 2008), p. 156.

3 J Goodare, *The Government of Scotland 1560–1625* (Oxford, 2004), p. 217.

4 Grant, 'Franchises' p. 161.

5 W C Dickinson (ed.), *Court Book of the Barony of Carnwath* (SHS, 1937), p. xiv.

 | DOI:10.1163/9789004472549_002

by grants of land directly from the crown carrying certain rights of jurisdiction devolved directly from royal authority. Once created, baronial jurisdictions were permanent and indivisible from the caput of the lands granted in fief.[6] Thus, it was possible for a baron to dispone his lands yet retain jurisdiction over them if he kept the caput. In the case of most grants the dignity of barony carried rights and privileges including basic, yet extensive, rights of civil and criminal jurisdiction. This jurisdiction was roughly equivalent to those of the sheriff, the officer in the royal courts. The jurisdiction of the baron courts is usually described by charters of infeftment in the terms '*cum furca et fossa soc et sak thol et them et infangandthef*' (with pit and gallows, the right to judge in suits over the domain, exact tolls and apprehend thieves caught red handed).[7] This was essentially a general jurisdiction to police tenants and hold courts, although the extent of the baron's jurisdiction varied according to the exact terms of the grant. The right upon the baron to pit and gallows was the hallmark of his ultimate jurisdiction. The ability to sentence his vassals upon pain of death underpinned the baron's authority and in turn ensured the effective exercise of the powers delegated to him.

Higher than the dignity of barony was that of regality. The first charters making grants of land in free regality date from the reign of Robert I.[8] Much has been made of the quasi-regal powers bestowed upon lords of regality by the kings of medieval Scotland. They could exclude the King's officers from operating upon their lands. They had the very important power to repledge those who resided upon their land from the sheriff and justiciary courts, with the result that residents of the regality could effectively only be tried in the regality court. They could hold justice and chamberlain ayres, and even issue their own brieves from the regality chancellery. Most potently, charters erecting regalities often purportedly gave lords the power to pursue those accused of the four pleas to the crown: rape, arson, robbery and murder. Lords of regality have often been described as being 'quasi Kings',[9] and their regalities as 'kingdoms within kingdoms'.[10] Historians often express both awe and disgust when discussing the powers of these medieval lords. For instance, Dickinson writing in 1897 stated that '[the creation of regalities] opened the door to unlimited petty tyranny, and, especially in the case of the great Lords of Regalities, it erected

6 P McIntyre, 'The Franchise Courts', Introduction to Scottish Legal History, 20 *Stair Society* (1958), pp. 374–383, p. 374.

7 According to W K Dickson, 'Heritable Jurisdictions', 9 *JR* (1897), pp. 428–444, pp. 429–30.

8 Grant, 'Franchises,' p. 167.

9 G Mackenzie, *Observations*, James II, Parliament II, Act 43 (Edinburgh, 1686).

10 Dickinson, 'Heritable Jurisdictions', p. 443.

imperia in imperio which easily might, and sometimes did, become so powerful as to be a serious danger to the State'.[11] For this reason, as Grant puts it, 'Scottish franchises – especially the late medieval regalities, equivalent to English palatinates – have not had good press from past historians'.[12] However, recent historians such as Grant view the medieval regalities differently.[13] Indeed, whilst attempted checks on the granting of new regalities and a curtailment of their powers were repeatedly made during the fifteenth and sixteenth centuries, the very survival of so many jurisdictions into the eighteenth century, along with the continuing creation of new regalities, hardly suggests that regalities were political entities posing a real threat to the crown in Scotland.[14]

In terms of jurisdiction the powers of regalities also appear to have been sensationalised by scholars in the past. Goodare has argued that regalities were not competent to hear the pleas to the crown, pointing to the fact that no seventeenth-century jurists can be found to support this claim.[15] Rather, he argues they were just glorified baron courts. The most powerful contemporary proponent of this view was Mackenzie. In his *Laws and Customs of Scotland* (1678) Mackenzie argued that regalities were 'inferior jurisdictions', occupying a place in the judicial system below that of the central courts.[16] As a result they had no jurisdiction over the pleas to the crown, thanks to an act of parliament of James VI which states that no inferior judges shall hear the pleas of the crown.[17] However, Stair appears to have been uncertain as to the status of bailies of regality, stating that the Courts Act of 1672 does not determine whether bailies of regality were restricted in their jurisdiction; they were simply competent in all crimes committed in their regality.[18] Furthermore, Stair states that, 'regality courts are the kings courts, the difference being that he

11 Dickinson, 'Heritable Jurisdictions', p. 440. See also P McIntyre, 'The Franchise Courts', p. 380, 'the lords of regality used the privileges they wrested from the weak Kings of the fourteenth century Scotland to establish an alternative system of government'.

12 Grant, 'Franchises', p. 155.

13 Grant's argument forms part of the re-evaluation of the relationship between the monarch and the noblemen of Scotland which has featured in the work of historians such as Boardman, Brown and Wormald.

14 Dickinson, 'Heritable Jurisdictions', p. 440.

15 Goodare, *The Government of Scotland*, pp. 183–5.

16 G Mackenzie, *The Laws and Customs of Scotland: in matters criminal: Wherein is to be seen how the civil law, and the laws and customs of other nations doth agree with, and supply ours* (Edinburgh, 1678), p. 402.

17 *RPS* 173, Parl 13, K Ja VI.

18 Stair, J Dalrymple Viscount of, *Institutions of the Law of Scotland: deduced from its originals, and collated with the civil, canon and feudal laws, and with the customs of neighbouring nations in iv books* (Edinburgh, 1693), iv, xxxvii, iv, p. 944.

had gifted the profits of the court to the lord of regality'.[19] If this was the only difference between the royal courts and those of regality, there seems to be no reason why regality courts should not have been competent to entertain the pleas to the crown. Putting the theoretical jurisdiction of regality courts aside, that no cases involving the pleas to the crown are readily found suggests that it was unlikely that regality courts heard such pleas in practice, although given the lack of research into regality court records this is uncertain.

Criticism of heritable offices in Scotland intensified during the sixteenth and seventeenth centuries and there were further attempts to check the power of regalities; James VI wrote in *Basilikon Doron*, that he believed heritable jurisdictions were one of the greatest obstacles to effective government in Scotland and charged commissioners to consider means for reducing the number of heritable offices.[20] However, the crown lacked the finances and possibly the political will to make serious headway in reducing the number of heritable jurisdictions, and efforts at reform largely targeted the sheriffdoms.[21] In a land where the opportunities for patronage were few and far between, such privileges were valuable, and an appropriate means for the sovereign to reward his supporters. The granting of a charter in free regality always had the aim of furthering central influence and cementing loyalty to the crown, as we shall see in the case of the Grant family. This helps to explain why the crown continued to grant away such important rights for so long in Scotland.

Nonetheless, the balance of power between the crown and the localities began to shift decisively during this period. This change was largely a result of the development of several important institutions at the heart of Scotland's administrative structure. These included, the privy council, the register of sasines, the office of the justice of the peace, and most importantly, the College of Justice. The college was from its establishment a supreme civil court.[22] Crucially for the process of centralisation, it was able to advocate cases from inferior jurisdictions (including regalities) upon the application of one of the litigants (this is a process which was later replicated in criminal processes). Advocations were in regular use by the 1530s and the assertion of superior jurisdiction by the College of Justice began a gradual erosion of the

19 Ibid, p. 387.

20 J P Sommerville (ed.), *King James VI and I: Political Writings* (Cambridge, 1995), p. 29.

21 See K M Brown, *Noble Power in Scotland from the Reformation to the Revolution* (Edinburgh, 2011) pp. 107–120 for discussion of attempted reforms to heritable offices during the seventeenth century.

22 M Godfrey, *Civil Justice in Renaissance Scotland: the Origins of a Central Court* (Leiden, 2009), pp. 40–93, and pp. 94–160.

power of regalities.[23] However, it is important that the immediate impact of this process is not overstated. The hands of the crown in matters of local government remained effectively tied, as despite developments at the centre, they remained dependent upon noble families and landowners. Direct interference was effectively out of the question and the practical limitations of royal government and central administration at local level are obvious.[24]

A more immediate threat to the system of franchise jurisdictions in Scotland came with the invasion of Cromwell and the establishment of the Commonwealth. The new Commonwealth was fragile and a centralised state was expected to help the three kingdoms to hang together.[25] The decentralised Scottish judicial system was incompatible with this new ideal and thus it underwent a complete overhaul under Cromwell, with all heritable jurisdictions purportedly being abolished on 12 April 1654. Administration of the law in the provinces by the new order alone was found to be difficult and in practice baron courts continued to sit.[26] With the Restoration, the Cromwellian reforms were abolished. The subsequent revolution of 1688–90 did not challenge the system of franchise courts. In fact, evidence such as the large number of new jurisdictions (including the regality of Grant) created following the revolution suggest that the reverse is true. The expansion of central state power at the expense of regional power in the localities and a diminution of the political role of local magnate families is a theme investigated throughout this book.[27]

23 Godfrey, *Civil Justice in Renaissance Scotland*, p. 192.

24 Brown, *Noble Power in Scotland*, pp. 98 and 119–20.

25 L M Smith, 'Sackcloth for the sinner or Punishment for the crime? Church and Secular Courts in Cromwellian Scotland', in J Dwyer, R A. Mason and A Murdoch (eds.), *New Perspectives on the Politics and Culture of Early Modern Scotland* (Edinburgh, 1982), p. 118.

26 See the Grant family's baron courts: NRS, Baron Court Extracts, GD248/76/2.

27 This is a topic that has been the subject of a great deal of research by historians of early-modern Scotland in recent years. Goodare, *The Government of* Scotland; J Goodare, *State and Society in Early Modern Scotland* (Oxford, 1999). K M Brown, J Wormald and A Grant have also considered the relationship between local power networks and the centre: K M Brown, *Bloodfeud in Scotland, 1573–1625* (Edinburgh, 1986); K M Brown *Noble Power in Scotland from the Reformation to the Revolution* (Edinburgh, 2011); J Wormald, *Lords and Men: Bonds of Manrent in Scotland, 1442–1603* (Edinburgh, 1985); Grant, 'Franchises'. The power dynamic between the Highlands and central government from the 1630s to the revolution of 1688 are provided by D Stevenson, *Alasdair MacColla and the Highland Problem in the Seventeenth Century* (Edinburgh, 1980) and A Kennedy, *Governing Gaeldom, the Scottish Highlands and the Restoration State* (Boston, 2014). Whetstone has studied this theme following the union, A Whetstone, *Scottish County Government in the Eighteenth and Nineteenth Centuries* (Edinburgh, 1981) and Hindle for England: S Hindle, *The State and Social Change in Early Modern England, c.1550–1640* (London, 2000).

In 1707 England and Scotland completed a political union. Article XX of the treaty of Union ensured the continuing existence of heritable jurisdictions, stating that 'all heritable Offices, Superiorities, heritable Jurisdictions, Offices for life, and Jurisdictions for life, be reserved to the Owners thereof, as Rights of Property, in the same manner as they are now enjoyed by the Laws of Scotland, notwithstanding of this Treaty'.[28] Many of the most committed supporters of the post-revolution regime were holders of heritable jurisdictions. The government had no wish to alienate these men by targeting their jurisdictions at the Union.[29] Additionally, the power and apparatus of central government in Scotland was still ill-equipped to administer the Scottish localities effectively. Yet, scarcely forty years after the treaty was signed, its terms supposedly inviolable, legislation for the abolition of heritable jurisdictions was being debated in parliament.

What changes to the political climate had taken place in the intervening forty years, to allow parliament to breach one of the key articles of the Union? The most immediate factors were rebellion, and a need to satisfy anti-Scottish sentiment stemming from the 1745 Jacobite uprising. Indeed, since the union, and especially in the wake of the '15, Whig writers in England voiced concern that the system of landholding and heritable justice had placed the people of Scotland in bondage and threatened the protestant succession in the British Isles. For example, Logan wrote 'that the protestant religion and succession and civil liberties of Great Britain are in imminent danger by these superiorities and heritable jurisdictions is evident'.[30] There arose a popular (mis)conception that the archaic system of heritable justice, exercised by many clan chiefs in the barbaric Highlands of Scotland, was to blame for the uprisings and that a lack of impartial justice in the area was responsible for the political unrest generally.[31] Such opinions were rapidly spread by lively pamphlet literature. One such pamphleteer wrote: 'There is no dispute that, the late rebellion, had their [sic] source in the tyrannic and unlimited power of the heritable Lords'.[32] Of

28 *RPS*, 1706/10/257.

29 N Davidson, 'The Scottish path to capitalist agriculture 1: from the crisis of feudalism to the origins of agrarian transformation (1688–1746)', *Journal of Agrarian Change*, 4 (2004), pp. 227–268, pp. 254–5.

30 W Logan, *A View of the Present State of Scotland in Regard to the Tenures and Slavish Dependencies of the Subjects of that Part of North Britain* (London, 1733), p. 14.

31 A MacKillop, 'Military Recruiting in the Scottish Highlands 1739 – 1815: The Political, Social and Economic Context' (Unpublished Ph.D. thesis University of Glasgow, 1995), p. 64.

32 Anon, *An ample disquisition into the nature of Regalities and other Heritable Jurisdictions, in that part of Great Britain called Scotland, As now under the consideration of Parliament* (London, 1747), p. 19.

regalities in particular the same author had this to say: 'these lords of regality are sovereign' and each lord 'can command his clans, on pain of death to take up arms against the sovereign'.[33] Another pamphleteer summed up opinions, 'it might perhaps appear that this [the existence of heritable jurisdictions] was one of the original causes of the late rebellion, as well of all the commotions that happened in Scotland … since the revolution'.[34] Whilst heritable justice was more common in the Lowlands than the Highlands, Scotland's heritable jurisdictions were a convenient target for a government who needed to be seen to be taking action in the wake of the rebellion.

The bill for abolishing heritable jurisdictions was the focal point of the post-Culloden legislation. It at first appeared that baron courts would be the target of the bill and regality courts retained.[35] The Lords of Session were opposed to any kind of abrogation of heritable powers at all and recommended their retention.[36] At the first vote on the bill in the commons Ludovick Grant of Grant (the chief of clan Grant) was one of the few Scots to vote in favour of the bill, thus helping the administration to win the vote; however, the margin in favour of abolition was surprisingly small.[37] Lord Milton, who was the Lord Justice Clerk and a close friend of the Duke of Argyll, who initially led a principled stand against the act,[38] voiced the opinion that by seeking to abolish jurisdictions the administration was looking for a scapegoat,

> There is one great mistake you are all in at London, as if the heritable jurisdictions were the cause of the rebellion and therefore ought to be suppressed in order to prevent future rebellion, whereas upon my honour and conscience I do not believe that ten men were added to the rebellion [by the heritable jurisdictions].[39]

However, the main ambition of the Heritable Jurisdictions Act was probably the consolidation of judicial power in the royal courts; this also offered new opportunities for patronage, especially in the sheriff courts, which had been

33 Ibid, p. 23.

34 Anon, *An enquiry into the causes of the late rebellion and the proper methods for preventing the like misfortune for the future* (London, 1746).

35 F Jewell, 'The Legislation relating to Scotland after the Forty-Five' (Unpublished Ph.D. thesis University of North Carolina at Chapel Hill, 1975), p. 156.

36 Ibid, p. 170.

37 Ibid, p. 198.

38 R L Emerson, *An Enlightened Duke; The Life of Archibald Campbell (1682–1761), Earl of Ilay, 3rd Duke of Argyll* (Kilcerran, 2013), pp. 305–8.

39 Jewell, 'The legislation relating to Scotland after the Forty-Five', p. 188.

the ambition of the Scottish, and then British governments, since at least the time of James VI. It is perhaps best to see the Heritable Jurisdictions Act as the conclusion of this agenda.

The 1747 legislation enacted that proprietors were to be entitled to 'reasonable and just' compensation for the abrogation of their jurisdictions.[40] Any person who could prove that he or she had been lawfully possessed of a heritable sheriffship, deputy sheriffship, regality, stewartry, constabulary, justiciary, bailliary or clerkship for life, over a period of at least forty years prior to 11 November 1746 was invited to enter a claim or claims for compensation to the court of session by 11 November 1747.[41]

The Duke of Argyll fought for the retention of baron courts, arguing that they abounded in the Lowlands to no ill-effect.[42] However, the barons' jurisdiction was greatly reduced, and barons were not compensated for the reduction of their jurisdiction. The Lord Advocate was responsible for raising objections to the claims entered by jurisdiction holders. Claimants were required to provide documentation supporting their claim from their charter chests: charters of erection, parliamentary ratifications, sasines, infeftments and assignations. Some jurisdiction holders also provided court books as evidence.[43] If the court was satisfied that the claimant was in lawful possession of the jurisdictions claimed, the claimant was then asked to provide evidence that they were in exercise of their jurisdiction. Additionally, some indication of the value of the lands was requested to help calculate compensation for the jurisdictions claimed. Compensation for regalities was determined on the following basis, 'The regality to be stated at 1 ½ years purchase of the valued rent and such of them as have been faintly exercised at ¾ of the valued rent'.[44] The Lords of Session awarded compensation for 115 jurisdictions, forty-nine of which were regalities, although initially 124 rights of regality were claimed.[45] The £152,237. 15. 4. sterling awarded by the court of session to compensate former jurisdiction holders marked the biggest injection of political capital into Scotland

40 Lords of the Council of Session, *Copy of the Report and Certificate Made to his Majesty in his Privy Council, Pursuant to the Act of Parliament ... for taking away and abolishing the Heritable Jurisdictions* (London, 1748), p. 4.

41 Ibid.

42 Jewell, 'The Legislation relating to Scotland after the Forty-Five', p. 192.

43 For instance, see NRS, Claim of the Earl of Galloway in respect of the Stewartry of Garlies, CS4/9, no fo. numbers.

44 NRS, Claims anent Heritable Jurisdictions, CS4/12.

45 Whetstone, *Scottish County Government*, p. 4; NRS, Claims anent Heritable Jurisdictions, CS4/12, no fo. numbers.

since the Union.[46] The largest recipients were those who were in possession of a sheriffship. Amongst these the Duke of Argyll, who received £21,000 stg, was the largest beneficiary, receiving nearly three times the compensation awarded to anyone else.

The abolition of Heritable jurisdictions in 1747 has long been accorded the status of a watershed moment in Scottish history by many historians, but for differing reasons. The historiographer royal, T C Smout describes heritable jurisdictions in the following terms in one of the most widely read elementary texts: 'Chiefs of the early eighteenth century could hold a private court in which they were effectively judge and jury in their own cause, but the rights of this jurisdiction, though still considerable, did not extend any longer to executing the guilty'.[47]

When we consider the views of other historians, such as Rosalind Mitchison, several different arguments emerge. Mitchison has criticized these rights of jurisdiction: 'There would be no guarantee of good justice so long as the Heritable Jurisdictions survived',[48] whilst Bruce Lenman wrote that 'Arguably this [1747] is a date which should rank with the Union of the Crowns in 1603 and the Union of the Parliaments of 1707 in the slow destruction of the traditional Scottish polity'.[49] Murray Pittock has claimed, 'It was the abolition of Heritable Jurisdictions in 1747 which brought this social order [regional clan power] to its knees, not earlier cultural or political change'.[50] The basis for these claims is uncertain, as no archival research is offered as evidence of their validity. Claims such as these probably owe their origin to Whig propaganda of the eighteenth century. So compelling is the belief in the processes of modernisation leading to the end date of 1747 that evidence is not required.

Others have seen heritable jurisdictions as casualties of a less precisely described modernisation. Stephen Davies wrote in 1980, 'by 1747 regality was a moribund institution in judicial terms'.[51] His view is shared by others who believe that the franchise courts had come to be viewed as increasingly anachronistic, rather than a threat to good governance. In the words of Peter

46 A I Macinnes, *Clanship, Commerce and the House of Stuart 1603–1788* (East Linton, 1996), p. 216.

47 T C Smout, *A History of the Scottish People, 1560–1830*, (London, 1972), p. 314.

48 R M Mitchison, 'The Government and the Highlands, 1707 – 1745', in N T Phillipson and R M Mitchison (eds.), *Scotland in the Age of Improvement* (Edinburgh, 1970), p. 44.

49 B P Lenman, *The Jacobite Risings in Britain 1689–1746* (London, 1980), p. 278.

50 M Pittock, *The Myth of the Jacobite Clans: The Jacobite Army in 1745* (Edinburgh, 2009), p. 36.

51 S Davies, 'Courts and the Scottish Legal System 1600–1747: the case of Stirlingshire', in V Gatrell, B P Lenman and G Parker, *Crime and the Law: The Social History of Crime in Western Europe since 1500* (London, 1980), p. 146.

McIntyre, 'it became increasingly evident, however, that they [heritable jurisdictions] had long outlived their usefulness'.[52] The decline of the franchise courts is directly linked to the rise of effective central bureaucracies, not only in Scotland, but across Europe in what has become known as the 'century of centralisation'.[53] The notion of heritable justice was inconsistent with centralisation and enlightened thought, which were key themes in life and politics in eighteenth-century Scotland. However, the realities of providing justice in the far-flung districts of Scotland were often not accounted for by intellectual ideals. The narrative of centralisation, concluding with the 1747 act, is a neat and convenient way to encapsulate the changes that eighteenth-century society was supposedly undergoing.[54]

The truth is far removed from this neat narrative. The sweeping power-grab of the 1747 act did nothing to transform the communications and transport links with the Highlands, saying nothing of the region's social structure, and

---

52 McIntyre, 'The Franchise Courts', p. 362.

53 J Blum, '*The Internal Structure and Polity of the European Village Community*', The Journal of Modern History, 43:4 (1971), pp. 542–576 p. 545; and J Hayhoe, *Enlightened Feudalism: Seigneurial Justice and Village Society in Eighteenth-Century Northern Burgundy* (Rochester, 2008). Hayhoe argues that the emergence of strong central courts in the 'century of centralisation' did not mean that seigneurial jurisdictions were overtaken in terms of importance in certain localities in France which is similar to the situation in the Highlands.

54 The social and political history of the Highlands in the eighteenth century has been extensively studied by Historians. Major research of this period has often focussed on two emotive topics which have remained of national importance. The first is, the ever-popular subject of Jacobitism, the second is the topic of improvement and its links to the demise of the clan system. Important works include: T M Devine, *The Scottish Clearances. A History of the Dispossessed* (London, 2018); R A Dodgshon, *From Chiefs to Landlords: Social and Economic Change in the Western Highlands and Islands, c. 1493–1820* (Edinburgh, 1998). Similarly: R M Mitchison, *Lordship to Patronage: Scotland 1603 – 1745* (Edinburgh, 1983). The transformation of the Highland economy in the later eighteenth century has largely focused on the western Highlands or those areas with Jacobite sympathies. However, in recent years historians such as, J R Barrett, *The Making of a Scottish Landscape: Moray's Regular Revolution 1760–1840* (Croydon, 2015); D Taylor, *The Wild Black Region: Badenoch 1750–1800* (Edinburgh, 2016) have expanded the reach of existing knowledge during this period by considering events in Moray and the Grampians in influential new local studies.

E R Cregeen, I F Grant and A McKerral had tentatively suggested that tacksmen were not the monsters that history had often painted them to be; however, the notion had not been researched thoroughly until Taylor's work. Cregeen in particular, has made detailed studies of the changes to tenure in Argyll and the impact this had upon the role of the tacksmen there, see: E R. Cregeen, 'The tacksmen and their successors: a study of tenurial reorganisation in Mull, Morvern and Tiree in the early eighteenth century', *Scottish Studies*, 13 (1969), pp. 93–144.

thus, the emasculated baron courts continued to be important in these areas, even into the nineteenth century. Emerson writing of Argyll's objections to the 1747 act summarises the situation well: 'The jurisdictions had a thousand-year-old history and were part of a complex social fabric. Their abolition should not be a hurried matter'.[55]

1.2 Seigneurial Justice: Scotland in a European Context

The Scottish experience of seigneurial jurisdictions did not exist in isolation and there is scope for comparison with other European jurisdictions, particularly the French seigneurial courts of the ancien régime. The law and language of feudalism, and subsequently of seigneurialism, was the same across Europe, where the infeudation of lands was commonly accompanied by rights of jurisdiction in favour of the superior. As in Scotland, these superiors were typically referred to as barons. The extent of their rights varied greatly according to the type of jurisdiction, the regalian powers of the Neapolitan barons, Scottish Lords of regality and English palatinates being at the apex, but less prestigious manorial jurisdictions were the norm. Such local jurisdictions were one of the defining features of lordship and, in turn, of localities across the continent. The decline of seigneurial courts was a gradual process; they are often regarded as casualties of the ongoing centralisation of European state government and administration. For instance, the reduction of the power of patrimonial courts took place much earlier in centralised England than in the rest of Europe, with only the impoverished manor courts being common by our period. In contrast, the rest of the continent's jurisdictions were only swept away during the hundred-year period from 1748–1848, during which time nearly all were abolished: in Scotland, the regalities fell by virtue of post-Jacobite legislation in 1748; in France, feudal courts were dispatched by the revolution of 1789; Napoleonic reforms led to their abolition in the kingdom of Naples in 1806;[56] however, it was not until 1848 that the patrimonial courts of Austria and Germany disappeared.[57]

---

55 Emerson, *An Enlightened Duke*, p. 307.

56 A M Rao, 'The Feudal Question in the Kingdom of Naples' in, A Forrest and P H Wilson eds. *The Bee and the Eagle; Napoleonic France and the End of the Holy Roman Empire, 1806* (Basingstoke, 2009), p. 227.

57 H Kuzmics and R Axtman, *Authority, State and National Character: The Civilizing Process in Austria and England 1700–1900* (Aldershot, 2007), p. 189.

Across Europe historians have traditionally paid little attention to these local courts, especially in the period leading to their disappearance. Social and legal historians have tended to view the development of European history through the distorting lens of growth at the centre. Where attention has been paid to the localities it is usually in terms of how central bureaucracy has exerted control over those regions rather than the way that local communities administered themselves. Legal historians have been guilty of concentrating on the great central courts and above all criminal justice, forgetting the role that local courts played in the ordering of civil society. The fixation with ongoing modernisation and centralisation probably stems from attitudes towards local justice which developed during the Enlightenment, wherein progress was seen to be good and a system of justice dependent upon seigneurs to be bad.

In recent years there has been lively discussion of seigneurial jurisdictions in France and a re-evaluation of the work of these courts is underway. Maligned by some contemporary writers and judges, the system of seigneurial courts was lambasted. Garnot has summarised their complaints (which were perpetuated by nineteenth and twentieth century writers): 'un personnel incompétent, une activité déclinante, une procédure opaque et fluctuante, des peines disproportionnées, sans parler d'une sujétion aux seigneurs dans le but d'opprimer les paysans, tels sont les principaux griefs qui sont faits aux justices seigneuriales'.[58] To the historian of Scottish franchise courts these criticisms sound all too familiar.[59] Similar criticisms, mostly eighteenth century in origin, abound across Europe. However, in light of more detailed research into the records left by the seigneurial courts of the ancien régime and other jurisdictions, historians now believe that these courts were in fact tailored to serve the needs of the inhabitants of rural localities and provided them with fast, efficient and cost-effective justice.

French historians such as Mauclair have undertaken studies similar in nature to the one in this book, by detailed investigation into a single jurisdiction. Thus, Mauclair's, *La justice seigneuriale du duché-pairie de La Vallière, 1667–1790,* considers the work of three seigneurial courts in the West of France at Château-la-Vallière, Saint-Christophe and Marçon.[60] His findings are

58 'Feckless officials, declining activity, inconsistent and opaque procedure, disproportionate punishments, without mentioning that the seigneurs exercised jurisdiction with the goal of oppressing the country folk, these are the major criticisms which are made against seigneurial justice'.

59 B Garnot, 'Une réhabilitation? Les justices seigneuriales dans la France du XVIIIe siècle', *Histoire, économie, et société*, 24:2 (2005), pp. 221–232, p. 221.

60 F Mauclair, *La justice seigneuriale du duché-pairie de La Vallière, 1667–1790* (Tours, 2006).

strikingly similar to what is to be discerned from the records of the regality of Grant; that until the end of the ancien régime seigneurial courts were actively engaged in a very wide range of social, economic, and judicial matters. They were fast, effective, inexpensive (compared to the royal courts), and carried real advantages for the inhabitants of the countryside especially.[61] Following a swathe of new research, the same can now be said of other parts of France. Of the seigneurial courts of Northern Burgundy, Hayhoe has uncovered that certain *cahiers de doléances* emanating from villages in the region, actually argued that the continuation of seigneurial courts there was 'crucial' in assisting communities to regulate their own affairs.[62] Villagers there valued the courts as a local service, even when they disliked the control that the seigneur exerted over the court.[63] Evidence of a sophisticated local legal culture emerges from Hayhoe's research. In 1741 the lord of the village of Jullenay, a village with two feudal courts, complained that his villagers always claimed *déclinatoire* when he initiated court proceedings against them, arguing that they were subject to the jurisdiction of the village's other court.[64] Given that both courts belonged to the same landowner, this plea can be viewed as an effective delaying tactic employed by locals to interrupt proceedings against them. As shall be seen from our examination of the Scottish court records, locals across Europe displayed an adeptness in exploiting feudal courts and their procedures to their own advantage.[65]

When we look to southern Italy, and the Kingdom of Naples, we find that barons with regalian powers also held sway. The similarities with Scotland are once more striking. As with the early-modern Highland clan chiefs, the Neapolitan barons split their time between the administrative centre of Naples and their baronial fiefs. Living in castles which (as with castle Grant in Strathspey) were a symbol of feudal rule, it was here that the halls of justice were to be found, along with the place of imprisonment. The barons administered their fiefs through a system of courts, operated by baronial officials

61 Ibid, pp. 321–326.

62 J Hayhoe, *Enlightened Feudalism; Seigneurial Justice and Village Society in Eighteenth-Century Northern Burgundy* (Rochester, 2008), p. 213. For the English-speaking historian, Hayhoe's work is the most accessible study. In French, the most comprehensive is the collection of essays on village justice in, François Brizay, Antoine Follain, and Véronique Sarrazin, eds. *Les Justices de village: Administration et justice locales de la fin du Moyen Âge à la Révolution* (Rennes, 2002).

63 Ibid, p. 195.

64 Ibid, p. 21.

65 See Chapter 8.

and captains. These courts were both paternalistic and self-serving.[66] Through them the barons were able to exert social control over their vassals, and also dictate the economy of the fief; regulating food supplies and production.[67] Although the use of a court in this way may appear alien to those familiar with modern justice systems, the use of franchise courts in this manner was ubiquitous in Scotland and France.[68]

Feudal franchise courts belonging to seigneurs were common from the far south of the continent to the north. For instance, in Sweden an increasing number of patrimonial courts were established during the seventeenth century.[69] The creation of new manorial courts there was used as a means to appease the nobility and has parallels with the increase in the number of jurisdictions in Scotland during the same period. Sweden did not have a deep feudal heritage, unlike neighbouring states in Germany and Denmark, and the spread of fiefs came late. As a result, the Swedish baronies were less numerous than equivalent jurisdictions in other countries and much larger in size; they were also completely assimilated within the system of royal courts.[70] Much remains to be discovered about Sweden's seigneurial courts; but, as with similar jurisdictions across Europe it is recognised that little attention has been paid to the role of Sweden's seigneurial courts, which is therefore ill-understood.

This evidence suggests that the regality of Grant may be a valuable comparator, providing guidance upon what was happening elsewhere, not only in Scotland, but also across Europe during the same period. This is because rural, agrarian communities across Europe in the seventeenth and eighteenth centuries shared many similarities in social structure, hierarchies, economy, and culture. At the heart of this way of life was the communal agrarian community, situated on the seigneurs' land: the French *villes et villages*, the Italian *terre et casale*, the English village or hamlet, and the Scots clachan, baile or toun. Each of these communities was to an extent self-regulating; however, events often demanded that the seigneurial court step in to help manage affairs and resolve

66 A Tommaso, *The Continuity of Feudal Power; The Caracciolo Di Brienza in Spanish Naples* (Cambridge, 1991), pp. 109–140.

67 Rao, 'The Feudal Question in the Kingdom of Naples', p. 229.

68 See Chapter 6 and Éric Gasparini, 'Justice seigneuriale et régulation sociale : l'exemple de quelques seigneuries comtoises dans la seconde moitié du xviiie siècle', in François Brizay, Antoine Follain, and Véronique Sarrazin, eds. *Les Justices de village: Administration et justice locales de la fin du Moyen Âge à la Révolution* (Rennes, 2002), pp.259–68.

69 H Pihlajamak, 'On forgotten jurisdictional complexities: The case of early-modern Sweden' in S P Donlan and D Heirbaut (eds.), *The Laws' many bodies: Studies in Legal Hybridity and Jurisdictional Complexity, c. 1600–1900* (Berlin, 2015), p. 128.

70 Ibid, pp. 131–4.

disputes in the community. Again, these problems were similar in nature, primarily concerning the ubiquity of credit, property disputes, and the distribution and management of community resources. For these matters the authority of the seigneur and his officials was paramount. Here we also find similarities. Inhabitants of bailes in Strathspey would undoubtedly have recognised the *juges et procureurs fiscaux* of the French feudal courts, although across Europe the lay magistracy was not necessarily in the hands of men of similar backgrounds and social standing.[71] In Scotland judges in the feudal courts tended to be amateurs who enjoyed the respect of the community; in France they were absentee professionals.[72] What these men all had in common was that they helped to provide effective resolution of disputes and assisted to operate the administrative machinery necessary to manage life in the localities.[73]

Whilst these courts were evidently integral to the way of life in European localities, there appears to have been large regional variations in their popularity and legitimacy with locals. Thus, residents of the Charente-Inférieur department complained that seigneurial justice was slow and expensive.[74] This was a common complaint across Europe, where rashes of overlapping and conflicting jurisdictions, absentee judges, and infrequent court sessions, complicated and delayed resolution. Inhabitants of the Kingdom of Naples were often frustrated by delays when engaging in litigation against their overlords, the barons, concerning baronial rights and dues. So slowly were these cases handled that at the beginning of the nineteenth century there are believed to have been somewhere in the region of 30,000 cases of this type pending in the Neapolitan baron courts.[75] Other tensions arose. In Northern Burgundy vassals disliked the increasingly intensive way seigneurial courts were used to maximise the seigneur's income.[76] The increasing use of seigneurial courts to exploit the lands of the landowners is another feature which was common across Europe during the decline of feudalism, when landowners began to embrace commercialism at the expense of paternalistic modes of estate management. The complaints of French vassals were echoed in Strathspey where tenants disliked the way that forests were being managed commercially to the detriment of the tenants.[77] Whilst the majority of cases in seigneurial courts

71 See chapter 2.
72 Hayhoe, *Enlightened Feudalism*, pp. 33–7.
73 Hayhoe, *Enlightened Feudalism*, pp.211–212.
74 A Cribhaugh, "Local Justice and Rural Society in the French Revolution." *Journal of Social History* 34 (2000): 327–50, p. 328.
75 Rao, 'The Feudal Question in the Kingdom of Naples', p. 231.
76 Heyhoe, *Enlightened Feudalism* p. 216.
77 See chapter 7.

MAP 2 Map of Scotland showing the (de-facto) territorial extent of the regality of Grant. 1. Strathspey; 2. Urquhart; 3. Mulben; 4. Laggan
SOURCE: THE AUTHOR

had nothing to do with the feudal superior and concerned relations between the vassals, it must be remembered that these courts were still the tool of the seigneur; they protected his property rights, enforced his regulations, and policed his vassals.[78] Whilst many seigneurs appear to have regarded the provision of justice to their vassals as a paternalistic or civic duty, others must have done so primarily out of self-interest, though perhaps, this was a reasonable price to pay for justice.

78 Hayhoe, *Enlightened Feudalism*, p. 61.

1.3 The Regality of Grant

Strathspey is a region in the Highlands of Scotland which runs the length of the river Spey, from Aviemore in the south to Ballindalloch in the North (at a point some twenty-five miles from where the Spey enters the Moray Firth) [see Map 1] This is a wide valley of fertile river haugh lands, extensive forestry, and vast tracts of moorland. The chiefs of Grant first made their home here in the fourteenth century.[79] Over the next 350 years they gradually managed to acquire the whole of Strathspey and the neighbouring valley of the river Dulnain. Further afield they also acquired possession of the lands of Glenurquhart by Loch Ness, Mulben in Banffshire, and Laggan on the border between Badenoch and Lochaber, in addition to part of the burgh of Elgin. Many of the lands and baronies were erected, by a charter granted to Ludovick Grant of Freuchie by King William II in 1694, into a single regality, that of Grant. The charter received parliamentary ratification two years later. This made the regality of Grant one of the last regalities erected in Scotland, but not the last; the regality of Dudhope was the final new regality, being ratified in March 1707.[80] The regalities of Grant and Dudhope, were only two of a slew of erections granted as a show of royal favour during the reigns of William, Mary, and Anne. The charter granted to the laird of Grant was a means of both rewarding and compensating a loyal servant of the government at little cost to the crown. Additionally, enhancing the judicial powers of a northern magnate,

---

79 Fraser, *Chiefs of Grant*, Vol I, pt. I p. xxix. The clan Grant has been the subject of several studies mainly concerned with the genealogy of the family. Fraser's *Chiefs of Grant* published in 1883 remains the starting point for studies relating to the family. He made little use of the Grant family's court records in his history, probably because the records reveal relatively little about the family itself. The *Chiefs of Grant* is partisan, of which the historian must be wary, as this led Fraser to suppress important parts of the clan's history. Several later historians have published histories of the Grant of Grant family, but they largely reproduce in less depth Fraser's research. See, A Kennedy, Earl of Cassilis, *The Rulers of Strathspey: A History of the Lairds of Grant and Earls of Seafield* (Inverness, 1911); I F Grant, *The Clan Grant: the development of a Clan* (Edinburgh, 1955). As a counterpoint to Fraser's documentary research, the other major Victorian work on Strathspey which remains important is William Forsyth's, *In the Shadow of Cairngorm* (Aviemore, 1999) [1900]. This text draws upon several diverse sources of history, relying heavily upon the oral traditions of the area, but also makes use of archival evidence such as kirk session minutes to create an invaluable record of the traditions, culture and popular history of Strathspey. In this respect Forsyth's work has never been emulated.

80 *RPS*, A1706/10/65, Dudhope contained a burgh of regality within Dundee rebuking the myth that heritable jurisdictions were a feature of the Highlands rather than the Lowlands by the eighteenth century. The penultimate regality, the regality of Primrose, was also located in the Lowlands, in Midlothian.

who was loyal to the new regime, may have been an extension of government policy of pacifying the Highlands. Ludovick Grant of Freuchie was an ardent supporter of the revolution, sitting as a member of the Convention of Estates called together by William in 1689, and adding his subscription to the minute declaring the assembly in the name of William to be lawful.[81] He was subsequently elected as a member of the committee for settling the Scottish government. Ludovick's support of the new monarch proved to be especially valuable in the ensuing war of 1689–90, when a significant part of the campaign was fought on lands held by the laird of Grant in Strathspey. Victory in the final battle of the rebellion, when the government routed the rebel forces at Cromdale on 1 May 1690, owed its success to Grant's clansmen, who acted as scouts for the government troops, alongside another 300 who were serving in General Sir Thomas Livingstone's regiment at the time.[82] The information they provided enabled Livingstone's troops to ford the Spey under cover of darkness and take the Jacobite forces by surprise, several hundred of whose escape was only aided by thick fog coming down from the Cromdale hills to their rear, by which way they were able to make their escape into Strathavon and thence into Gordon country[see Illustration 1].[83]

Whilst the laird's actions had placed him in a favourable position politically, they had come at a dear cost financially. Besides the cost of raising his own regiment, Ludovick Grant had also had government troops quarter on his lands in both Strathspey and Urquhart. Incursions by Jacobite forces onto his estates had caused much damage to his and his tenants' stock and grain; this exacerbated the financial troubles both lord and tenant were suffering thanks to the economic and climatic disasters of the 1690s.[84] A parliamentary commission

81 *RPS, 1689/3/18*; Fraser, *Chiefs of Grant*, Vol I, pt. II, p. 309.

82 Fraser, *Chiefs of Grant*. Vol I, pt. II, pp. 317–8.

83 Ibid, pp. 318–9.

84 Ludovick's financial troubles were exacerbated by the nationwide economic and climatic disasters of the 1690s. See, K J Cullen, *Famine in Scotland: The Ill Years of the 1690s*, (Edinburgh, 2010). This book will contribute to our understanding of the effects of this crisis. For other important studies of the wider Scottish economy, the discussion of which this study contributes to, see, I D Whyte and K A Whyte, Debt and Credit, 'Poverty and Prosperity in a Seventeenth Century Scottish Rural Community', in R M Mitchison and P Roebuck (eds.), *Economy and Society in Scotland and Ireland, 1500–1939* (Edinburgh, 1988); L A Ewan, 'Debt and Credit in Early Modern Scotland: The Grandtully Estates 1650–1765' (Unpublished Ph.D. thesis the University of Edinburgh, 1988); M H B Sanderson, *Scottish Rural Society in the Sixteenth Century*, (Edinburgh, 1982); I D Whyte, *Agriculture and Society in Seventeenth Century Scotland*, (Edinburgh, 1979); N Davidson, *Discovering the Scottish Revolution 1692–1746* (London, 2003); N Davidson, 'The Scottish path to capitalist agriculture: from the crisis of feudalism to the origins of agrarian transformation (1688–1746)', *Journal of Agrarian Change*, 4 (2004), pp. 227–268.

ILLUSTRATION 1 The Braes of Cromdale, where the final action of the battle of Cromdale was fought. From left to right: the farm of Easter Lethendrie, tenanted by David Blair, regality clerk; the farm of Burnside, tenanted by John Grant in Burnside, bailie of regality; and the farm of Comedge, one of the townships involved in a boundary dispute in 1719. Beyond are the Cairngorms
SOURCE: THE AUTHOR

appointed in 1695 to consider the losses he had suffered during the rebellion estimated the damage to be in the region of £12,000 sterling and put his case to the crown for consideration.[85] No compensation was forthcoming, nor would it be for Ludovick's successors who, continued to press Grant claims for compensation throughout the next century. Instead, Ludovick was forced to accept the meagre rewards that came his way, these being a bishop's rent rebate, the sheriffdom of Inverness and his regality.

In fact, the gift of a regality appears to have been promised to Ludovick by James VII following Argyll's short-lived rebellion in 1685. This grant was probably intended to maintain the chief of Grant's support for the Stuart crown and was the reward for promptly marching with 300 men of his clan in support of the government campaign against Argyll. The Seafield Muniments show that Sir John Nisbet, a former Lord Advocate, and Sir James Dalrymple, first Viscount Stair, were consulted by Ludovick Grant in 1686 regarding changing his baronies and other lands into a regality.[86]

85 Ibid, p. 322.

86 NRS, Grant Legal Papers, GD248/18/3.

A regality offered Ludovick Grant enhanced political authority within his own lands and the wider region of Inverness-shire and Moray. A crucial aspect of this enhanced authority was freeing the laird of Grant from the superiority of the regality of Spynie, to which the laird of Grant had previously owed suit and which had been competent as an appeal court from the Grant baronies. The regality of Spynie was originally an ecclesiastical regality, held by the bishops of Moray until the Reformation. Thereafter it passed into the patrimony of the Airlie family and then ultimately to the Dukes of Gordon.[87] Spynie held the superiority of several lands purchased by the Grants in Strathspey. Besides requiring Grant to pay suit at Spynie head courts, the regality court of Spynie also occasionally convened on Grant lands. For instance, in April 1686, John Cumming, bailie depute of the regality of Spynie, held a court at Ballintomb.[88] The imposition of Spynie's superiority in this manner seriously undermined the laird of Freuchie's authority. In an era in which status and authority were of paramount importance, the avoidance of such courts may have been one of the primary benefits of a regality for the Grants.

Whilst the bailies of the regality of Spynie ceased to have jurisdiction within the regality, so did the sheriff of Moray. The sheriffdom of Moray was held heritably by the Dunbar family of Westfield. Dunbar of Westfield sought reduction of the regality of Grant in a court of session case in November 1697.[89] He argued that the King was not competent to grant new regalities outwith parliament, especially where such a grant was to the prejudice of his rights as heritable sheriff of Moray. Westfield's counsel concluded by remarking that 'regalities are always mentioned as one of the grievances [of princes]; and in the Highlands they were yet more dangerous'.[90] In reply, Grant's counsel argued that if all regalities erected since 1455 were actually required to be granted in full parliament then there would scarce be a jurisdiction in the Kingdom which could claim to have cleared this hurdle. The Lords of Session advised that Westfield could not simply reduce the laird of Grant's regality, 'because the concession of a regality contains many things which the Sheriff could lay no manner of claim to,– such as the having a chapel and chancery, the right of the single escheat, &c.; so that the Sheriff could quarrel it no farther than it interfered with his heritable jurisdiction, and encroached on his property'.[91] However, given that the case raised important issues, the Lords decided to refer

87 L Shaw, *The History of the Province of Moray* (Elgin, 1827), p. 186.

88 NRS, Grant Legal Papers, GD248/18/2, fo. 19.

89 (1697) 4 Bro. Sup. 386.

90 Ibid, p. 389.

91 Ibid, p. 392.

the issue to parliament to consider as an important matter of government, despite the Lords stating that 'the Parliament would think it a strange question to be remitted to them, Whether the King had power to grant a regality, where so many concerned in such jurisdictions had a vote'.

The matter was referred to parliament with the petition of Westfield being heard by parliament in August 1698. The case was continued for some time until it drops from the parliamentary record. Although it appears that Westfield probably abandoned his objections to the erection of the regality in his sheriffdom, the ongoing uncertainty over the status of Grant's regality was to endure for several years. Notably, it was upon this basis that Grant's attempt in 1700 to repledge his vassals, the notorious bandits, Peter and Donald Brown, from Banff sheriff court was repelled.

Having eventually overcome this serious legal challenge, the Lairds of Grant were able to enjoy their newly expanded jurisdiction. They and their bailies were now theoretically competent to 'sit as judges in all actions civil and criminal, except lese-majeste and treason, etc'., and had the lucrative right to 'benefit of all escheats falling within the bounds of the regality by reason of rebellion, putting to the horn, etc'.[92] In addition, the Castletoun of Freuchie was erected into a burgh able to hold thrice-yearly fairs and a weekly market at the regality cross. Ancillary to this was the important right of replegiation. The Grants of Freuchie were also able to change their designation from the Grants of Freuchie to the Grants of Grant, and their Castle from Ballachastel, to Castle Grant.[93] The erection of Ludovick Grant of Freuchie's several baronies into a single regality was also a matter of considerable utility. This is alluded to in the charter of erection,

> Considering how convenient and commodious it would be to the said Ludovick Grant, his vassals and tenants, and whole inhabitants of the said lands and baronies, to have the same erected into a free regality, and to have a free burgh of regality, with fairs and weekly markets, in respect that the lands above written lie at a great distance from the chief burghs of their respective sheriffdoms, and that all lie near the Castletoun of Freuquhie: Therefore their Majesties dissolve the foresaid lands and baronies from all sheriffdoms, stewartries, regalities, earldoms, lordships, baronies, and other jurisdictions whatsoever, to which they or any part of them pertained or was annexed, or of which they were formerly parts and

92 *RPS*, 1696/9/192.

93 Ibid.

> pertinents, and unite, erect, create, and incorporate all and sundry the foresaid town, lands, and baronies above enumerated into one whole and free regality, with free chapel and chancellery, and power of justiciary, now and in all time coming to be called the Regality of Grant.[94]

Of the lands held by the Grants of Freuchie, the following were incorporated into the new regality of Grant: the baronies of Knockando, Kirdells, Mulben, Freuchie, Cromdale, Urquhart and Corriemony, the lands of Glenchernich, Ballindalloch, Muldaries, Bridgeton of Spey and a tenement in Elgin. Conspicuously absent were the Lordship of Abernethy, the lands of Curr, Clury, Tullochgorum in Inverallan and the lands of Gallovie, Aberarder and Tullochcroam by Loch Laggan. This was because these lands were part of the regality of Huntly.[95] Regardless of this, the Grants treated the territorial extent of their regality with some degree of fluidity in practice, with all lands in their patrimony being treated as if they were properly part of the regality [See Map 2]. The frequent acquisition and sale of lands by the Grants meant that latitude was necessary if not legal. However, the treatment of lands not mentioned in the charter as being part of the regality was seized upon by Alexander Boswell, his majesty's advocate, who objected to Sir Ludovick Grant of Grant's claim for compensation of £5000 in January 1748 stating that 'with respect to the value claim'd it is excessive; the Claimant has subjoin'd a List of the lands contained in the Charter of Erection … the four last articles in this List, do not appear to be in the Charter of Erection'.[96] Luckily for the Grant family, this jurisdictional slip had gone unnoticed throughout the previous half-century. The resulting compensation of only £900 paid to Sir Ludovick Grant was the only material consequence of this mistake.

94 Reproduced and translated in Fraser, *Chiefs of Grant*, Vol III, pt. II, p. 476.

95 *RPS*, Ratification in favour of George Gordon Duke of Gordon, 1685/4/92.

96 Defences and Objections for His Majesties Advocate in behalf of the Crown v. The Claims of Sir Ludovick Grant of Grant, (08/01/1748).

CHAPTER 2

The Clan Grant and the Regality Court

The regality court of Grant was adapted to suit the needs of rural society in Strathspey. In Strathspey, society was still based around the clan system in the early-eighteenth century. Understanding the links between the clan system and the court is integral to comprehending the nature of the court and how it operated. This chapter seeks to define the significance of heritable jurisdictions in clan society. In particular, it will show how the laird and his gentry sought to make use of the regality court to enhance their status and manage the clan.

2.1 Strathspey in the Early Eighteenth Century

The Grant lands in Strathspey exhibited the typical features of Gaelic Highland society associated with the clan system. This society was ordered by the following social structure: the clan chief at the apex, below whom were the clan gentry, whom were ordinarily tacksmen or wadsetters, with ties of fictive or actual kinship to the chief.[1] Lesser in rank than the chief and tacksmen were tenants and subtenants cultivating cooperative runrig ferm touns. The clan Grant also had lesser septs, such as the clan Phadrick, who were incorporated into the body of the larger clan. The clan had its traditional hereditary office-holders: bailie, piper and standard bearer, along with its bards and musicians.[2] Gaelic was the common language of the people in parishes of the regality upstream of Tulchan, many of whom were monoglot.[3] Although such features characterised life in Strathspey, falling on the eastern margins of the Highlands proper, the area was especially open to Lowland social and cultural influences. For this reason the Grant chiefs identified with the lairds of Lowland Banff, Moray, and Inverness-shire: Forbes of Culloden, Rose of Kilravock, Gordon of Huntly,

1 C W J Withers, *Gaelic Scotland: The Transformation of a Culture Region* (London, 1988), p.77.

2 Withers, *Gaelic Scotland*, pp. 5 and 76; E R Cregeen, 'The Changing role of the House of Argyll in the Scottish Highlands', in N T Phillipson and R M Mitchison, *Scotland in the Age of Improvement* (Edinburgh, 1970), p. 7.

3 Indeed, the proportion of Gaelic speakers in these parishes remained at 50% into the mid-nineteenth century. Gordon J (ed.), *The Second Statistical Account of Scotland*, vol. xiv (Edinburgh, 1845), p. 439.

 | DOI:10.1163/9789004472549_003

Fraser of Lovat, with whom they spent time associating. In fact, they probably did not regard themselves as Highlanders at all (despite Ludovick Grant reputedly being dubbed 'His Highland Majesty' in parliament by the Duke of York in 1681).[4] It seems the same was perhaps true of their tenants. Depositions to the baron court in the wake of the first Jacobite rebellion described when the 'Highland army' was in the country.[5]

Land in Strathspey was organised by davochs, medieval units of land assessment used to allocate economic resources amongst inhabitants. These units of land, which are still visible in the landscape as modern-day farm units, were also used as a means of assessment for tax and common burdens.[6] On the parts of the Strathspey estate pertinent to Castle Grant, davochs were typically let directly to multiple tenants, each holding a written tack from the laird. Each tenant had a share of land in one of the several townships of the davoch. These shares were usually discussed in terms of divisions into auchten parts, oxgates or sten parts.[7] The extent of each davoch, and the amount of arable and grazing land in each, varied greatly across the regality.

Davochs were 'self-contained' units, in the respect that they contained all the resources required by the community to sustain their activities throughout the year.[8] These resources were allocated to land holders within the davochs by the fraction of land that they held, giving each a share of the total economic resources of the davoch.[9] This also applied to the arable land; thus, in the multiple-tenant townships, farming proceeded by runrig. The township's arable was divided into narrow strips known as rigs. This arable land was not always contiguous and might be dispersed around the land of the township. Tenants also had access to the township's common grazing and beyond that shieling and hill grazing. Their livelihoods depended upon this additional and extensive rough grazing. It was not uncommon for tenants in multiple-tenant farms to be absentee, residing in one township whilst also holding land in another township or davoch.[10] This they might farm 'in their own hand' or

4 Kennedy, *Governing Gaeldom*, p. 32; Fraser, *Chiefs of Grant*, Vol I pt. II, p. 302.

5 Grant Court Book 1, 1690–1701, 22/11/1690, p. 17; 24/11/1690, p. 18; 24/11/1691, p. 24. Murray Pittock tackles the issue of 'what is a Highlander?': M Pittock, *The Myth of the Jacobite Clans*, pp. 31–36.

6 A Ross, *Land Assessment and Lordship in Medieval Northern Scotland* (Turnhout, 2015), pp. 13, 61, 68 and 152–176.

7 Ibid, p. 64.

8 Ross, *Land Assessment*, p. 68.

9 Ibid.

10 See for instance Gregor Burgess holding land in Achnagallin and Achnahannet. NRS, GD248/158/3.

sub-let. Burdens levied upon davochs were also applied as fractions according to the land held by each tenant there. These burdens included both national levies, for taxation and military service, along with local services owed to the laird, such as leading [i.e. collecting] peats and providing men for tilling and reaping.[11]

The further from Castle Grant, the less the influence of the laird. In the outlying areas, the prevalence of the tacksmen was both a cause and an effect of this lessening of the laird's authority. The parish of Duthil was where this manifestation of the clan system and landholding was most obvious. There, almost all the land was let by the laird of Grant to the gentlemen of his clan; these tacksmen then sub-let the land to their own sub-tenants to farm as multiple tenant runrig farms. These sub-tenants owed loyalty primarily to their tacksman before their laird. It was to the tacksman that they paid their rent, and to him that they discharged their labour services. Like their multiple-tenant counterparts in Strathspey they farmed the land in runrig but enjoyed no security, holding their land at the will of their tacksman.[12] The tacksmen themselves usually kept the best land to be farmed 'in their own hand' at the mains [i.e. home farm], whilst living from the rents paid to them by the sub-tenants (although in some cases tacksmen did not have a tack of the entire davoch or might become absentee tacksmen by renting other davochs or even lands on other estates). As members of the clan gentry, managers, factors, bailies, and authority figures, as well as military officers of the clan and independent companies these men were of the utmost social, cultural, and economic importance.

The advantages of the tacksman system for the laird were several. Firstly, it eased the collection of rentals.[13] Whilst in the lands adjacent to Castle Grant it was a small matter to have tenants drive their rent in kind to the granaries, corrals, or have a collector tour the townships, this process was more difficult in the outlying lands. The task was simplified by making tacksmen responsible for the payment of their subtenants' rent. Tacksmen were also responsible for converting a sub-tenant's payment in kind into cash for payment to the laird, thus saving the laird the trouble of marketing surplus rent in kind. These men also discharged important economic functions to the advantage of their followers such as loaning seed, cattle and implements along with extending credit to help sustain agricultural production on their tack-lands.[14] Tacksmen

11 Ross, *Land Assessment*, pp. 152–171.

12 By the mid-eighteenth century there is evidence that many sub-tenants held the lands sub-set to them by written tack. NRS, Estate Papers, GD248/533/2, fo. 8.

13 R A Dodgshon, *Land and Society in Early Scotland* (Oxford, 1981), p. 281.

14 Cregeen, 'The tacksmen and their successors', pp. 102 and 131.

also played a political role in securing the support of the clan for their chief. This was an important aspect of maintaining law and order within the regality. A further advantage of having tacksmen for the laird was that as tacksmen's, and especially wadsetters', tenure of their lands lengthened they increasingly sought to improve their lands to augment their income. These improvement schemes required no initial capital outlay on the part of the laird. Much reclamation of land and construction of modern stone houses took place in this manner on the Grant estates.

There were, however, serious downsides to the tacksman system. The high rents that tacksmen demanded from their subtenants, compared to the tack duty of the land payable to the laird, meant that the landowner lost a substantial income through these middlemen. Many davochs were held by the same family over several generations. These davochs comprised the tacksmen's *duthcas,* the ancestral dwelling place of their family.[15] In an attempt to cement their hold upon their family land, many tacksmen seized the opportunity to contract wadsets over their tack-lands. Wadset was a mortgage of heritable property, completed by conveying the property to the creditor until such time as the original sum was repaid. Contracts of wadset between the lairds of Grant and their clan gentry proliferated from the lairdship of John Grant, fifth of Freuchie, in the early seventeenth century and continued until the mid-eighteenth century. John Grant's practice, subsequently continued by his successors, was only to wadset lands to kinsmen so that the chief's political influence over his lands was supposedly undiminished.[16] These families became known as the 'old wadsetters', many of whom held onto their land for over a century before the wadsets were redeemed in the later eighteenth century and the clan gentry were destroyed by a closed bidding system for the lands which had once comprised their *duthcas*. The final three families to retain their wadset lands were the Grants of Tullochgorum, the Grants of Lurg and the Grants of Tulloch. The Grants of Tullochgorum had particularly strong ties to their wadset lands, having first obtained a wadset of Tullochgorum in 1614. The persistent poverty of their Grant superiors enabled them to obtain several prorogations of the original wadset, delaying the eventual redemption until 1777, when after 163 years of continuous quasi-ownership the Grants of Tullochgorum were reduced to the status of tenants.[17]

Much has been written of the military role of the tacksmen as officers of the clan. By the eighteenth century this element of their function was undoubtedly

15 Taylor, *The Wild Black Region*, p. 20.

16 Brown, *Noble Society in Scotland*, p. 94.

17 Fraser, *Chiefs of Grant*, Vol I, pt. I, p. lxix.

minor compared to their economic and managerial roles in clan society.[18] However, the formation of the independent companies, hunting and hosting, and most importantly the necessity to guard the shielings and marches of Strathspey, presented opportunities for the Grant tacksmen to exercise a traditional military role into the mid-eighteenth century. Even following the '45 and the consequent diminishing of their cultural and military functions, the tacksmen did not simply disappear and continued as the lynchpins of society and the economy in the region until the end of the eighteenth century.[19]

Below tacksmen and tenants in the social hierarchy were the subtenant farmers who had a stake in the land but often no written tack. In most cases the only difference between these husbandmen and the multiple tenant farmers was that the subtenant farmers had a tacksman as their superior rather than the laird. Alongside the subtenant farmers were several other classes who had a more limited stake in the land. Primary amongst these were the malanders, day-labourers who laboured for a wage and usually rented a house along with grazing to support a cow and a few hens from the tacksman or tenant. In return for this they paid a small rent and were expected to labour for the tenant for a certain number of days each week. Labouring on the land alongside the malanders were tied or 'fied' agricultural labourers who had no stake in the land at all. Similarly, there was also a large class of domestic servants, usually young and unmarried, who moved regularly between employers, with limited prospects and opportunities.[20] Living in the townships alongside the husbandmen and their labourers were the rural tradesmen and merchants. Weavers,

18 Macinnes, *Clanship, Commerce and the House of Stuart 1603–1788*, pp. 1–190.

19 Taylor in his study, *Wild Black Region*, has re-evaluated the role of tacksmen in the eighteenth century. E R Cregeen, I F Grant and A McKerral had tentatively suggested that tacksmen were not the monsters that history had often painted them to be; however, the notion had not been researched thoroughly until Taylor's work.

20 In recent years there has been much written about the experience of the Scottish peasantry and how their everyday lives and relationships were controlled, particularly by the reformed kirk and its system of moral discipline administered by the kirk session. See, R M Mitchison and L Leneman, *Girls in Trouble. Sexuality and Social Control in Rural Scotland 1660–1780* (Edinburgh, 1998); R M Mitchison and L Leneman, *Sin and the City: Sexuality and Social Control in Urban Scotland 1660–1780* (Edinburgh, 1998); E Ewan, 'Women and Daily Life in Late-Medieval Scotland', in Y G Brown and R Ferguson (eds.), *Twisted Sisters: Women, Crime and Deviance in Scotland Since 1400* (East Linton, 2002). Of particular relevance to this study is Cornell's, 'Gender, Sex and Social Control'. Her thesis takes a broader approach to the notion of social control than other comparable studies by considering all available court records for a region rather than the kirk sessions alone. This builds a picture of how the entire system of social control exercised by the central government, judiciary, landed classes and kirk hung together as a whole within the shire of Haddington.

brewers, shoemakers, millers, and tailors plied their trade in the small townships whilst also sometimes undertaking some small subsistence agriculture to supplement the income from their trades.[21]

These people were housed in cruck houses walled and roofed largely in turf, roughly half-a-dozen houses to a township. It is likely that the houses of the gentry were little different in outward appearance from those of their dependants in the early years of the eighteenth century, the only differences being that they were larger, better furnished and set apart from the main township.[22] The township was surrounded by unfenced infield land which was intensively cropped in runrig. Crops cultivated among the arable rigs of the ferm touns were mainly oats, barley and bere.[23] Whilst grain was the main crop cultivated (it was a convenient cash crop with which to pay for rent, wages and services), the lower classes subsisted primarily on dairy produce from their cattle, sheep and goats for most of the year.[24] This was supplemented by grain and salted meat during winter time.[25] The wealth of all classes in Strathspey was reliant upon the extensive hill-grazings where cattle could be fed during the spring and summer months. Cattle were the most valuable produce of this pastoral society, because of milk production, the possibility of sale to Lowland dealers, and the production of manure. These uplands also provided the stone, feal[26] and divots for building walls and houses as well as the peat moss to keep the home-fires burning.

---

21 Barrett, *The Making of a Scottish Landscape*, pp. 36–60.

22 See what it is believed to be a rare surviving tacksman's house from the early-eighteenth century that survives in at Corriemony in the former regality. https://canmore.org.uk/site/86689/corrimony-corrimony-grange-cruck-framed-building.

23 Barrett, *The Making of a Scottish Landscape*, pp. 37–8.

24 Taylor, *Wild Black Region*, pp. 56–7; A Simmons (ed.), *Burt's Letters from the North of Scotland* (Edinburgh, 1998), pp. 204–5.

25 The most important work on this subject is A Gibson and T C Smout, *Prices, Food and Wages in Scotland, 1550–1780* (Cambridge, 1995). Useful comparators with the urban economy can be found in works such as: M Lynch (ed.), *The Early Modern Town in Scotland* (London, 1987); P S M Symms, 'Social Control in a Sixteenth Century Burgh: A Study of the Burgh Court Book of Selkirk' (Unpublished Ph.D. thesis University of Edinburgh, 1986).

26 A turf or sod used in building construction, "Fail *n.*[1], *v.*[1]". *Dictionary of the Scots Language*. 2004. Scottish Language Dictionaries Ltd.

2.2 The Lairds of Grant, the *Fine* and the Regality Court of Grant

2.2.1 *The Lairds of Grant*

The duties of the lairds of Grant as chiefs of clan Grant were economic, defensive, patriarchal, and judicial. In the late seventeenth and early eighteenth-century chiefs were still expected to fulfil these duties personally. Only by competently exercising these duties could the chief hope to maintain the political allegiance and cohesion of his clan.[27] The provision of justice was at the heart of the relationship between lord and vassal, chieftain, and clansman. As lords of the regality of Grant the chiefs of clan Grant also had expectations placed upon them by central authority to maintain law and order by using the powers devolved to them. Naturally, the Grant lairds also sought to use their powers of jurisdiction to further their own ambitions and interests upon their lands. The way that the Grant lairds used their court was a direct result of these competing expectations.

The erection of the Grant estates into a regality by King William II vested rights of jurisdiction personally in Ludovick Grant of Freuchie and his heirs. Whilst it was common practice for jurisdiction holders to appoint bailies to exercise these judicial powers on their behalf, the laird and his family sometimes presided over their court in person. Even so, Mackenzie argued that lords of regality were not permitted to sit themselves in their own court but were to exercise justice exclusively through a nominated bailie.[28] It seems that either Mackenzie was incorrect or that the Grant lairds provided a rare exception. Of other jurisdictions the following has been written: Barron says, in his introduction to the SHS transcript of the baron court of Urie, that 'the baron did not preside, at least in later times, in person';[29] whilst Dickinson's study of Carnwath shows that the baron did occasionally preside there during the first half of the sixteenth century.[30] It is recorded that the laird of Grant or his heir exercised the right to preside in their regality court on seventeen separate occasions. Ludovick Grant of Grant, styled thus after the erection of the regality, frequented the bailie's chair more often than the other Grant lairds of the period, sitting eight times.[31]

There are patterns to the appearances of the lairds in the regality court. They appeared most often during the winter months when they made their

27 Cathcart, *Kinship and Clientage*, pp.61–4.
28 Mackenzie, *The Laws and Customs of Scotland*, p. 409.
29 Barron, *Baron Court Book of Urie*, p. viii.
30 Dickinson, *Court Book of the Barony of Carnwath*, p. lxxviii.
31 Grant Court Book 1, p. 149; Grant Court Book 2, pp. 15, 25, 88, 107, 118, 120.

increasingly brief returns from political and social life in Edinburgh and London. They took responsibility for important decisions, in some cases delaying hearings until they could attend in person; however, routine matters were also dealt with. By the eighteenth century the Grant lairds appear to have preferred to spend only two months of the year in their homeland, residing for the rest, initially in Edinburgh, and then later in London.[32] Alexander Grant of Grant, second lord of the regality, was seldom in Strathspey after getting command of a regiment, his chamberlain writing to him in somewhat despairing terms in May 1717: 'I am very sorry your Lordship beginns to think of not coming home since your presence would contribute more to your business then all mortals however your lordship is best judge in this matter'.[33] Litigants in the regality court also found themselves troubled by the laird's absence. This was due to the bailie deputes' practice of deferring judgement in cases which were complicated or involved the laird's property until the outcome could be determined personally by the laird. For instance, on 13 May 1715 Bailie Dalrachney sentenced two men guilty of burning moor and woodlands, 'to be incarserat at the prison of Castle Grant and to be maintained upon their masters charges until the said laird of Grant be known how to proceed in the said matter'.[34] It could be many months until the laird returned home to deal with the matter or could correspond by letter. The possibility of having to wait months for the resolution of their case clearly vexed pursuers:

> The judge having found the mala fama sufficiently prove by report refers the future decision of the affair to the lord of the regality upon which the pursuer protested that fearing of the lord of the regality is at a distance that he may grant warrand to the other three baillies of the country to sitt with this judge as assessors to determine there anent in case the lord of the regality has no tyme to cognose.[35]

---

32 NRS, Grant Correspondence, GD248/49/2/16 A letter addressed to James Grant of Grant in September 1761, 'I left Moy on Saturday morning and lay that night at Castle Grant – alas! The latter place is in sad disrepair … your father [Ludovick Grant] was there for 2 months last summer' The correspondent goes on to lambast Sir James Grant of Grant, the young James' late grandfather: 'Sir James seems to have been a well-bred, genteel man, but so extremely indolent, so much engaged in London, and so inattentive to his proper concerns, that he certainly left the fortune of the family £15,000 worse than he found it'. Unfortunately, the letter is unsigned.

33 NRS, Papers of Alexander Grant of Grant, GD248/18/4/41.

34 Grant Court Book 3, 13/5/1715, p. 76.

35 Grant Court Book 4, 28/11/1723, p. 78.

Whether the business before the court was a serious matter clearly demanding their personal attention, or was routine and easily handled by a subordinate, it appears the purpose of the laird's appearance was the same: to show themselves to their dependants whilst playingthe role of paternalistic landlords, exercising this function with diligence as the following examples show.

Ludovick Grant succeeded to the Grant estates in 1665 upon the death of his father James. He returned to assume the management of his Highland estates in 1668 after completing his education at St Andrews. He first appeared as a bailie at courts in 1674, 1675 and 1676 on each occasion sitting alongside one of his baron bailies.[36] Two of these courts were justice courts convened to try notorious thieves, one of whom was executed upon the orders of the laird. In these cases, Ludovick was clearly sitting to show that the laird took the responsibility for upholding the law on his lands with the utmost seriousness, by dispensing justice in some of the most important cases personally and showing himself to his vassals. This is a practice that was repeated in later cases. Appearances in person also served to impress the importance of his own estate policies upon his tenants.[37] For instance, in March 1700 Ludovick presided as lord of regality over his own court when an important act for the preservation of forestry on his estate was enacted by him and his bailie.[38] By appearing personally Ludovick was also playing upon ties of kinship. His tenants were more likely to obey the orders of their clan chief if they were issued in person.

It was customary for the laird to appear alongside one of his bailies when presiding over the court. There are only two exceptions to this in the Grant court books. Both examples relate to the slaying of Francis Grant younger of Logie, son of John Grant the laird of Logie and Moyness in 1700.[39] Alexander Grant, newly appointed as bailie principal of his father's regality, presided alone to decide the fate of the killers and the distribution of the escheat; a month later he presided again to determine the punishments to be handed down to three women who tried to aid the killers.[40] Alexander's appearances in these cases are very significant. They demonstrate their seriousness, requiring the judgement of the laird and clan chief, being as he was the ultimate source of justice

36 NRS, Baron Court Extracts, GD248/76/2, fos., 123,112, 120.

37 The Grants of Grant were not alone in continuing to appear as bailies in their own court. Sir Archibald Grant of Monymusk presided over a head court of his barony in October 1734 to warn tenants against meddling with his woods; Hamilton, *Selections from the Monymusk Papers*, p. 219.

38 Grant Court Book 1, 7/3/1700, p. 149.

39 Grant Court Book 1, pp.155–9.

40 The case is discussed in greater detail in chapter 5 'Criminal Jurisdiction'.

in the regality. Furthermore, by taking difficult decisions upon themselves the lairds were able to use their own personal authority to give greater legitimacy to the decisions they took as bailies in their court. An execution was no small matter and the laird took the full responsibility for the decisions.

Display was also clearly important in the lairds' decision to preside over their regality court. During June 1720 James Grant presided over three courts alongside his bailie Dalrachney. James was infeft in the Grant estate in November of the same year and the timing of his appearances in court is important. They suggest that James was either trying to learn something of the operation of the court prior to his taking charge of the Grant estates, or that the laird in waiting was showing himself to the people of his regality. The three courts he attended were held over the course of a fortnight at Duthil, Rothiemoon and Milntoun respectively. The only parish missing from James's tour was Inverallan.[41] The impression made by James' appearance in these farm touns, presiding inside ordinary houses can easily be imagined.

2.2.2 *Bailies of the Regality of Grant*

By the eighteenth century the office had gained greater importance as the lairds spent increasingly little time in Strathspey and relied on their bailies to manage affairs in their absence. For this reason, the bailie of the regality court was the most important office holder both in the court and arguably in the wider landed estate. A commission of bailiary was the greatest gift of patronage that a clansman or gentleman could receive from their laird. These appointments also recognised that the laird of Grant did not necessarily exert effective control over all his territories thanks to the practice of wadsetting. In such areas as the upper Dulnain valley and in Abernethy, the cadet families of Dalrachney and Lurg assumed the role of bailies largely thanks to their status of quasi-heritors in their respective domains.

Preserved in the court books of the regality of Grant is a letter of bailziary.[42] This is the commission appointing the bailie principal of the regality, in this case Alexander Grant of Grantsfield, cousin of James Grant of Grant. This letter of bailziary was handed by the incoming bailie of the regality to the regality clerk to give formal proof of his credentials to act as bailie. The letter was then read aloud to the people assembled in the court. This commission is the ideal starting point from which to consider the role of the bailies of the regality of Grant. The commission sets out in precise terms the expectations placed upon

41 Grant Court Book 4, 2/6/1720 p. 33–4, 14/6/1720 p. 35, 16/6/1720 p. 36.

42 Grant Court Book 5, 11/12/1723, pp. 3–5.

a bailie of regality. Firstly, the commission makes clear that the laird could personally vouch for the candidate's ability to perform the office of bailie. Stating that the proposed bailie is, 'known to me, and that I have entire confidence in him and faithfullie carefully and diligently without partialitie discharge his office'. Secondly the candidate was required to have qualified himself in law by swearing all the relevant oaths. Emphasis was placed on the bailie being of, 'affection to the present government'. In 1723 ,when Grantsfield was appointed bailie, fears of Jacobitism were at fever pitch, as had been the case intermittently since 1689.[43] The purpose of such state oaths was to encumber the consciences of office bearers so as to ensure their faithful adherence to the sovereign.[44] The effectiveness of such oaths was primarily dependent upon the religious connotations associated with the swearing of oaths.[45] Grantsfield was required to swear three oaths: one of allegiance, another of assurance and finally one of abjuration.[46] This Grantsfield duly did, swearing the three oaths at Castle Grant on 18 December 1723, under the watchful eye of the laird.[47] None of the other bailies of the regality of Grant are recorded as having sworn these oaths, despite it being a legal requirement that all persons named as bailies of regality had to take the oath and assurance. This is probably attributable to missing records.

The commission also sets out in detail the powers bestowed upon the bailie of regality. Once qualified the bailie was empowered to: 'affix and affirm, hold and continue courts of the regality'. In practice this meant that the timing and location of a court were left entirely to the discretion of the bailie. The bailie was entitled to choose and elect the lesser officers of the regality court, 'with power also to my said bailie to substitute appoint and ordain bailzie deputes under him for exercing in the said office of bailiary in his absence as need requires and to creat other members of court as need requires and proper for ane regality court, for all which he shall be answerable'. This was of foremost importance, given that it was these men who would be doing most of the day-to-day work in the court, the office of bailie principal being to an extent an

43 Intriguingly Grantsfield was later suspected of Jacobitism. He appointed James Petrie, a known Jacobite, as his sheriff-substitute of Aberdeen in 1744. Later in 1746, his house was surrounded and searched by Government troops. D Littlejohn (ed.), *Records of the Sheriff Court of Aberdeenshire,* Vol III (Aberdeen, 1841), pp. 110–111.

44 A Raffe, Scottish State Oaths and the Revolution of 1688–1690, in S Adams and J Goodare (eds.), *Scotland in the Age of two Revolutions* (Woodbridge, 2014), p. 174.

45 Ibid, p. 188.

46 *RPS* 1689/6/11; 1690/4/161; 4 Ann C. 8.

47 Grant Court Book 5, 18/12/1723, pp. 11–12.

honorary position.[48] In practice the court records show us that it was customary for the incoming bailie principal to continue the existing members of the court in their roles. Grantsfield did exactly this upon taking up his commission on 11 December 1723: 'The said day the said bailzie continues the samen clerk and officers formerly constitute in each parish of the said regality'.[49] Bailie deputes also had to receive a commission which they were required to show to the clerk of the court, as in 1725 when 'John Grant of Delrachney bailzie depute of Glenchernick, Inverallan and Cromdale conform to his commission produced there anent ordinary members of court continued'.[50] Some bailie deputes, such as John Grant of Dalrachney, became the mainstay of the court; however, other deputes and substitutes had only a single appearance as bailie. In addition, these bailie deputes, could in turn could be replaced by substitutes. Bailie substitutes' commissions usually specified the number of courts that they could hold and the powers which they had been delegated:

> Mungo Grant of Mullochard bailie substitute of the said parish ... conform to ane act of deputatione grantit be the said bailie principal to the said substitute empowering him to hold ane six courts within the said parish three or four days at ane sederunt before Candlemas next reserving to decern for mealles and duties ryotes debtes and other matters debait as the said deputation initiat at this present court.[51]

We can make some assumptions about how bailie deputes were chosen. Certain families in the regality, namely those of Dalrachney, Lurg and Tullochgorum, appear to have held their positions as bailie deputes on a quasi-hereditary basis. Bailie principals simply respected this status quo when choosing deputes. On the other hand, these families were in their own right quasi-heritors within their respective domain thanks to the practice of wadsetting by the Grant lairds and their appointment as deputes was probably a recognition that these men held power and control over their respective parts of the regality. Awarding them the right to preside over courts was a pragmatic recognition of the conditions that existed on the ground: the most powerful and influential tenants deserved to exercise judicial power and could do so most effectively.

The other powers delegated to the bailie reflect those powers awarded to the lord of regality in his charter of erection:

48 For instance, Grantsfield only appeared in court on three occasions during his tenure.
49 Grant Court Book 5, 11/12/1723, p. 2.
50 Grant Court Book 5, 20/07/1725, p. 54.
51 Grant Court Book 3, 27/11/1711, p. 17.

> Cause with witnesses to all assizes and to pronounce and give furth decreets sentences and dooms theron. Cause execute the samen according to law, transgressors to punish, delinquents and absents to fine and amerciat, escheats fynes and amerciaments of court to uplift and exact, and to emit edicts for choosing curators during minoritie to all persons concerned and requiring the samen within my said regality, and duely and lawfully cause execute and proclaime brieves ... and to repledge.

The letter of bailziary reveals the perquisites that the laird of Grant's bailie could expect to receive for the execution of his office:

> And lastly my said bailie for his faithful administration in the said office of bailziary is to have this present letter of bailziary all the bailzie darraiks and herezalles of Strathspey during his encumbency as said is (reserving for my own use [i.e. the laird] and desposal so much of the said bailie darraciks and so manie of the said herezals as I shall judge proper and convenient)

The bailie darracks was a labour service owed by Grant tenants to the bailie. The service does not appear in tenants' written tacks; however, the specific nature of the burden is revealed in a letter written by William Lorimer (tutor and advisor to Sir James Grant of Grant) in 1763:

> The tenants have always been in use to pay to the chamberlain bailey-darachs services to the bailey or factor, one day for leading his peats, one day for shearing or cutting down his crop, one day for tilling, one day for spreading his dung, every tenant pays this according to what land he possesses.[52]

The court records show people being fined for non-performance of this duty. The herezald was the bailie's right to claim the best article of a deceased tenant's livestock.[53] This calp was effectively a tax paid by dependants of the Grants in return for enjoying the protection of the laird and the benefits of membership of the clan during their lifetime.[54] The OSA entry for Abernethy

52 NRS, Letter from William Lorimer to Sir James Grant, GD248/38/1.

53 On Tiree herezalds were payable by sub-tenants to their tacksman, who in turn owed herezald to the Dukes of Argyll upon their own decease. It is not clear if this was the case in Strathspey, Cregeen, 'The tacksmen and their successors', p. 106.

54 Cathcart, *Kinship and Clientage*, p. 87.

claims that herezalds ceased to be uplifted by the Grants as of 1738.[55] The only reference to be found in the Seafield Muniments to herezalds is in the estate accounts from 1680, where it is recorded that livestock to the value of £203,6,8 was claimed by the laird from eighteen deceased tenants.[56] This unfortunately gives us no indication if any share was left for the baron bailies after the laird had taken his part. In addition to these perquisites the bailie of the regality was entitled to one tenth of fine money exacted upon ecclesiastical delinquents.[57] It is unclear if the bailie was entitled to a similar proportion of other fines uplifted in the course of his judicial business. Equally unclear is whether bailies were permitted to keep a share of goods escheated by criminals convicted in the regality court. The OSA claims that the bailies of the regality were well known to have kept all fines and escheats determined by the court; however, the writer, Rev. John Grant, is often unreliable. The historian William Cramond, who wrote a short history of the regality, disputed the claim made by Rev. John Grant as ridiculous, but it is unclear whether Cramond had found any factual basis from which to attack the assertions made in the OSA.[58] Regardless, it is debatable whether these benefits were regarded as the main attraction of performing the office.

The offices of bailie and chamberlain were often combined on Grant's Strathspey estates. This meant that the incumbent was also in receipt of a £200 p.a. salary in addition to the bailie's perquisites. Men, such as James Grant of Gelloway, who held both the office of bailie and chamberlain and exercised both personally must have found most of their time taken up by these roles, leaving little time left over for attending to their own land holdings. That Gelloway had his own chamber at Castle Grant (which continued to bear his name long after his death) is further indication of the large amount of time that bailies expended at the service of their laird.[59] Nonetheless, despite potentially small financial gains, and the risk of neglecting their own affairs, the office of bailie was prestigious. In Strathspey, the bailie appears to have ranked above all the other gentry in the clan and on the estate beyond the immediate family of the laird. There may also have been a sense of duty attached to helping uphold law and order. On a practical level appointment as bailie allowed them to exercise a close level of control, not only over their own rental or wadset

55 Sir J Sinclair (ed.), *The Statistical Account of Scotland, Abernethy and Kinchardine, Inverness*, Vol. XIII (Edinburgh, 1794), at 152.

56 NRS, Grant Legal Papers, GD248/18/1, fo. 16.

57 Grant Court Book 2, 08/12/1703, p. 17.

58 Cramond, *The Court Books of the Regality of Grant*, pp. 4–5.

59 Fraser, *Chiefs of Grant*, Vol. I, pt. I, p. xlii.

lands, but over the entire Strathspey estate. Arguably this power only increased over time as the Grant lairds came to spend increasingly large amounts of time in Edinburgh and London. In this sense the bailie was more than a judicial officer: he was the laird's representative.

2.2.3 *The* Fine *of Clan Grant: John Grant of Dalrachney*

A case study of John Grant of Dalrachney, who made the most appearances of any of the bailies of the regality of Grant during the period of study, reveals much about the men who discharged the role of bailie and the society in the regality during the period.

John Grant of Dalrachney made his first appearance as bailie of Glenchernick and Duthil on 18 November 1705, taking over the role from Duncan Grant of Mullochard. He would continue to act as a bailie until his death over thirty years later.[60] In common with all but three of the bailies recorded as presiding over the regality court, John Grant of Dalrachney was a member of the extended Grant kin group and was a distant cousin of the Laird of Grant, being descended from John Grant of Freuchie the fourth laird. The Grants of Dalrachney were a cadet branch of the Grant family, first holding lands in Glenchernick during the early part of the seventeenth century. These were added to over the next hundred years elevating them to amongst the most powerful of the cadet branches of the clan by the early eighteenth century. The power and local influence of cadet branches of the Grant family, such as the Grants of Dalrachney, are important when considering why certain men were selected as bailies. Nearly all the other bailies of the regality share a similar family history to the Grants of Dalrachney within their own respective demesnes.

The practise of bestowing patronage upon these branches of the clan was part of a wider pattern of behaviour exercised by the clan chiefs to engender amity and loyalty between the disparate branches of the clan and above all to their chief. The closeness of these cadet branches of the clan to the laird's family can be illustrated by several social conventions practiced between the laird and his bailies. For instance, in the case of the Grants of Dalrachney, they were

---

60 Fraser states that John Grant of Dalrachney died in 1735. Correspondence between Colonel Lewis Grant of Dunphail and his brother Sir James Grant of Grant in March 1735 certainly suggests that Dalrachney was seriously ill: 'I came here [Inverlaidnan] last night and found Dalrachnie very ill of a severe cold and shortness of breath, he began to droop fast and really Im affray'd … that he will not last long'. (NRS, Letter on local politics, GD248/47/4, fo. 50). However, court petitions continued to be addressed to John Grant of Dalrachney into 1736. (NRS, Baron court petitions, GD248/431/4, fo. 1).

selected by Ludovick Grant of Grant to be the foster family to one of his sons who lodged with the Dalrachney family in the 1690s; the practice of fostering cemented ties of kinship within the clan and was a mark of the social respect afforded to the cadet branch by their superiors.[61] Francis Grant, who was one of the younger sons of Sir James Grant of Grant, also lodged with Dalrachney in 1729.[62] In another instance, Alexander Grant younger of Grant agreed to be one of the curators of the third son of James Grant of Gelloway, bailie from 1690–1702.[63] A further mark of the affection and respect that the heads of the cadet branches of the clan enjoyed is evidenced by the striking series of portraits of the clan commissioned by Alexander Grant of Grant and his brother James between 1713 and 1726. Amongst the portraits of close family and clan gentry, the artist Richard Waitt produced portraits of several bailies: John Grant of Dalrachney, Robert Grant of Lurg, Mungo Grant of Mullochard, Patrick Grant of Tullochgorum, George Grant of Clury, Alexander Grant of Grantsfield and John Grant of Burnside in Cromdale. These portraits hung alongside paintings of the lairds and their family in the gallery at Castle Grant. That the laird of Grant wished to surround himself by images of his trusted office-bearers, as he was surrounded by them in the day-to-day administration of his estate, is surely a display of the esteem in which these men were held.[64]

The Grant lairds had working relationships with the cadet families stretching back over several generations. Many of the notable cadet branches held estate offices on what seems to have been a hereditary basis. Thus, in the case of John Grant of Dalrachney his grandfather (also John Grant of Dalrachney), was factor and bailie of Glenchernick earlier in the seventeenth century, whilst John's son Alexander was also subsequently a bailie of the regality of Grant.[65] Several generations of the Grants of Lurg, Tullochgorum and Gelloway also performed the role of bailie on what appears to have been nearly a hereditary

61 S Nenadic, Lairds and Luxury, *The Highland Gentry in Eighteenth-century Scotland* (Edinburgh, 2007), pp. 46–7; Cathcart, *Kinship and Clientage*, pp. 80–82. J Logan, *The Scottish Gael; Or, Celtic Manners, as Preserved Among the Highlanders: Being an Historical and Descriptive Account of the Inhabitants, Antiquities, and National Peculiarities of Scotland; More Particularly of the Northern, Or Gaelic Parts of the Country, where the Singular Habits of the Aboriginal Celts are Most Tenaciously Retained*, Vol. I (Inverness, 1876), p. 177; NRS, Estate Accounts, GD248/108/16, fo. 8.

62 NRS, Estate Papers, GD248/113/7, fo. 19.

63 NRS, Bond to James Grant of Gellovie, GD80/369.

64 For more on these portraits see: M B Jones, *I, Richard Waitt, picture drawer: Portraits of a Highland Clan* (Grantown-on-Spey, 2017).

65 Fraser, *Chiefs of Grant*, Vol I, pt. II, p. 526.

basis [See Figure 1].[66] Additionally, men such as Dalrachney were able to obtain patronage for family members by virtue of their office. For instance, in 1706 Dalrachney was able to award the job of the collector of a tax to fund a bounty for vermin hunters to his brother Alexander.[67] This was a lucrative position; half of all the money uplifted was allocated to pay Alexander's fee. Robert Grant of Lurg managed to obtain the same position for his sons James and William in 1727.[68] In this way the gentry found it possible to advance the interests of their family.

John Grant of Dalrachney was a tacksman and wadsetter. Of the twenty-four bailies recorded in the court records twenty were tacksmen on the Strathspey estates, with eleven of those holding their lands by wadset (the remaining four were lairds in their own right in other parts of Moray). Both tacksmen and wadsetters exercised a cultural and social role in the community that was indispensable to the Grant chiefs.[69] Creegan has written that tacksmen were the 'native leaders and natural cement of Highland society'.[70] In many ways Dalrachney epitomised this class of powerful and independent men. Dalrachney was infeft in the wadset lands of Kinveachy-robie and Lethendry-chule in 1705, the same year that he first appeared as bailie. It is suggested that his elevation to the status of wadsetter was the cause for his appointment as bailie, (he later added the wadset lands of Lethendry-veole, Meikle and Little Dalrachnies, Forigens, Wester Duthil and Biannach to his possessions).[71] This was also the case with other bailies such as George Grant of Clury, who became a bailie after he contracted wadsets for the lands of Kinveachy and Lethendry-chule in 1724 (after they had been redeemed from Dalrachney).[72] The documents surviving from the appointment of Alexander Grant of Grantsfield as

66 The close links that certain Strathspey families had with the court is also seen in other roles besides that of bailie. For instance, the Blair family had a relationship with the baron and regality courts enduring for several generations. James Blair, son of the clerk David Blair, was appointed as the Procurator fiscal of the regality in 1712, when he first appears in the court records. He continued to perform the duties of fiscal over the next 15 years. Whilst, in 1722, when David Blair ceased to be clerk of the regality, Ludovick and John Blair had one appearance each as clerk of the court.

67 Grant Court Book 2, 09/12/1706, p. 84.

68 Grant Court Book 5, 11/11/1727, p. 135–6.

69 Taylor, *The Wild Black Region*, p. 156.

70 Cregeen, 'The tacksmen and their successors: a study of tenurial reorganisation in Mull, Morvern and Tiree in the early eighteenth century', p. 96.

71 NRS, Papers relating to the granting of wadsets to Grantsfield and Dalrachney 1723, GD248/163/5 Dalrachney was infeft in wadset lands of Kinveachy and Lethendrie in 1705 in terms of a disposition from Patrick Grant of Dalvey granted in 1701.

72 NRS, Rental of Glenchernick, GD248/23/1/5.

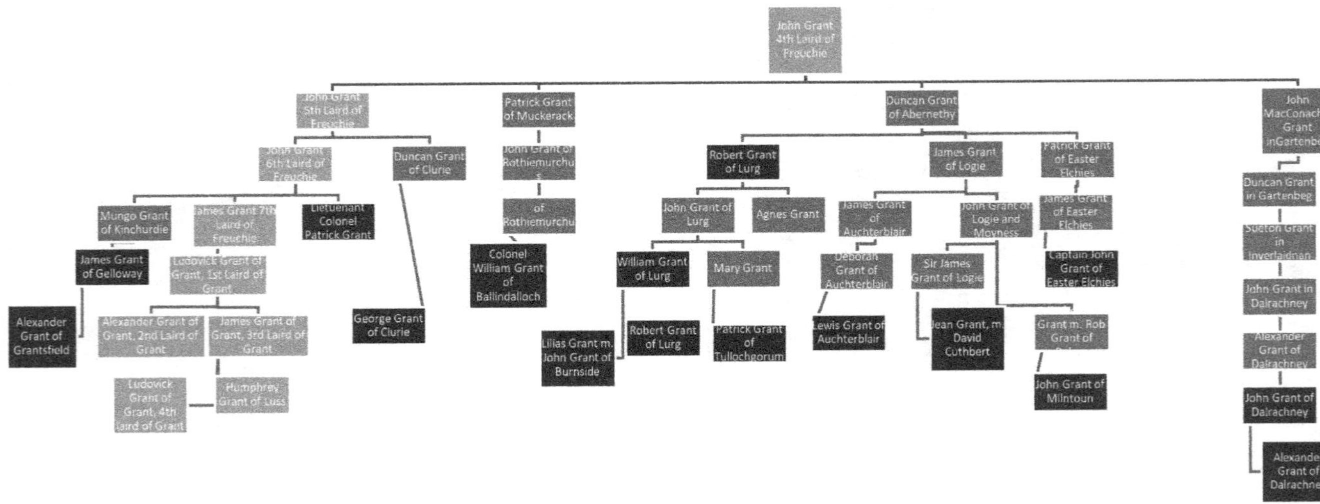

FIGURE 1 The Bailies of the Regality of Grant (marked in black)
SOURCE: THE AUTHOR

bailie in 1723 suggests that commissions of bailziary sometimes accompanied contracts of wadset.

The source of the gentry's power really lay in the practice of subletting. The practice of subletting their tack and wadset lands meant that most of the population of the regality were in fact tenants of the tacksmen rather than the laird, giving the tacksmen direct control over their dependants who made up most of the regality's inhabitants.[73] Tacksmen were responsible for organising their subtenants. Of course, the most important part of this management meant uplifting rentals and their conversion into cash for payment to the laird, they also ensured that military and labour services were discharged. This managerial role, and their status as cultural and social leaders of the clan and estate, gave the wadsetters and tacksmen an authority over, and knowledge of their subordinates which was invaluable to the operation of the court. The status of bailies as social and cultural leaders of the community is reflected in a memorial sent to Alexander Grant of Grant, probably in 1715 or 1716: 'a baillye and chamberlane may be appointed with convenience from London ... such measures ought to be taken to engage the whole country to concur in the execution of the law for the preservation of the family'.[74] Clearly the role of bailie was essential to the continuance of Grant control over Strathspey. It was understood that a bailie needed to command the respect of the people whilst also enjoying a degree of popular support. This is one of the respects in which it may be argued that the government of the community was participatory. In turn the tacksmen, as with gentry across Europe, were arguably the group of people with the greatest interest in the effective operation of the regality court, as an effective legal system was for them especially desirable, as they required it to help control their subordinates and protect their property rights.[75] For these reasons tacksmen, in theory, were the only men who could reasonably be expected to be able to exercise the office of bailie on a day to day basis.

Many of the clan gentry were wealthy men, largely by virtue of the rental income derived from their subtenants. By dividing and sub-letting the majority of their rental lands the tacksmen were able to live effectively rent free, whilst still retaining the best portion of the land to farm in their own hand. Participation in the cattle trade and military service provided other revenue streams for the Strathspey tacksmen. Wadsetters, on the other hand, paid no rent at all (besides some who paid small augmentation rents to the laird to compensate for inflation). In the case of Dalrachney, by 1710, he had

73 Taylor, *The Wild Black Region*, p. 21.

74 NRS, Memorial anent disorders in Strathspey, GD248/22/4/21.

75 C W Brooks, *Law, Politics and Society in Early Modern England* (Cambridge, 2008), p. 280.

thirty-eight subtenants and their families on his wadset lands alone, realising an annual rental for him of some £725, none of which went to the laird.[76] All of Dalrachney's lands were in the parish of Duthil which had a total rental of some £2000. When we consider that nearly all the land in the parish of Duthil was wadset to various gentlemen at that time, both the power of the gentry and the diminution of the Grant rentals becomes clear.

The intermediary role of the gentry in the collection of rentals did not go uncriticised. One anonymous, mid-eighteenth-century visitor to Strathspey made his dislike clear in a letter to the laird of Grant:

> Oh that word wadset cutts me to my very soul-I hope heaven will allow me so many days on this Earth as to see every vestige of wadsets on your estate effaced and destroyed. They are vermin that waste your substance and tyrrants that live on the blood and marrow of the poor.[77]

Whilst the source of the gentry's wealth came at the expense of both their laird and subtenants, the gentry remained the main source of credit both for the Grant lairds (through money lending and wadsetting) and also for their subtenants.[78] The social status of wadsetters such as Dalrachney, was underpinned by the fact that they were in the position to lend money to men of higher standing such as the laird of Grant. The Grants of Delay, Lurg and Burnside in particular, were major creditors of the laird and their appointment as bailies was in part thanks to their willingness to lend and sometimes forgo repayment. These appointments illustrate how the bailies and gentry had their own financial interests in the success of the Grant estates; a success they could help promote by effective use of the courts. This is further emphasised by the appointment of several major creditors from outwith the regality as administrators and bailies of the Grant estates in 1711 to recoup loans made to the laird of Grant. These men included Colonel William Grant of Ballindalloch and Alexander Duff of Drummuir.

John Grant of Dalrachney was the most successful of all the Strathspey wadsetters, crowning his possessions with a long nineteen-year tack of the lands and toun of Inverlaidnan in 1711; in the following year this tack was extended to fifty-seven years. This enabled him to unite all the lands held by his forebears which would become the base for his family throughout the eighteenth

76 NRS, Estate Rentals, GD248/67/1.

77 NRS, Grant Correspondence, GD248/49/2/16.

78 See, for instance, the wife of Gartenmore lending to sub-tenants, NRS, Declarations of Mullochard's witnesses against Lord and Lady Grant, GD248/22/2/35, fo. 3.

century.[79] Such was his success that he became the first of the Strathspey gentry to construct a modern stone mansion with a slated roof upon his lands [see Illustration 2].[80] Buildings and land acquisitions such as those seen at Inverlaidnan, betray the underlying quest for status which underpinned the very nature and purpose of wadsetting for the Strathspey gentry. It was a means for social climbing, the first rung on the ladder to the ultimate goal of landownership. Their social role as bailies only served to further enforce their notions of status and role as the leaders of the community.

This quest for status inevitably threatened the social position of the laird. For instance, John Grant of Dalrachney was in regular correspondence with other north east landowners such as the Duke of Gordon, for whom he was also acting as a bailie. In these letters Dalrachney is frequently referred to as 'the laird of Dalrachney'.[81] Such social aspirations must have piqued the Grants of Grant who were, after all, the real lairds of Dalrachney. Whilst the wadsetter-bailies were predominantly kinsmen of the laird and relations were usually friendly, the necessity of courting them as an essential source of credit and as managers on the estate could lead to antagonism between laird and bailie. As a result, the wadsetters were increasingly viewed as a necessary evil by the lairds who viewed the financial success of the wadsetters with envy and who believed it had been accumulated to their prejudice. An agreement reached between Sir James Grant of Grant and Alexander Grant of Grantsfield in 1723 reveals the uneasy relationship between the lord of regality and his bailie John Grant of Dalrachney.[82]

79 NRS, Minute Book of the Managers of the Grant Estate, GD248/37/1, p. 121.

80 NRS, Letters on local politics, GD248/151/11. Dalrachney entered into a contract with Alexander Grant of Grant in November 1711 to complete a 'ston house ... not exceeding eight hundred merks' within two years or surrender the tack of Inverlaidnan. However, it seems that the construction of the house had still not commenced in January 1717 as Dalrachney wrote to Alexander Grant of Grant at this time complaining that drawings for the planned house sent to him by Alexander were too expensive and worth more than his right in the land (NRS, Grant Correspondence, GD248/170/3, fo. 39). It seems the insistence that wadsetters such as Dalrachney and Clury build stone houses, was an attempt by Alexander Grant to improve his own estates without incurring any immediate cost, by playing upon the social aspersions of the wadsetters. At length, the house at Inverlaidnan was completed, and Prince Charles Edward Stuart stayed in the house as a guest of John Grant of Dalrachney's son Alexander on the night of 15 February 1746. The house of Inverlaidnan was ruinous by the mid-nineteenth century. It appears that Alexander Grant also made agreements with other wadsetters such as George Grant of Clury to construct stone houses on their wadset lands. (NRS, Grant Correspondence, GD248/170/1, fo. 81).

81 NRS, Letter from Dalrachney to the Duke of Gordon, GD44/28/14, fo. 52.

82 NRS, Papers relating to the granting of wadsets to Grantsfield and Dalrachney 1723, GD248/163/5.

ILLUSTRATION 2 The ruins of John Grant of Dalrachney's mansion at Inverlaidnan. This was first stone house in Strathspey and symbolic of the prestige and wealth accrued by Dalrachney. Following a fire it was partially rebuilt by his son Alexander. Prince Charles Edward Stuart passed a night here in 1746
SOURCE: THE AUTHOR

The power and lands accumulated by John Grant of Dalrachney had come to be resented by Sir James Grant of Grant the new laird. James sought to break the power of the old wadsetters, who were haemorrhaging money from the estate's rental books. The new laird planned to start with Dalrachney 'considering that the said John Grant of Dalrachnie ... hath exorbitant advantages by the said wadset rights. The annual rents of the moneys for which the said lands are redeemable being far under and bearing no manner of proportion to the rent of these lands'.[83] For several years the estate records show that the lairds of Grant had desired to redeem the lands alienated by them through extensive wadsetting. However, they could not find sufficient capital to redeem the wadsets outright. In 1723 a plot was hatched to undermine the regality's most powerful wadsetter.

83 NRS, Papers relating to the granting of wadsets to Grantsfield and Dalrachney 1723, GD248/163/5.

Sir James Grant and his son Humphrey Grant made a contract with Alexander Grant of Grantsfield, a distant cousin, who was the son of former bailie James Grant of Gelloway, whereby Grantsfield paid to redeem the wadsets of Lethendrie, Kinveachy-robie, meikle and little Dalrachnies, the half davoch of Wester Duthil, two auchten parts of Binanach croft, and Lynesail all held by John Grant of Dalrachney. In return Grantsfield would receive a nineteen-year tack of these lands and be appointed as bailie principal of the regality of Grant.[84] On 20 February 1724 Dalrachney was informed that his wadset lands were to be redeemed at Whitsunday and that he was to go to the parish churches of Cromdale and Duthil to receive the redemption money owed to him.[85] Thereafter he was to be offered short tacks of his former wadset lands pending Grantsfield's own infeftment. On the final day of February 1724, Sir James Grant's procurator, Dalrachney, William Grant of Delay, and Patrick Grant of Dalvey gathered at Dalrachney's mansion at Inverlaidnan to retour Sir James Grant in the wadset lands formerly held by Dalrachney. Dalrachney subsequently appeared at Duthil church to accept payment of the sum of the redemption money owed to him. However, Dalrachney was not prepared to be deprived of his *duthcas* without a fight: he refused to appear at Cromdale kirk and proceeded to dispute the legality of the redemption by arguing that the redemption premonition was invalid.[86] It transpired that only two years previously in 1722, Sir James Grant had made a contract with Dalrachney prolonging Dalrachney's possession of his wadset lands and barring James from initiating a redemption of the lands for nineteen years. Amidst the legal wrangling Grantsfield had already taken infeftment in Dalrachney's wadset lands of Wester Duthil, Lethendrie-chule, Kinveachy-robie and was now in possession; however, despite this the laird was forced to back down and renounce the contract with Grantsfield. Dalrachney was regranted his former lands in wadset, with the lands of Deshar being offered as compensation for the lands of Wester Duthil, Lethendrie-chule and Kinveachy-robie which Dalrachney accepted as having been redeemed.[87] Thus, far from being undermined, John Grant of Dalrachney found his position stronger than ever. It would be another fifty years until the lairds of Grant finally succeeded in dislodging the Grants of Dalrachney from their corner of the regality. This episode demonstrates the fragile relationship between the wadsetter-bailies and the lairds of Grant. The

84 Ibid.

85 Ibid.

86 NRS, Papers relating to the granting of wadsets to Grantsfield and Dalrachney 1723, GD248/163/5.

87 Ibid.

system of land tenure combined with the cultural, social, and judicial authority of men such as Dalrachney meant that the wadsetter-bailies were virtually immune to threats from the laird to their position in society.[88]

Following the debacle involving Dalrachney's wadset lands, Grantsfield made no further appearances as bailie and was quickly replaced as bailie principal by Colonel William Grant of Ballindalloch who was instated for a second time as bailie principal in June 1725.[89] Dalrachney extended his wadset lands still further, contracting wadsets for the lands of Granish, Miln of Aviemore, Docharn, Elan, Crofts of Inshtomach, Tullochgribanbeg, Delbuach and the davoch of Aviemore in 1727. Dalrachney himself also assumed the role of de facto bailie principal, with his son Alexander as his main depute.[90] At the same time that Dalrachney was acting as bailie of the regality of Grant he was also a bailie of the regality of Huntly within the lordship of Badenoch. This is further evidence of the power and respect afforded to the man chosen to be the representative of both the laird of Grant and the Duke of Gordon in Badenoch and Strathspey respectively.[91]

2.3 Conclusion

It has been written that 'for every Highland clan the hereditary right or power to do justice was the indispensable key to discipline, cohesion and effectiveness'.[92] To an extent this is true; however, the regality court of Grant reveals much more about the relationship between clanship and heritable justice in the early eighteenth century.

The chiefs of clan Grant had a complex relationship with their rights of jurisdiction. For them the exercise of their rights of jurisdiction was at once: a paternalistic duty, an opportunity to foment political support amongst the gentry of the clan, a means to exercise control over their dependants, a chance for chiefly display and to a small extent a source of income. Contrary to what has been written of other jurisdictions, the Grant chiefs personally presided

88 See parallels in Badenoch in the 1770s, Taylor, *The Wild Black Region*, p. 156.

89 Alexander Grant of Grantsfield was appointed as J.P. of Aberdeenshire and a baron bailie to Sir Archibald Grant of Monymusk in May 1732; Hamilton, *Monymusk Papers*, p. 209. He would later go on to be appointed as sheriff principal of Aberdeen.

90 By the 1730s John Grant of Dalrachney was styled simply as, 'Bailie of the Regality of Grant' in court petitions.

91 See for instance, Dalrachney acting as bailie at a court at Ruthven in 1727, NRS, Court Books of the Regality of Huntly (Lordship of Badenoch), RH11/40/5, p. 121.

92 Lenman, *The Jacobite Risings in Britain, 1689–1746*, p. 141.

over their regality court reasonably often. Sometimes they did so alone or more often alongside one of their bailies or bailie-deputes. The most important appearances in the court of the lairds were when they presided over serious cases to show they took ultimate responsibility for justice in the regality and over their people. On occasions when the laird was not able to be present personally, as was usually the case, and instead one of their bailies was hearing a case, the bailie would often refer difficult decisions back to the laird for his personal consideration. The personal authority and justice of the laird obviously continued to carry a very great deal of importance. It is possible to go so far as to say that their personal authority carried as much weight as their powers of jurisdiction.

The gentry of the clan Grant are integral to gaining an understanding of the court. For them, perhaps even more so than the landowner, the regality court was of great significance. These men were the ones who had the most to gain from the effective operation of the court. Realistically, they were also the only people in society with the cultural and social authority to dispense justice over the body of sub-tenants who made up the wider body of the regality.

The gentry's role in the provision of justice suggests that we should re-evaluate the role of tacksmen in the eighteenth century. Taylor in his recent work, *The Wild Black Region,* presents strong evidence that tacksmen were crucial to the economic, cultural, and social success of several estates in Badenoch. His argument runs contrary to the popular conception that tacksmen were anachronistic parasites who were swept away by improvement and the demise of the clan system to the benefit of landowner and peasant. This revision of the role of the gentry is also true of Strathspey in the early eighteenth century. Even gentlemen who did not receive court or estate commissions as chamberlains, bailies or tax collectors had ample opportunities to participate in the operation of the regality court and in turn the governance of the community, for instance, by voting upon acts of court and economic regulations or by sitting on assizes. In this way it is arguable that the gentry were the effective managers of Strathspey and were largely responsible for directing and executing economic and social policies on the Grant estates. This was in addition to the gentry filling new roles as agents of central government: as J.P.s, commissioners of supply and serving in the independent companies.

Whilst the gentry of the clan were essential if the court was to operate effectively, the political interplay between laird and gentry was complicated by the practice of wadsetting. What was initially intended as a quick means by which the lairds of Grant could secure much needed cash whilst maintaining political influence turned into a poisoned chalice. The very men on whom the success of the estate and clan relied were at the same time a necessary evil – wealthy social climbers with their own political following. For the gentry, commissions of bailziary in the regality court, were like commissions as officers, integral to securing their own social status within the region. The Grant chiefs were wary of the social aspirations of these men who wielded so much control and independence, yet lacked the money or power to keep the wadsetters in check. Redemption of most of the wadsets was largely initiated only after the regality was abolished. This consolidation of land holding back into the hands of the Grant chiefs from the mid-eighteenth century onwards was perhaps aided by the dilution of the political and legal role of the gentry.

CHAPTER 3

The Regality Court and Its Procedures

This chapter describes the procedures which dictated how the regality court of Grant functioned, from the appointment of its officeholders to when and where courts were held.

3.1 Court Officials

3.1.1 *Clerks of the Court*

The reader of the court records of the regality of Grant, or indeed the wider Grant papers in the period from 1690 to 1722, cannot fail but to become well acquainted with David Blair the clerk to the court. It is in his scrawling, near illegible, antiquated secretary hand that the work of the court is recorded and preserved for the benefit of the modern-day researcher. Blair appears to have spent some time as a clerk depute to the sheriff court of Banff before being appointed as clerk to the courts in Strathspey.[1] He received his commission as clerk to the courts of Ludovick Grant on 2 January 1690 from the new bailie of Strathspey, Lieutenant Colonel Patrick Grant: 'The said day the said baylie did elect and choose ane David Blair not[ary] publict to be clerk to the said court who gave my oath de fideli administratioune'.[2] Thereafter Blair's story is indelibly interwoven with that of the court.

As clerk, Blair's duties were numerous and indispensable to the functioning of the court. His main duty was to take minutes of what passed in court. These notes were later written up into the actual court book which was the property of the clerk and resided in the clerk's custody; this is clear as it says so on front cover of each court book. The court record was of foremost importance. Should a case be appealed to the privy council or to the justice court, the court record was required. Should central government wish to investigate the work done by the court, for instance for the purposes of compensation in 1748, the court record was required. It was often necessary to refer to old cases, in which instances the court record was again required. The court books also formed an economic and administrative record, vital for the chamberlain,

1 Grant Court Book 1, January 1686, p. 5.

2 Ibid, 02/01/1690, p. 11.

 DOI:10.1163/9789004472549_004

procurator fiscal and others involved in the administration of both court and estate. If bearing responsibility for keeping a full and accurate record of court proceedings was not enough to occupy the working hours of the clerk, he was also responsible for functions entailed in the office of notary public, such as executing and witnessing deeds and notarial instruments. Taking advantage of his legal training as a notary, the clerk was able to advise the bailie on points of law when the need arose. Additionally, the clerk had to take the roll of suitors present in court at the start of each sederunt and might also be called to ingather any fine money at the bar.

The clerk was also attached to the laird's estate and was thus responsible for helping to compile rentals, accounts, sasines, tacks, or any document that might be required in the day to day operations of a Highland estate. Blair added to these duties by acting on occasion as the Grant family's law agent in the region, and as such can be found in the sheriff court records of Banff in 1700 attempting to repledge Patrick Brown on behalf of Ludovick Grant in the famous case against James MacPherson and the Browns, who were sentenced to hang by the sheriff for committing several robberies at markets in the north-east.[3]

The type of men who filled the role of clerk becomes clear when we delve deeper into the life of David Blair. The poll tax roll from Inverness-shire in 1699 records that Blair paid £4 in poll tax for his 5000 merks worth of stock.[4] With an ox being worth approximately twenty merks and a hogg or wedder sheep £1 in 1700, it can be appreciated just how wealthy Blair was, 5000 merks being approximately equivalent to 250 oxen or 3300 sheep. This meant that Blair was the second largest payer of the poll in the parishes of Cromdale, Inverallan and Abernethy, putting his wealth above tacksmen such as Patrick Grant of Tullochgorum (later a bailie of the regality court) and Ludovick Grant of Wester Tulloch who are also recorded in the poll tax roll. The estate records reveal that Blair drew a salary of £40 per annum, much less than his stock would have us expect. This means that men such as Blair must have been earning significant sums from their own private business contracted as notaries. The clerk also received a separate fee for each court action, boosting his earnings. David Blair was in such a strong financial position in the mid-1690s as to be able to lend money to Ludovick Grant of Grant.[5] He was also able to take advantage of the

3 J Stuart (ed.), 'Process against the Egyptians at Banff 1700', *Miscellany of the Spalding Club*, Vol III (Aberdeen, 1843), p. 175.

4 https://scotlandsplaces.gov.uk/digital-volumes/historical-tax-rolls/poll-tax-rolls-1694-1698/poll-tax-records-inverness-shire-item-1/6 E70/6/1/6.

5 NRS, Estate Accounts, GD248/83/2.

economic and demographic crisis of these years by entering into a tack of lands left waste by his neighbour John Grant in Ballachule.[6] Blair's status was such that in a petition of the heritors, wadsetters and liferenters of Invernessshire in 1701 he styled himself as David Blair *of* East Lethendrie.[7] However, for all his aspirations, Blair appears to have over-reached himself. In the estate rentals Blair is found to be owing £92. 19. 4. for failing to pay his rent in 1699 and 1700, just after he acquired his neighbour's waste lands.[8] Blair's financial malaise did not ease in the early years of the next decade, when he was unable to pay his whole rent in 1703, 1704, or 1705.[9] By 1706 he is styled as David Blair in Achroisk. Whether this change in tenancy constituted a move up or down in the world for Blair is unclear. Whilst the arable land in Achroisk was undoubtedly better than that higher up in Lethendrie he would not have had access to the extensive hill ground which enabled him to run so much stock.

Regardless of Blair's financial difficulties (which would appear to have been by no means unusual amongst his peers) he obviously enjoyed respect and status in the community. He was also evidently well regarded by his employers, accompanying them on hunting trips, with his hunting rifle being kept in Castle Grant for this purpose.[10] His appointment as a birlawman in November 1705 is also evidence of this.[11] Blair was obviously a man respected by both gentleman and commoner. In his role as a birlawman and constable, Blair is recorded as holding a court of the 'lands of Cromdale' alongside his fellow birlawman and elder Alexander Grant in Burnside of Cromdale to enforce economic acts of the regality court.[12] It is unclear whether this court was in fact a birlaw court. This was not the only time that Blair presided over a court; on another occasion he examined witnesses in a case concerning the ownership of a stray horse.[13]

Blair ceased to appear as clerk in 1722. His handwriting by this point has evidently become increasingly frail, suggesting he was of old age and possibly

---

6 NRS, Estate Accounts, GD248/108/16, fo. 3.

7 *RPS*, A1700/10/30.

8 NRS, Estate Accounts, GD248/108/16, fo. 3.

9 Ibid, fo. 9.

10 Fraser, *Chiefs of Grant* Vol 1, pt. 1, p. xlii. Inventory of guns and weapons in the Grant Armoury showed a long rifle engraved "Clerk to the Laird of Grant". David Cuthbert also had a gun in the Castle at this date.

11 Grant Court Book 2, 15/11/1705, p. 57.

12 Grant Court Book 2, 12/01/1705, p. 60.

13 Interestingly this court record is not in the hand of David Blair but another man, with Blair being unable to preside over the court and act as clerk at the same time. Grant Court Book 3, 06/10/1714, pp. 62–4.

infirm. Two of the men succeeding David Blair as clerk in 1722 were Patrick Blair and John Blair.[14] Whilst it is unclear whether these men were related to David Blair it seems highly likely. John Blair was a notary public and was the notary from whom Dalrachney took instrument of sasine in 1701 in Inverness.[15] However, neither man held the post of clerk beyond one sederunt of the regality court and appear to have been something of a stop gap replacement for the recently departed David Blair. The fourth court book, like its predecessors belonging to David Blair, finishes at Martinmas 1722. The front cover of the fifth court book reads, 'This book belongs to Alexander Cumming clerk of the Regality of Grant'; a permanent replacement meant a new court book belonging to the new incumbent.

3.1.2 *Procurators Fiscal*

Procurators fiscal played a prominent role in the regality court of Grant. The role of a fiscal was originally to ingather fines paid in court; however, over time the fiscal developed into a public prosecutor, helping to preserve the impartiality of the bailie presiding in a case.[16] Evidence of both roles can be found in the court books. The fiscal's main duty was to prosecute in criminal cases, acting in the public (read laird's) interest to uphold public authority and standards, whilst ensuring that any fine money that might be incurred as a result of the action was successfully uplifted.[17] Pursuers in criminal cases might pursue a prosecution independently (if they were the only party adversely affected and wished to seek compensation) or with the concurrence of the procurator fiscal of the regality where the offender had disturbed the laird's peace.

The original purpose of the fiscal, the ingathering of fines, remained a central element of the fiscal's function throughout our period of study. Fiscals, like bailies, often had a patrimonial interest in the sentence money paid to the bar, as in many jurisdictions their remuneration was usually drawn from this, though it is unclear whether this was the case in the regality of Grant.[18] John Finlay has written that fiscals were often unskilled, and by no means needed to have any kind of legal training. Thus, the ability of fiscals varied considerably.[19]

---

14 Grant Court Book 4, 31/07/1722, p. 84; 20/10/1722, p. 87. We also find another Blair: Alaster Blair sitting as bailie at a court held at Duthil; Grant Court Book 5, 15/12/1724, p. 40.

15 NRS, Papers relating to the granting of wadsets to Grantsfield and Dalrachney 1723, GD248/163/5.

16 J Finlay, *Legal Practice in Eighteenth Century Scotland* (Boston, 2015), pp. 319–20.

17 Ibid, p. 346.

18 Finlay, *Legal Practice in Eighteenth Century Scotland*, p. 348.

19 Ibid, p. 353.

In relatively remote areas such as Strathspey it would be reasonable to assume that fiscals were unlikely to be sophisticated lawyers. Their office generally required little knowledge of the law; for example, in the records fiscals were often responsible for the custody of strayed livestock until the rightful owner could be found.[20] The fiscal was also responsible for declaring that stray livestock had been recovered, in order that the rightful owner might have the chance to reclaim his property.[21] Inhabitants of the regality finding stray livestock were directed to hand the animal over to the fiscal.[22] Anyone who suffered loss as a result of waif livestock straying onto their land was able to claim reparation from the fiscal, a problem undoubtedly of great importance in a rural subsistence economy.[23] Other duties performed by the fiscal included the enforcement of suit and presence in the regality court.

There were several active fiscals within the regality at any given time, each responsible for their own parish. The first fiscal mentioned in the records is Gregor Grant in Culreach, who was continued in the role by bailie Lieutenant Colonel Patrick Grant at a court in January 1690.[24] He was procurator fiscal for Abernethy in 1696, and was still acting in the roll in 1711, demonstrating that it was possible to enjoy longevity in the post. Like the clerk David Blair, Gregor Grant was also appointed as a constable in 1712, showing that fiscals were drawn from the same group of trusted tenants as clerks and other public offices within the regality.[25]

3.1.3 *Officers*

The court's officers also feature prominently in the court records. Whilst much is clear about the functions of this office, there is little information about the men who held it. The officer was essentially responsible for the smooth running of the court, by ensuring that people complied with summonses and court decisions. Thus, it was the officer's duty lawfully to summon parties to court and to deliver precepts of removing to tenants whose tack was about to expire. On the court day he undertook the symbolic fencing of the court and was also responsible for calling the suitors and any parties and witnesses to the bar. If they failed to appear the officer called their name at the courthouse door three times, after which they were declared absent.[26] In the fencing of the court the

20 See Grant Court Book 5, 05/07/1728, 29/07/1728, pp. 147 and 152B.
21 Grant Court Book 3, 01/06/1715, p. 80.
22 Grant Court Book 4, 02/12/1720, p. 44.
23 Grant Court Book 5,17/05/1728, p. 145.
24 Grant Court Book 1, 02/01/1690, p. 11.
25 Grant Court Book 3, 25/11/1712, p. 31.
26 Dickinson, *Court Book of the Barony of Carnwath*, p. lxxxv.

officer was sometimes described as 'officer and dempster'.[27] Thus, the court officer was responsible for pronouncing the doom or sentence as laid down by the bailie. Following the court it was the officer's task to put into execution any court judgement involving arrestments and poindings and this might sometimes include apprehending and imprisoning those convicted or suspected of offences.[28] It was in the execution of these duties that we most frequently find court officers appearing in the court books, particularly when they were 'deforced' or forcibly prevented from carrying out their duty. The officers were also responsible for riding throughout the regality to make the date of the next court known and to publicise any new acts of court at places of worship and other gathering points. The regality officer was often also called upon by the kirk sessions of the regality to perform the same tasks but on behalf of the ecclesiastical court.[29]

The regality had several officers acting within Strathspey at any given time, as for instance, two officers compear as witnesses at a court in July 1697.[30] The area was too large for one man to carry out the role alone. The multiplicity of duties incorporated into the role could only have been carried out by a knowledgeable local person who enjoyed the cooperation of his peers, but also had a good knowledge of process and procedure within the court. The role of officer carried a great deal of importance: when he failed in his duty the work of the court was frustrated.[31] It is also clear from this record that officers were not necessarily literate men, which could clearly prove problematic in executing their duties effectively. In the high court case of Mungo Grant of Mullochard v. Ludovick Grant of Grant, one of the officers questioned in the precognition claimed he could neither read, write, nor speak English, a situation which was to help the laird circumvent due legal process.[32] It is unclear whether these individuals were literate in Gaelic; however, this seems unlikely.

Some of the court officers received a salary; however, most appear instead to have been paid a fee for each summons, poinding or arrest that they carried out.[33] In addition, the officer of the parishes of Cromdale, Inverallan and

27 Grant Court Book 1, 21/11/1690, p. 17.

28 Dickinson, *Court Book of the Barony of Carnwath*, p. lxxxvi.

29 This can be seen in the Kirk Session Minutes of the Parish of Abernethy: HA, Kirk Session of Abernethy Minutes, CH2/1054.

30 Grant Court Book 1, 20/07/1697, p. 112.

31 See chapter 8 'Land Tenure' for the implications of officers failing in their duty.

32 NRS, Declarations of Mullochard's witnesses against Lord and lady Grant GD248/22/3/35, fo. 2.

33 In 1719 Lewis Grant officer in Abernethy was paid a salary of £26. 13. 4., the same as William Cumming the laird's piper. However, in the same accounts Thomas Grant

Advie got possession of the 'officer's croft' near Castle Grant as payment for his services.[34]

3.1.4 *Birlawmen*

Birlawmen enjoyed an unusual position in the community. They held an office which allowed participation in the legal system, yet they drew their authority from being ordinary members of the community.[35] Birlawmen were appointed and sworn in open court, usually with four men serving in each parish.[36] For instance on 8 December 1703, four men were, 'appointed birlawmen of the lo[rdshi]p of Glenchernick ffor poyndings, apprysings and devisions of land and parting thereof or suchlyk betwixt neighbours … and to be payed by the imployer for each day'.[37] Whilst they were appointed with the approval of the laird or bailie, it was integral to the effectiveness of the role of the birlawmen that they acted by consent of the local community they served; this is what made their office unique. Evidence from other areas of Scotland and England, for the birlawman was a figure found in village communities across early modern Europe, suggests that birlawmen were elected by the community.[38] The participatory nature of the office allowed them to enforce measures for the good of the community and resolve neighbourly disputes in a conciliatory manner, acting as a bridge between the regality court and the local communities in the ferm touns. As birlaw courts were not courts of record, little material directly relating to their activities exist. What we know of their duties in Strathspey comes from the regality court books and estate records; however, this leaves us with only a shadowy understanding of their role. It appears that their principal duties in Strathspey included: the valuation of goods and gear at poindings, where two birlawmen were customarily paid to act as assessors; valuing holdings and goods in disputes over rent and compensation; settling boundary disagreements; entering tenants into possession of their holdings by witnessing the tenant labouring the ground; and enforcing court regulations.

---

officer in Castle Grant did not receive a salary for his position. NRS, Estate Accounts, GD248/113/7.

34 NRS, Rental of Cromdale Parish 1727, GD248/158/3/27.

35 For further see, D Sellar 'Birlaw Courts and Birleymen', in *Stair Society* Vol. 62, Miscellany VII (Edinburgh, 2015); and Dickinson, *Court Book of the Barony of Carnwath*, Appendix A, "The Burlaw Men", cxiii-cxvi.

36 This was also the case in Argyll. Sellar, 'Birlaw Courts', p. 167; and also, in northern England, A J L Winchester, *The Harvest of the Hills: Rural Life in Northern England and the Scottish Borders, 1400–1700* (Edinburgh: Edinburgh University Press, 2000), p. 45.

37 Grant Court Book 2, 08/12/1703, p.18.

38 Sellar, 'Birlaw Courts', pp. 176–7; Winchester, *The Harvest of the Hills*, p. 42.

The birlawmen were despatched to deal with issues where their own mediation was judged to be a more appropriate means of resolving local issues rather than taking them to law. They had the power to poind and fine; furthermore, in Strathspey they were instructed to appoint their own officers to be paid out of the fine money they uplifted.[39] Of the birlawmen in northern England, Winchester has written that enclosure and the disappearance of the commons led to their demise.[40] However, in Strathspey the process of enclosure and improvement in the second half of the eighteenth century appears to have brought extra work for the birlawmen who were often called to resolve boundary disputes on the new improvements which were notoriously poorly demarcated.[41]

3.2 How, Why and When Were Courts Convened?

3.2.1 *When?*

Court cases in the regality court of Grant were initiated by a written petition or bill of plaint from the pursuer to the bailie. The petition took the form of a letter giving a detailed description of the complaint or issue and the outcome sought by the pursuer:

> I John Geddes second lawful son of the deceist Thomas Geddes in Auchnahannet who am past 14 years of age humbly craves shows that there is an edict duly execute at my instance for choosing curators anent managing my affairs during my minority and charged to compear to this dyet therefore craves John Grant chamberlain of Strathspey and Lachlan Cameron in Auchnahannet may be admitted to act and do for me as any curators chosen be me for managing my affairs.[42]

Such a petition would often set in motion the process of holding a court because the regality court of Grant was generally convened as and when its services were required by commoner, gentry or laird alike.[43] If the case was sufficiently serious, as in the example given above, the bailie would convene a

39 Grant Court Book 2, 15/11/1704, p. 57.

40 Winchester, *The Harvest of the Hills*, p. 148.

41 NRS, Petition of William Cumming 1775, GD248/44/4/15.

42 NRS, Petitions to the Bailie of Grant, GD248/431/4, fo. 5.

43 Dickinson states this was also how the barony of Carnwath operated, Dickinson, *Court Book of the Barony of Carnwath* p. lxxvii.

regality court specifically to deal with that sole complaint. On the other hand, minor complaints such as resting debts and bloodwitts would be dealt with in the course of the general business of the court at the next scheduled court day. Sometimes courts were convened regardless of whether any plaints had been submitted to the bailie.[44] In such cases, petitioners were able to raise a complaint on the day in the courthouse; this might include handing up indictments for criminal cases. On occasions this system led to court days when no business was heard. This ad hoc system meant that in practice several months could pass between sederunts of the court should no urgent business require its services.[45] The absence of set court days was reflected in tenants' tacks. In the regality of Grant, tenants' tacks simply required tenants to give suit when required: 'and the said Alexander [tacksman] obliges himself and his ser[van] ts to give his suit and presence to the said Ludovick his courts of the said baronies upon lawful citation'.[46] Thereafter the parties were summoned to appear upon the appointed day by a written summons and bill delivered in person by the court officer. Witnesses and suitors also had summonses served upon them by the court officer.

Despite the irregular occurrence of courts, some trends in the distribution of court days do emerge. Firstly, the distribution of court days throughout the year relates to patterns in the agricultural calendar. Two of the quietest months in the agricultural year were the months of November and December; the greatest number of courts were held during these two months, with eighty and seventy-four court days respectively being recorded for the years 1695 to 1729. The greater number of courts in November especially, reflects the fact that the term day of Martinmas fell during this month and the court was required to meet to settle the payment of rents and other pecuniary obligations falling due following the harvest. There must also have been a backlog of cases which were not dealt with during the busy weeks of the harvest. July and June were the next busiest months for court days; this was another quiet period in the agricultural calendar, coinciding with the shieling period. April saw the fewest court days, with only eleven regality court days being recorded in this month during our period of study [See Table 1].[47]

---

44 For instance, Court at Ballintomb, Grant Court Book 3, 19/07/1716, p.95.

45 This study is based on surviving entries into the regality court books. It is obvious by comparison with other sources that the court books are not a complete record of the meetings of the regality court of Grant, and that, for whatever reason, many sederunts of the court were not recorded in the main court books.

46 NRS, Tack of Kylintra 1674, GD248/533/5, fo. 19.

47 Period of study being 1695–1729 inclusive. No records remain for 1718 and for some other years the records are incomplete.

TABLE 1 Court days by month

Month	Number of court days 1695–1729
January	50
February	57
March	16
April	11
May	28
June	66
July	69
August	23
September	12
October	16
November	80
December	74

Courts were infrequently held during the busiest months in the agricultural calendar: March and April were the months of ploughing and sowing, whilst September and October were the months of harvest. People found it easier to attend court when there was less work demanding their attention. A consequence of less work was increased idleness which often manifested itself in misdemeanours such as assaults, which also led to an increase in the number of courts during these times in the year.[48] Presumably people also put off their civil business until these quiet periods.

The second important trend revealed is that the number of court days was not decreasing over time [see Table 2]. Rather, the number of court days appears to have increased during the late 1720s. This tells us that there was still a healthy amount of business coming before the regality court of Grant.

Sederunts could last for several days. For instance, the court convened at Culnakyle in Abernethy during February 1696 sat for three days from 20 February to 22 February. A single meeting of the regality court could last for several days but be held in different locations; in 1697 the court sat for two days at Culnakyle on 29 and 30 November. The following day it sat at Lochend of Gaich before the business of court was carried on to the following day, 2

48 Grant Court Book 1, 13-22/02/1696, pp. 66–70.

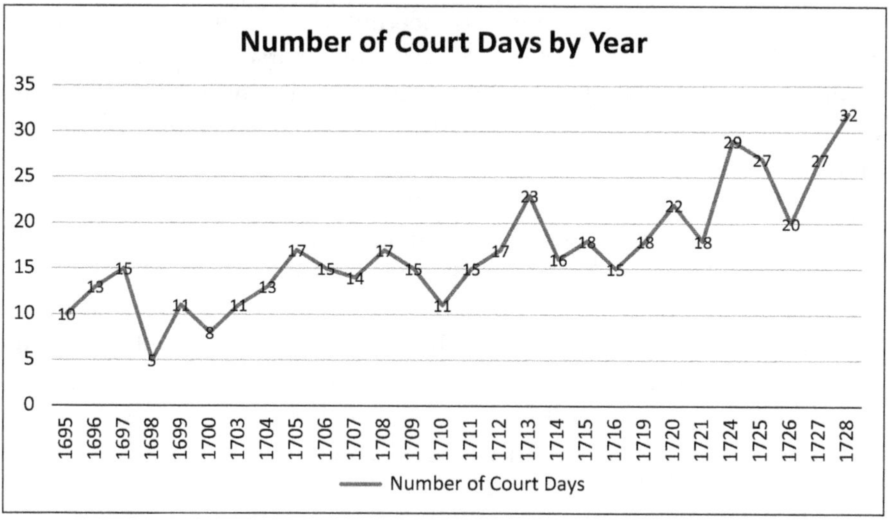

TABLE 2 No court records survive from 1702 or 1718, although other sources reveal that courts were held in these years. The other years for which very low number of courts days are recorded fall upon the years when court books were ended or begun: 1701, 1717, 1722 and 1723. It seems that some of the records from these years are missing as a result. The year 1729 is also incomplete. These years have been omitted from the chart

December, in Grantown, where the business before the court was finally concluded.[49] Occasionally two sederunts of the court were required to be held on the same day; these sederunts could also be held in different locations. For instance, on 13 May 1715 a head court of the regality visited both Culnakyle and Rothiemoon on the same day.[50] Culnakyle and Rothiemoon were neighbouring davochs, and their respective ferm touns were roughly a mile apart, meaning it was an easy task for the court to transfer from one township to the other. In early 1729 John Grant of Dalrachney held a morning session at Castle Grant, before the court then adjourned four miles to Ballintomb, around an hour's walk away, the court recommencing at three o'clock in the afternoon there.[51]

3.2.2 *Where?*

Besides fixing a date and time for the court it was also important to appoint a place for it to be held. The location of the next court would usually be

49 Grant Court Book 1, pp. 124–5.
50 Grant Court book 3, p. 76.
51 Grant Court Book 5, pp. 160–1.

announced at the end of the previous sederunt. In addition, the officer would ride throughout the relevant parts of the regality apprising people of the next sitting of the court. The choice of the location for the court fell to the discretion of the bailie, as can be seen from the commission appointing Grantsfield as bailie in 1723:

> With full and ample power, warrand and commission to him, as my said bailie to affix and affirm, hold and continue courts of the regality within the house of Castle Grant or any other place or places in the said regalitie he shall judge fit and proper for the better and more speedie administration of justice and accommodation and ease of the leidges residing within the bounds of the said regality and [illeg] that may repair thither and be concerned there as oft as need bees and as matters require.[52]

Some flexibility in appointing the location in which the court was to sit could be advantageous. A good example from within the parish of Abernethy can be found when the regality court convened at Comedge to resolve a boundary dispute. By sitting on the land at the heart of the dispute, it can be appreciated how well equipped the court was to resolve such disputes; physical evidence was readily at hand, and witnesses were much more likely to compear with the court meeting locally. Such practice had not been unusual in medieval Scotland where courts regularly resolved boundary disputes upon the disputed ground.[53] Within the township selected the court might be held either indoors or in the open air depending upon the season and number of people paying suit.

All jurisdictions in Scotland had to have a nominal caput where the jurisdiction was vested. In the regality of Grant the caput was the Grant's power base at Castle Grant[see Illustration 3], old caput of the barony of Freuchie.

Freuchie has a long-standing connection with the provisions of justice in the area; this is a feature common to most court sites in Strathspey where long continuity of practice is evident. Many court locations in the regality had been used as assembly sites for millennia. The primary example of a court site with ancient usage as an assembly point is Ballintomb (place of the hill) situated in the parish of Inverallan. This was the rallying point for clan Grant and the main place of assembly for courts in Strathspey. The long drumlin (often described as the moor of Ballintomb or Tom nan Carragh)[54] rising directly

52 Grant Court Book 5, 11/12/1723, pp. 3–5.

53 O O'Grady, 'The Setting and Practice of Open Air Judicial Assemblies in Medieval Scotland: a Multidisciplinary Study' (Unpublished Ph.D. thesis Glasgow, 2008), pp. 345–6.

54 Meaning hill of the pillars, referring to the standing stones.

ILLUSTRATION 3 Castle Grant, until 1696 known as Ballachastel. This was the seat of the lairds of Grant and caput of the regality. It continued in the ownership of the family until eventually sold in 1969
SOURCE: THE AUTHOR

above the Spey to the east, and above flat farmland to the West, had long been the location where courts were held within the old Lordship of Inverallan [see Illustration 4]. Before the erection of the regality court in 1696, Ballintomb was used by the Grants to hold united courts for all their lands and baronies in the area,[55] along with being the site chosen to hold their justice courts.[56] Eighty-nine courts are recorded at Ballintomb from 1658 to 1675 with a further 100 court days recorded there between 1690 and 1729.

The Grants were the last in a long succession of people in Strathspey to recognise the prominence and importance of Ballintomb, which sits at an important ferry point across the Spey (linking the parish of Abernethy with Inverallan) and at the junction of roads along the Spey and Dulnain valleys.

55 Dickinson states that whilst a baron might hold several baronies he was obliged to hold separate courts unless there had been a formal grant from the crown re-erecting the baronies as a united whole: Dickinson, *Court Book of the Barony of Carnwath* p.xxxvii. This was clearly not adhered to by the Grant family when they held a court of Strathspey. On the other hand, Dickinson also asserts that it was common practice for barons to hold several baron courts at once: Dickinson, *Court Book of the Barony of Carnwath*, p. li.

56 NRS, Baron Court Extracts, GD248/76/2, fos. 112 and 123.

ILLUSTRATION 4 One of the standing stones upon Tom nan Carragh, the court site for Ballintomb. The stones at Ballintomb were the rallying point for the clan and the site chosen to hold justice courts, along with being the site of common execution.
SOURCE: THE AUTHOR

Thus, Ballintomb was positioned at the focal point of movement and communication in the area [see Illustration 5]. The earliest evidence of Ballintomb's use as a place of assembly is during the megalithic period. Three standing stones survive upon the moor of Ballintomb. It is believed that the alignment of these stones was intended to mark the sunsets on the winter mid quarter days of Martinmas and Candlemas.[57] Intriguingly the mid quarter days were often dates when head courts were held next to the standing stones, suggesting a tantalising link between the megalithic and early modern periods in Strathspey. The practice of holding courts close to megalithic monuments was also to be found elsewhere in the regality, such as at Milntoun of Castle Grant, whilst in the 1660s there are several references to a court tantalisingly named 'The court of the fourstane'.[58] Until recently there stood a stone circle of four stones at Lynagowan by the Via Regia (a once major medieval road connecting

57 D Scott, 'Astronomical Survery of Three Groups of Standing Stones in Strath Spey, Scotland', *Journal of the History of Astronomy*, 15 (1990), pp. 56–8.

58 NRS, Baron Court Extracts, GD248/76/2, Fo. 60.

ILLUSTRATION 5 The moor of Ballintomb with Abernethy forest and the Cairngorm mountains in the distance. The arrow indicates the probable location of the regality gallows. The strategic positioning of Ballintomb is immediately clear, being visible to travellers from miles around.
SOURCE: THE AUTHOR

Strathspey with the Moray coast), just beyond the northern boundary of the parish of Cromdale. Much of the parish of Braemoray, where the stone circle was located, belonged to the Grants and this would appear to be the four stones that the court referred to.[59]

3.3 The Court Day

On the day of the court all those who had been warned 'generally or particularly' to attend the court that day, by having notice served upon them by the court officer, were required to be present in court by 10 am if it was a morning sederunt, or 3 pm if it was an afternoon sederunt.[60] Defenders who had been cited to appear but were not present in court by these times were then 'cried' three times by the court officer. If they did not appear in court by the third

59 I Keillar, 'Edinkillie Stone Circle', *Discovery and Excavation: Scotland*, (1972), p. 30. The site was later cleared in the 1970s; https://canmore.org.uk/site/15764/lynagowan.

60 Grant Court Book 2, 03/08/1705, p. 54; and Grant Court Book 5, 1729, p. 161.

call, then they were declared contumacious. This resulted in fines of £5 for servants and labourers, £10 for husbandmen/small tenants and £100 for gentry. Defenders who were contumacious were allowed a further three court days in which to appear and answer to the charges laid against them before being held to have confessed or ceded the case to the pursuer as in absentia upon their fourth absence.

The presence of those others warned to attend court was confirmed by the calling of the court roll by the clerk. Any found to be absent from this list were fined on the same scale as for defenders who were contumacious. The duty of suit and presence, the requirement that a tenant presented himself in person in court on specified days, was of great importance to heritable justice. Suitors composed the bodies of all such courts in Scotland. Although the bailie or less frequently the baron himself presided over the court, decision-making in criminal cases (during the first decade of this study) fell to the body of suitors, thus subjecting those indicted to the judgment of their peers.[61] It appears that tacks granted to tenants of the Grants did not specify certain days when the tenants was expected to give suit and presence, instead they were required to give suit when cited.[62] Courts were also advertised to the people of Strathspey at church and presumably by word of mouth. However, sometimes these provisions were insufficient and the inhabitants of the regality had to be warned to attend court by a pronouncement in the regality court itself. For instance, in July 1721 the lord of the regality of Grant, Sir James Grant, appeared in person at a court held at milntoun of Castle Grant and craved an act of court ordering that his vassals in Mulben, 'should be obliged upon the forsaid Tuesday of this instant to answer to ane head court of the said regalitie and give the suit and presence thereto'.[63] The laird of Grant must have had trouble getting the tenants of far flung Mulben, thirty miles down-river of Castle Grant, to attend courts in Strathspey. A similar problem was encountered with some even more distant inhabitants of the regality along Loch Laggan on the edge of Lochaber.[64]

The court could also pass by-laws determining or changing the times that a davoch had to give suit to the court. Thus, in 1724 the tenants of Balintomb were reminded that they were required by an act of court to attend at Milntoun of Castle Grant each year on the second Tuesday in June.[65]

---

61 Dickinson, *Court Book of the Barony of Carnwath* pp. lxxx and xciii.

62 NRS, Tack of Kylintra 1675, GD248/533/5, fo. 19.

63 Grant Court Book 4, July 1721, p. 65.

64 Vassals in Laggan failed to attend court when cited in July 1727 and were subsequently fined, Grant Court Book 5, pp. 125–6.

65 Ibid, 09/06/1724, p. 22.

References to suit and presence and contumacy appear most frequently in the final decade of the court records. This might suggest increasing reluctance by suitors to attend when they had no business of their own before the court. Unfortunately, there is insufficient evidence in the court records to test this hypothesis more fully. Contumacy was a persistent problem in the early eighteenth century in all Scottish courts.[66] The court records for the regality of Grant make it evident that this court was no exception to the general trend.

Following the calling of the suits the court was ceremonially fenced by the court officer, signified by the term, 'curia affirmata'. Only after the completion of this formality was the court legally competent to proceed as a court of law. This was the case for nearly all courts in Scotland, from parliament to barony but excluding the court of session.[67] The fencing of the court was an ancient ceremony, the purpose of which was to declare the inviolability of the court, its processes and judgements.[68] Thus, misconduct such as swearing in court was strictly frowned upon. John Grant in Mullochard discovered this to his cost in December 1693 when he was fined £5 for, 'his miscarriage and bad language before the court'.[69]

During the fencing of the court, the officer also had to designate which court was sitting. For several years following the erection of the regality in 1694 the court continued to be fenced as the 'Court of the lands, parishes and baronies of Strathspey'. The first time that the court was formally fenced as the 'Regality Court of Grant' was not until March 1700.[70] This court introduced important forestry legislation. During the next year the court was regularly fenced as a regality court; however, another two years were to pass until the next court designated as one of the regality was held to try a case of serous theft in December 1703. After August 1704 it was not until October 1707 that another court was fenced as that of the regality (to try two men accused of slandering the parish minister), the court being described as a parish or baron court during the interim. Thus, it appears that during the early years of the regality of Grant the court only sat as a full regality court to hear important cases. This changed after 1708 when the court was regularly designated as a regality court; however, even after this point the court frequently continued to sit as a baron or parish court. It is unclear why this distinction continued to be made. Davies argues that there were different types of regality: private

66 J Finlay, *Legal practice in eighteenth-century Scotland*, p. 347.

67 P J Hamilton- Grierson, 'Fencing the Court', *SHR* 21:1 (1923), pp. 54–62, p. 56.

68 Ibid.

69 Grant Court Book 1, 05/12/1693, p. 47.

70 Grant Court Book 1, 07/03/1700, pp. 149–150.

sheriffdoms and full regalities.[71] However, whilst practice in Strathspey could possibly be construed as evidence of this dichotomy, Davies' explanation is not convincing as he himself admits that even what he describes as 'full regalities' mostly operated as private sheriffdoms. A better distinction might be found along the lines of those regalities which were simply baronies with 'powers of regality' and those jurisdictions which had full regalian powers, regardless of whether they were actually exercised; this is a distinction which was drawn by the Lords of Session when judging the compensation claims of 1747.[72] All we can say with certainty from the Grant records is that the regality had greater powers than a barony but less than the session and high court of justiciary.

Following the fencing of the court, the bailie proceeded to business. In civil actions the petition of the pursuer was first read aloud in court. Any evidence or witnesses were then led by both parties, who swore oaths accordingly. Any witnesses giving evidence who resided beyond the boundaries of the regality were required to furnish evidence of their suitability as a witness. In practice this took the form of a testimony from their parish minister. In some cases, the letter of testimony was inserted into the court record.[73] The outcome of the case was usually decided by the bailie; however, in some difficult cases the bailie could refer the case up to the lord of the regality or choose to sit alongside several of the other bailies of the regality to hear the case. The bailie could decide to award the pursuer the remedy craved, modify the award or dismiss the case.

Procedure for minor criminal plaints was very similar to that employed in civil cases.[74] Typically pursuers sought restitution in addition to assythement, known as 'cost, skaith and damage', in both civil and minor criminal complaints.[75] The decision of the bailie regarding the petition was written on the reverse of the written bill and handed back to the pursuer in court. This answer then formed an extract which the pursuer could use to help enforce the bailie's judgement.

---

71 Davies, 'Law and Order in Stirlingshire', p. 250.

72 NRS, List of claims anent the Abolition of Heritable Jurisdictions, CS4/8 and CS4/9.

73 Grant Court Book 5, p. 151A.

74 Many acts which we would consider as crimes were rather regarded as delicts and thus required the payment of compensation to the victim rather than, or in addition to, a punishment to satisfy the King or lord. However, there were exceptions such as the pleas to the crown and other acts which required physical judicial punishment. Davies, 'Law and Order in Stirlingshire', pp. 63–70.

75 The issue of damages shall be dealt with more fully in ensuing chapters.

In serious criminal complaints prosecution proceeded by dittay handed in to the procurator fiscal prior to the court or in some cases during the sederunt itself:

> Intrand: John McEan Roy vic Coul vic Martin, Sorel McCaul vic Ewen vic Martin, Donald dow McJames vic Glashen
>
> The off[ice]r halving proclaimed three severall tymes if ther wer ane persone or persones that had anie dittayes to be gilven in ag[ains]t the persones above wri[tte]n to compear in tyme and place convenient and because none compeired therfor the bailzie judge above wri[tte]n has dismissed the said persones.[76]

The indictments were read before the court and the defender asked how he or she pleaded for each indictment. If he or she denied any part of the indictment, evidence was then led by the procurator fiscal and pursuer to prove the disputed points of the libel.

Until 1700 the outcome of such cases was always determined by an assize. Before the indictments were read out, the defender and their procurator were asked whether they had any complaints regarding the men chosen to sit on the assize.[77] If there were no objections then the fifteen men of the assize were called up to the bar to be sworn in groups of five. Assizors were selected before the court day and faced a fine of 100 merks if they failed to attend.[78] At a court convened to consider an indictment of theft on 20 July 1697 sixteen men rather than the usual fifteen were sworn to sit on the assize. The extra man was Robert Grant in Curr who was elected to be the assize's clerk. He was the laird of Grant's factor in Inverallan. Having an even number of assizors was not unusual in early modern Scotland. For instance, in the records of the baron court of Urie the number of assizors varied but never reached fifteen.[79] The men chosen to sit on assizes in early modern Scotland were not picked at random. Originally assizes in capital cases were restricted to men of property and from this pool of men, individuals were selected owing to their knowledge of the case and the position they held in society.[80] In the regality of Grant the

76 NRS, Baron Court Extracts, GD248/76/2, 24/07/1667, fo. 88.

77 NRS, Baron Court Extracts, GD248/76/2, 01/10/1675, fo. 112.

78 Grant Court Book 1, 13/08/1696, p. 88.

79 Barron, *Baron Court Book of Urie*, p. xi.

80 A MacDowall, Lord Bankton, *An Institute of the Laws of Scotland in Civil Rights: with observations upon the agreements or diversity between them and the laws of England* (Stair Society, 1993–5), p. 662. Alex II c. 3.

group of individuals who were selected to sit on assizes was drawn from the gentry and more substantial tenants, often holding large shares in multiple-tenancy townships. As a result, the number of men qualified to sit on assizes was relatively small; hence, we find the same men appearing frequently on assizes, which were particularly dominated by the tacksmen, the leaders of the community. Of the ten assizes recorded in the court books of the regality of Grant for which the names of assizors survive, sixteen individuals served on more than three of the assizes. Duncan Grant of Mullochard (later a bailie), and James Grant of Auchterblair (whose father and son were bailies and who himself was a chamberlain) served on seven assizes apiece. Other bailies who served on assizes were: John Grant of Dalrachney, William Grant of Lurg, William Grant of Delay and Patrick Grant of Tullochgorum. Important tenants who were not part of the clan gentry also appeared frequently, Robert Lawson in Port and Duncan Grant in Achnahannet appearing on five assizes each.

After hearing the evidence, the assize was asked to elect a chancellor to preside over their deliberations and deliver their verdict to the bailie. The assize was then directed to withdraw from the court to a nearby venue where they could be 'enclosed' until they reached a decision on each indictment. Places where the assize were often enclosed pending their decision included the Smith's barn and house in Ballintomb. The assize returned to court and their chancellor delivered their verdict to the bailie. Those found guilty were entreated to the mercy of the bailie who imposed a punishment accordingly. The sentence imposed by the bailie was delivered to the panel and the court by the dempster, who was often the court officer or sometimes the executioner.

All those who passed before an assize in the regality court of Grant were found guilty. In many cases this resulted in corporal punishment such as scourging, lugging or branding [see Table 3]. Those panelled before the court were clearly aware that being remitted to pass before an assize was almost certain to result in corporal punishment. With this in mind, plea bargaining was an attractive proposition for panels, as can be seen in a court at Culnakyle on 15 February 1699:

> Lybell and accusa[t]ine at the instance of Patrick Stuart in Dell ag[ains]t Johne Makacheill in Clacheg and Wm Girnrach the pursuers servant for the spuilzieing of his horse of the goods gear and monies lybelled upone the probatione ag[ains]t Makacheill and Girnrach his confession the bailie ordained them to pass under ane assyse and thereafter the said bailie being verie pressing with Makacheill and putting hire[81] to him to confess at last the said Makacheill declared he was rather willing to pay

81 "Here", at this point. *DSL*.

> the pursuer damage then to goe to the knowledge of ane inquest Because the said judge haid promised upon him ingenuitie of confessione to pass from corporal punishement and hereby declares that this process shal not infer any guilt upone him therefter ... and that the samen shall not be ane dittay ag[ains]t Makacheill.[82]

Panels usually only passed to an assize if they were of habit and repute as criminals, incorrigible and were likely to be found guilty of the crimes libelled.[83] The belief that assizes were guaranteed to return guilty verdicts is recalled in a satirical seventeenth century play describing the procedure of a fictional baron court. The baron court officer warns a belligerent tenant:

> Go get you gone in time, if you be wise,
> Lest you pass to the knowledge of assize.[84]

However, courts in Scotland were often reluctant to impose corporal punishment, it being a last resort. Corporal punishments were infrequently imposed by the laird of Grant's bailies and such punishments virtually disappear after 1700. In fact, only one assize is recorded in the court records after this point, for the theft of sheep in July 1721.[85]

Evidence suggests that where corporal punishments such as scourging and luggings and other executions were imposed, they were nearly always intended as a ritual spectacle intended to warn the population. A good example was the symbolic punishment handed down by bailie James Grant of Auchterblair to a thief in in 1670:

> The said day Jon roy McAlister roy is unlawed in ten punds Scottis for breaking the yards of Ballachastel and stealing of peats ... and also the said Jon Roy his lug is ordain to be nailed to the gat of Ballachastel for cutting and stealing of ane part of the lead of the battleing[86] of Ballachastel

82 Grant Court Book 1 15/02/1699, p. 138.

83 See Mackenzie, *Matters Criminal*, pp. 98–100, discussion of punishment of thieves (nearly all cases handled by assizes in the regality of Grant were thefts) and the reluctance to impose capital punishment.

84 P Anderson, *The Copie of a Barons Court, newly translated by whats-you-call-him, clerk to the same* (Edinburgh, 1680).

85 Grant Court Book 4, 18/07/1721, p. 66.

86 "Battaling", battlement. *DSL*.

> and ther to remain until he break the grip or that he hes libertie to goe away.[87]

Banishment was a more common punishment and was employed by the bailies until the abolition of the regality in 1748. Whilst the bailies of regality could in theory only banish convicted panels from the bounds of the regality, in practice they could be found trying to go beyond their jurisdiction. For instance, on 19 July 1697 the bailie James Grant of Gelloway banished William Gow for theft in the following manner:

> The said judge James Grant of Gelloway... by the mouth of the dempster doeth banish the said William Gow from the country of Strathspey and from all countries of Scotland be north the toun of Perth never to return ... under failie of putting the sentence of death upon him ... and to leave Strathspey within eight days ... and the said Wm Gow shall not return to any plaice in Scotland be north of the Tay.[88]

Clearly the bailie of the regality of Grant did not possess the jurisdiction to banish a thief from the whole of the north of Scotland by virtue of the powers of regality alone. On 24 July in the same year bailie Gelloway banished a thief from, 'Speysyd above the lands of Easter Elchies never to remain or travel in any place in Speysyd above Easter Elchies'.[89] Speyside upstream of Aviemore fell within the regality of Huntly, also beyond the jurisdiction the regality of Grant. Whilst these pronouncements may just have been aggrandisement upon the part of James Grant of Gelloway, they may also reflect that the erection of the regality owed its origins, at least in part, to continuing attempts to stamp out disorder throughout the Highlands. By banishing thieves beyond the boundaries of the Highlands the bailie of the regality may have been helping to execute government policy.

Banishment was particularly useful as a mode of punishment, especially if the felon's goods and gear were also escheat to the regality. This was because people in early modern Scotland did not tend to move far from the parish where they were born and required a testimonial from their parish minister if they were to do so.[90] This was obviously withheld in cases of banishment, marking the convict as a vagrant.

---

87 NRS, Baron Court Extracts, GD248/76/2, 19/08/1670, fo.14.

88 Grant Court Book 1, 19/07/1697, p. 110.

89 Ibid, 24/07/1697, p. 133.

90 Cullen, *Famine in Scotland*, pp. 157–9; Davies, 'Law and Order in Stirlingshire', p. 295.

TABLE 3 Punishments handed down by the regality court of Grant

Punishment	Number of panels sentenced (where known from 1694–1748).
Hanging	9
Banishment	27
Scourging	11
Lugging or nailing	14
Branding	1

SOURCE: GRANT COURT BOOKS 1 – 5; ABERNETHY KIRK SESSION MINUTES, CH2/1054

Inhabitants of the regality were prevented from harbouring the banished under pain of amercement, being warned to this effect in church and other public places. Regardless of the risks, the realities of trying to survive the upheavals of banishment could lead to people trying to return to their communities where friends remained who were willing to hide them.[91]

Panels convicted before the court were often imprisoned at Castle Grant. This was most frequently employed to detain those who were unable to pay a fine or find caution. Men and women facing a criminal process before the court were detained in the pit at Castle Grant before their trial. However, imprisonment was only a short-term measure to ensure compliance with the court's judgements or summonses. Anyone imprisoned was also required to pay for their upkeep during their incarceration.[92]

The most serious punishment of all was hanging. Nine men were sentenced to death in the regality court of Grant between 1694 and 1703 in response to the social unrest experienced during the ill years of the 1690s. Criminals were usually executed at the standing stones near Ballintomb, where most corporal punishments were also exacted. On 2 September 1697 a group of thieves, Thomas Innes, Gillander Stewart and Donald MacRobbie, were sentenced to death by bailie Gelloway:

> [the accused] to be carried from the court to the pit of Castle Grant and to remain till Tuesday next the 7th day of this inst September and upone the

91 Grant Court Book 1, 13/01/1701, p. 160.

92 Grant Court Book 3, 13/05/1715, p. 76.

> said Tuesday morning to be brought from the forsaid prison under guard to the gallowhill of bellintom at ten hours in the morning And upon the forsaid day to be all three hanged upone the gallows at bellintom betwixt two and four hours in the afternoon till they be dead and decernes Gregor Dow to be bound to the Gellows at the tyme of the execution and to have his left ear cut off and to be scourged and banished the country. And the forsaid execution to be done by the hands of Lachlane Browne. And this is given for doome.[93]

Lachlan Brown had been convicted a month earlier of stealing sheep and sentenced to be whipped. That we find him acting as executioner suggests that he accepted the role in return for the remittance of punishment against his own person. This had long been common practice in Strathspey. Among other references to this practice in the court records, we learn that in 1668 a criminal named Duncan Dow McJames 'has accepted of the office of dempster and hangman and … shall exercise his office of dempster and hangman when occasion shall offer and he shall be requyrit'.[94] This suggests that the regality did not have a hangman. With corporal punishments and executions being rare, this was true of other regalities. For instance, in October 1719 Alexander Murray wrote to the provost of Perth asking for the loan of Perth's hangman to hang thieves convicted by the regality court of Atholl.[95]

Whilst there is no direct evidence prior to 1748, it appears that meetings of the court were much more than a judicial assembly. For the scattered communities of Strathspey, they were, besides market and fair days, opportunities for the wider community of the regality to come together. For rural communities, court days were an important social event. Brooks writing about English manorial courts emphasises that 'conviviality' was part of the judicial process, with the provision of food and drink being a key part of seigneurial responsibility at these events. For this reason, the majority of these courts met at inns or alehouses.[96] It appears matters were similar in the Highlands. In the regality of Huntly in the Lordship of Badenoch (which marched with the regality of Grant) in 1748 the innkeeper asked for a reduction in her rent fearing a lack of custom following the Heritable Jurisdictions Act (in spite of baron courts continuing to be held there): 'the Regality [court] now being gone, which will

93 Grant Court Book 1, 02/09/1697, p. 120.

94 NRS, Baron Court Extracts, GD248/76/2, 16/07/1668, fo. 82.

95 L Leneman, 'A Social History of the Atholl Estates 1685–1785' (Unpublished Ph.D. thesis University of Edinburgh, 1982), p. 222.

96 Brooks, *Law, Politics and Society in Early Modern England*, p. 245.

occasion the Country people being seldome in Ruthven … Consequently there must be a Decay of Consumption from both the Country and Passengers'.[97] The later records of the baron court of Strathspey give us some idea of the socialising which went hand in hand with judicial proceedings. A bill to be paid by the laird of Grant accompanying the court records for a court held at Grantown on 16 June 1789 reads as follows:

> Dinner for six gentlemen, 4s.
> Three bottles of Port Wine, 7s 6d.
> Half a mutchkin of gin, 6d.
> Six bottles small beer, 1s 3d.
> A bottle of porter, 4 ½d.[98]

This shows how as late as 1789 the baron court was still being used as a forum for socialising amongst the gentry. Regality courts of old were presumably much larger events. With many people attending court as suitors, witnesses, pursuers and defenders, tradesmen and ale-house keepers must have done a roaring trade on court days in their township. For this reason, ale-house keepers actively petitioned the bailie to be allowed to host courts on their premises and this practice continued until the late eighteenth century.[99]

97 Taylor, *The Wild Black Region*, p. 47.

98 NRS, The Baron Court of Strathspey, GD248/372/6, no folio numbers.

99 NRS, Petitions, GD248/38/1/27.

CHAPTER 4

Actions for Debt

The collection of rents, debts, duties, and casualties was a primary function and concern of all franchise courts in Scotland. A number of historians have described the work of the baron and regality courts in their later years as being dominated by cases involving debts and rentals, the majority of other court business having fallen away.[1] Indeed by the eighteenth century many of these courts are believed to have existed solely to service this need. In the sheriff court, actions for debt were, and still are, the most common business to be found.[2] In the regality of Grant citations of tenants to make payments of their outstanding debts to the Grants are a regular occurrence in the court books. However, actions for the recovery of debts between tenants are much less common than might be expected given the overwhelming presence of such actions in other court records from the period.[3] Study of this mundane yet vital role of the court in the rural community can reveal much about both the court and society at the time.

4.1 Debt and Credit in Strathspey

Debt and credit were an everyday feature of life in Strathspey during the late seventeenth and early eighteenth century. People were in most cases both debtors and creditors. A study of 200 testaments in rural Angus by Whyte and Whyte has shown that, of the testaments studied, 70% of the deceased had debts of some kind, whilst 69% were creditors. Only 2% were not involved in any kind of credit.[4] It is likely that the situation was similar in Strathspey. A good example of a man who was at the same time both a debtor and creditor residing within the regality of Grant was the clerk to the regality court, David Blair. Estate records show that Blair had lent money to the laird, Ludovick

1 Gunn, *Records of the Baron Court of Stitchill*, p. xxiii; Davies, 'Law and Order in Stirlingshire', p. 252; Dickinson, *Court Book of the Barony of Carnwath*, p. xlvii.

2 Davies, 'Law and Order in Stirlingshire', pp.241 and 252.

3 See for instance, *Records of the Baron Court of Stitchill*.

4 ID Whyte and KA Whyte, 'Debt and Credit, Poverty and Prosperity in a Seventeenth Century Scottish Rural Community', in R M Mitchison and P Roebuck (eds.), *Economy and Society in Scotland and Ireland, 1500–1939* (Edinburgh, 1988), p. 72.

 | DOI:10.1163/9789004472549_005

Grant, on bond and, at the same time, was owed wages by him. However, Blair himself had large outstanding debts for rent owing to the laird.[5] The financial situation of David Blair was similar to that of many inhabitants of the regality, from richest to poorest.

Credit was clearly unrestricted by rank. The very poorest in society up to the laird of Grant himself were involved in credit arrangements spanning social divides. The estate accounts show the Grants were reliant on their tenants for loans, often on bond.[6] Gentlemen and wadsetters were themselves borrowing from their tenants and lending to the laird.[7] In turn, both gentry and smaller tenants were widely in arrears of rent.[8] Thus, what existed was a confusing web of interdependency founded upon debt and credit. The estate records show that most of the powerful gentlemen and wadsetters in the regality were consistently in arrears of rents and especially of their augmentation duties owed on their wadset lands.[9] This was despite such men often possessing significant assets. Study of the testament of one of the largest farmers and biggest beneficiaries of Grant patronage, Mungo Grant of Mullochard, who died in 1722, reveals that all of his wealth was locked within his farm stock and sown crops.[10] His only liquid asset was his twenty-four bolls of victual estimated to be worth £104 sc. No cash is recorded in his testament. The inventory of his goods and debts was taken in April. This explains why he was owing £160 to the laird and a further £115 to his servants. His ability to pay his way was dependent upon the success of his farming endeavours and the harvest. This is an important point to bear in mind when considering debt and credit in rural Scotland. Mullochard and many other farmers like him were reliant on the sale of produce after harvest and cash income from cattle sales to pay their bills in cash at the end of the farming year. Importantly the value of Mullochard's farm stock far exceeded his liabilities. Until the point in time when he was able realise these assets, he was able to make some payments in victual, for everything else he was reliant upon credit.

As the testament of Mullochard shows, cash was not in plentiful supply. The universal need for credit during this period is often attributed to a lack of specie in Scotland. Historians such as Craig Muldrew have argued that the lack of

5 See: NRS, Estate Accounts, GD248/83/2 and GD248/108/16.

6 NRS, Estate Accounts, GD248/10/16.

7 Ibid.

8 Ibid. A state of affairs which would continue throughout the eighteenth century.

9 "Augmentation duty" was the sum owed by wadsetters to the landowner, as a result of the value of the wadset lands increasing above the value for which they were originally wadset.

10 NRS, Inverness Commissary Court Register of Testaments, CC11/4/156.

coinage meant that whilst every day goods and services were valued in pounds, in practice, money was not the primary means for funding an exchange.[11] This situation was exacerbated by the nature of the rural agricultural economy, where, until the autumn harvest and cattle sales, there was little in the way of either cash or produce with which to settle debts or make payment. Instead, credit was used in most transactions. As a result, it seems that many debts were simply 'reckoned', with equivalent sums owing between parties simply cancelling each other out in most cases.[12] Cash was only necessary in settling any final outstanding payment after such sums had been definitively reckoned. As credit agreements must have happened with great frequency in Strathspey, it is natural that a large number must have been oral in nature, as must have been the case for most small debts. With little security for a creditor in such situations the principal factor at play in such agreements was trust and credit worthiness. These links of trust and credit bound communities together, with the economic fortunes of many parties being interwoven and interdependent. So why lend at all in such situations? With no banks it was almost certainly better to put your money to work through lending rather than leaving it sitting in a kist at home. Lending to others in the community was certainly a social experience. Extending trust and a helping hand through financial aid to others in the community was a neighbourly act: an expression of social ties and Christian values. Participation in the life of the community through the extension of credit was similar in nature to the act of standing caution for someone in court.[13] It was seen as a mechanism for inclusion within the wider economic and social community and also established the creditor as a person of good credit worthiness and thus, by implication trust.

Trust became a problematic basis for organising credit transactions when it was breached, leading to disputes and ultimately litigation. The details of many individual cases in the court records are scant, and the records themselves obviously form an incomplete picture of debt contracted, disputed, and litigated. There were several reasons for debts becoming contested. In many instances, repayment was probably impossible for the debtor. On other occasions, disputes over debts could arise from the poorly recorded nature of many credit agreements. As most debts were orally transacted with no paperwork or record, the timescale, and even the amount of money owed could easily become matters of disagreement between parties that could end in litigation.

11 Muldrew, *The Economy of Obligation*, pp. 100–101. Whilst Muldrew's study is concerned largely with urban England his conclusions are likely to be true of Scotland also.

12 Ibid, p. 108.

13 Falconer, *Crime and Community in Reformation Scotland*, pp 61–62.

This was further exacerbated by the long-term nature of many debts. Muldrew has argued that there was a general willingness to tolerate debts for long time periods rather than go to court to try and recover the money owed.[14] An example of such a longstanding debt in the regality court of Grant records survives from 1715:

> Jon Nairn in Kirktoun of Inverelane being p[u]rsued be Johne Grant in Lettoch for twentie pounds scotis … the deceist Duncan Grant in Lagan wes decerend by ane decreit befor the baron bailie of the parish of Cromdale in the 1684 year of God as cautioner confest for the deceist Patrick Grant in Gartonne and that because the said Johne Nairn wes exe[cut]or to the said Duncan and intromits with the defunctis means.[15]

There were a number of reasons why creditors might choose to refrain from court action for so long. Firstly, litigation was expensive. Secondly, if a debt was disputed because of the informal way in which it had been recorded, there was little chance of successfully litigating in the regality court. Litigation was a drastic measure. If the bailie found in favour of the creditor then the creditor may succeed in recovering the debt but at the cost to the debtor of ruining their credit, trust and standing within the community. If the debtor was a neighbour of the creditor it may have been better to live with the debt rather than ruin the debtor and threaten relations within the community. The court-book entry from 13 December 1696 clearly demonstrates the tensions that unpaid debts, and threats of legal action, could create within the community, 'it is found that [Duncan] Makandie beat and blood [John] Brachiter upone mouth and nose upone Brachiter his offering to poynd Makandy for ane debt'.[16] This entry also suggests that the mere suggestion of court action was perceived as a threat. This could go some way to explaining the relatively small amount of debt cases to be found in the court books. Perhaps the threat of initiating a court action was often impetus enough to prompt payment. It is of course to be remembered that the majority of debts were probably payed timeously or settled amicably. Equally, many disputes over debts must have been settled out of court, through mediation.

If creditors wanted more security in their lending they could lend on bond. Bonds were a much more secure form of lending as they had to be in legal

14 Muldrew, *The Economy of Obligation*, p. 200.

15 Grant Court Book 3, 29/11/1714, p.68.

16 Grant Court Book 1, 31/12/1696, p.101.

form attested to by witnesses, and in turn usually carried interest.[17] Because of these legal formalities bonds were usually considered to be water-tight evidence of a debt, and thus carried none of the risks that came with less formal credit arrangements.[18] Whilst the benefits to creditors were obvious, lending on bond also carried advantages for the debtor. Borrowing on bond, especially from an individual of some social standing, was likely to reflect well on the debtor's own credit worthiness as it was clear evidence of their liquidity.[19] The court records show that whilst bonds were a more secure form of credit, it did not guarantee timeous repayment. Bonds could also go unpaid for some time before litigation was initiated. For instance, it is noted in the final Grant court book that payment of a bond dated 28 November 1690 and later assigned in 1712 was still being sought as late as 1729.[20] In such cases what prompted creditors to seek repayment of debts?

The main trigger for seeking repayment of a debt was the death of the debtor. In the records left by the regality of Grant forty-nine cases involving debts are recorded, of these thirteen can be linked to the death of the debtor, whilst one was instigated by the death of the creditor. Of the former, the majority consist of a claim made against the executor or more usually executrix of the defunct's estate. The settlement of the estate of the wadsetter William Grant of Dallachaple following his death in 1707 led to a relatively large amount of litigation in the regality court.[21] His relict and executrix, Barbara Dunbar, appeared in court on three occasions, cited to make payment of debts owed by her deceased husband to four separate creditors.[22] Widows appearing in the court records as executrixes is one of the most prominent ways in which women featured in the workings of the court. This highlights the way in which a woman's connection with the law and her social status changed upon the death of her husband.[23] The case of Barbara Dunbar also highlights the position of relative power widows were placed in, if they were well provided for by their husband's estate. Barbara Dunbar was clearly placed in such a position, as the court book records that, by the time of the court actions involving her husband's estate, she was already remarried to David Cuthbert of Milntoun, who was bailie of

17 Muldrew, *Economy of Obligation*, p. 109 and Ewan, 'Debt and Credit in Early Modern Scotland', p. 50.

18 Muldrew, *Economy of Obligation*, p. 109.

19 Ibid.

20 Grant Court Book 5, p. 176.

21 NRS, Moray Commissary Court Register of Testaments, CC16/4/1.

22 Grant Court Book 2, pp.107, 108 and 124.

23 C Spence, *Women, Credit and Debt in Early Modern Scotland*, (Manchester, 2016), p. 14.

the regality of Grant in the parish of Cromdale from 1706 to 1709. He presided as bailie at the court on 17 February 1708 in which his wife was cited for debt. At the court held 14 June 1709 he was cited alongside his wife to make payment of debts they owed separately to the same creditor: 'The said day the said bailie gives de[cree]t at the instance of Johne Grant in Kylentra creditor for 138 merkes 6s. 8d. by the deciest Dellachaple against Barbara Dunbar the defuncts relict and executor confirmed and David Cuthbert her husband for his errears also compeared and confest the debt and allowed of the debt to be executed'.[24]

The role of the regality court in settling actions for debt prompted by the death of the debtor also reveals a conflict with the jurisdiction of the commissary courts. The commissary courts had a jurisdiction which included the confirmation of testaments, the registration of inventories and settlements, and other executry matters. Importantly they could also hear debt cases up to a value of £40. This jurisdiction over petty debts conflicted with the jurisdiction of baron and regality courts. A case of a debt arising in July 1713 shows the potential for jurisdictional conflict. The defenders John Dunbar and his wife Elspet Grant in Tomnabain argued that

> noe process could be sustained against his spouse and him befor any judge but before the commissar of Murray before whome his wyff was conformed executrix creditrix to her husband for fulfilling her contract of marriage and therefor not lyable for her husbands debts and that he had process of exoneration against all creditors depending before the said commissioners whereupon he appealed from this court to the said commissioners.[25]

The relict of Thomas Grant in Achnahannet, Jean Farquharson, also attempted to challenge the decision of the regality court by removing the case to the commissary court to evade her husband's creditors and show that the debt could not be proven:

> The said day compeared Jean Farqrsone relict of the deceased Thomas Grant in Achnahannet declared that she wes pursued … for her husbands debts by alledged creditors before this regalitie as intromissatrix with her deciest husbands meanes and exec[utry] And such all her intromission was necessary for presivation of her owne right of lyffrent forsaid be the

24 Grant Court Book 2, 14/06/1709, p. 124.
25 Grant Court Book 3, 24/07/1713, p. 43.

> contract of marriage twixt her husband and her and be other rightes maid to her be her said husband with that she was intended to remove from the bounds of the said regalitie tharefore she did appeall from this judicator to the com[missione]r of Elgin or murray for to be heard concernand her right and protestis that the creditors of her husband have not proven in this court or any.[26]

Both Jean Farquharson and Elspet Grant succeeded in having the cases against them removed upon appeal to the commissary of Moray, although I have found no record of the cases continuing before this court. Lorna Ewan discussed the jurisdictional clash between the baron courts on the Grandtully estates and the commissary court in Dunkeld in her thesis on debt and credit on the Grandtully estates in Perthshire 1650–1765.[27] She wrote that many cases falling within the jurisdiction of the baron court of Grandtully and other franchise courts were being heard by the commissaries in Dunkeld. The commissary court there frequently went beyond its jurisdiction and heard cases for debts larger than £40 sc. but only with the assent of the defender in the case. She identified that a large proportion of these debt cases above the value of £40 sc. were for rests of rents and similar official dues such as teinds.[28] Her explanation for the pursuit of such cases before the commissariat was primarily that the commissary court was perceived to be unbiased compared to the franchise courts, (although it is unclear why a jurisdiction holder would acquiesce in an action for rests of rent being heard in a court other than his own).[29] The evidence in the Grant court books suggests that this phenomenon was not found in Strathspey, with only two of forty-nine debt cases raised in the regality court of Grant ultimately being resolved by the commissary court. Concerns about the quality of justice in the regality court and of bias could explain why Jean Farquharson and Elspet Grant wished to have their cases heard by the commissary court. Nonetheless the commissary courts were the proper jurisdiction for the administration of estates, and the settlement of debts was clearly a part of this administration. Hence, the most important point to draw from these cases is that creditors valued the local regality court in pursuing such debts. Geography was probably a primary factor in their choice of jurisdiction: it being much easier to sue in a regality court held within their own parish rather

26 Grant Court Book 2, p. 135.

27 Ewan, 'Debt and Credit in Early Modern Scotland'.

28 Ibid, p. 168.

29 Ibid, p.169.

than having to undertake a seventy-mile round trip to plead before the commissariat in Elgin.

The debt cases recorded in the court records make up a small proportion of the overall work of the regality court of Grant as recorded in petitions and the court books. However, this is not representative of the role that debt played in the day-to-day working of the court. Several clues in the documentary evidence suggest that actions on debt were very common in the regality court. It appears that the officials in the court treated debt cases as common, one particularly revealing court entry reads: 'No pr[e]sentes exept actiones of debts betwixt tennant'.[30] The wording of the entry and the fact that no debt actions were recorded in the book for this day clearly suggests that debt cases were so common as not to be routinely registered in the main court record. Similarly, the court record from 1 July 1715 states that: 'This court for small debts and decreits' yet none are recorded.[31] Or on 21 November 1706, 'the court again sitting upone complaints for debtes'.[32] This entry again emphasises that litigation over debts must have been commonplace. This is supported by the baron court records from after 1748 abound with small claims for debts.[33] Many similar claims must have been made to the regality court which was its predecessor.

Another feature of the court books which tells us more about the way debts were treated by the court are working notes of debts jotted within the rear pages or inside covers of some of the court books. In the back pages of the final court book there is an entry for 7 June 1728 from a court held at Ballintomb. This entry does not fit the chronology of the rest of the court book. This suggests the entry was a rough note, of a type usually recorded elsewhere rather than in the court book. A list of nine debts is recorded:

> Mungo Stuart in Culchastle for ane debt rests 4s.
> James Smith in Cragan 14s.
> Wm Cumin's relict in Port £1 1s.
> Donald Stuart in Tulluch £5 7s.
> James Grant 10s.
> James McRobyvoir 12s.
> His brother's relict £1 4s.
> John Buy and Donald Grant for two bills 12s.
> John Gregorach 19s

30 Grant Court Book 2, 16/05/1707, p.85.
31 Grant Court Book 3, 01/07/1715, p. 83.
32 Grant Court Book 2, 21/11/1706, p. 80.
33 NRS, Baron Court Extracts, GD248/372.

> John Fraser in Cottortown for loosing his arrested goods in James Bain millers hand 12s.[34]

Similar entries are made in some of the other back pages of the court books. It is unclear whether these were debts owed to the laird or individuals. However, this entry is important as it gives an idea of the number of debts being pursued or recorded at an average court. Also, it suggests that there was a separate court register of protests and deeds where bonds, bills of process and other deeds, often relating to debts and obligations, could be registered. Several such registers survive from other regality courts.[35] The surviving court records of the baron courts which operated in Strathspey during the restoration era also contain few debt cases. I have identified only two actions during this period, which suggests that the use of a separate register was of long standing.[36]

Finally, it remains only to describe the practice used to pursue a debt before the regality court of Grant. A creditor was first required to make a complaint to the bailie, describing the reason for their petition and craving that decreet be granted against the defaulting debtor. The debtor would then be summoned by the officer to appear at the next sitting of the court. The process for making such a complaint or plaint is demonstrated in the following petition to the bailie:

> Petition:
>
> To John Grant of Delrachney Bailie of the Regality of Grant the petition of George Similaw Taylor in Mullochard against Ranald McKean his prentice
>
> Humbly shewes
>
> Where the said Ranald … Owes half of his prentice fee the first half was paid in hand and gave John Grant in Gartenbeg as cautioner for his faithful performance
>
> May it therefore please your lordship to decern the present debtor and cautioner in payment of the sum of 10 merks
>
> [On reverse:]
>
> Duthell Nov 21st 1728. Ordains the prentice and his cautioner to make payment and that the prentice should fulfil his service to the pursuer.[37]

34 Grant Court Book 5, 07/06/1728, p. 174.

35 For instance, NRS, Regality of Huntly, RH11/40/4, NRS, Regality of Dunkeld, RH11/28/10, NRS, Regality of Dunfermline, RH11/27/28-40.

36 NRS, Baron Court Extracts, GD248/76/2, fos. 29 and 122.

37 Papers of the Bailie of Grant, NRS, GD248/224/7, fo. 5.

In the example above it appears that the debtor and cautioner failed to compear in court and liability for the debt was inferred from their absence. Decreet was therefore granted in favour of the pursuer. The extracted decreet was simply written on the back of the petition by the clerk and handed back to the pursuer at the bar. The pursuer left the court with extracted decreet in hand.[38]

4.2 The Collection of Rents

> Every heritor may hold courts for causing his tennents pay his rent[39]

Rent arrears were the most common type of debt for which inhabitants of rural Scotland found themselves liable during the period of study.[40] Regality and barony courts were a key institution in running the Grant family's estates, the most important element of which was making sure that rents, duties and customs were paid. The chamberlain was responsible for the work of uplifting and ingathering rents, compiling rentals, and bringing legal proceedings against tenants who were in arrears in payment of rent. He had to work closely with the regality court. The chamberlain was perhaps second only in importance to the bailie, the most prestigious office in the hierarchy of estate servants. In fact, on the Grant Strathspey estates the offices of both bailie and chamberlain were often bestowed upon one man. James Grant of Gelloway received such a commission in 1695 and performed both offices until his death in 1702.[41] Following the death of Gelloway in February 1702, the office of bailie and chamberlain was again awarded as a joint commission, but upon five men rather than one, each to be responsible for the administration of justice and finances within each of their respective parishes.[42] The interplay between the offices of bailie and chamberlain was of great importance to the smooth operation of the estate. The chamberlain was responsible for all estate finances ingoing and outgoing and relied upon the courts to uphold his authority. By combining the two great offices of the estate, administration was greatly eased, as in practice

38 An extracted decreet meant the proper written evidence or warrant on which diligence or execution of a judicial decree proceeded, it did not need to be a copy of an actual entry in a public record. R Bell, *A Dictionary of the Law of Scotland* (Edinburgh, 1826), p. 394.

39 G Mackenzie, *Institutions of the Law of Scotland* (Edinburgh, 1730), p.33.

40 Whyte and Whyte, 'Debt and Credit, Poverty and Prosperity in a Seventeenth Century Scottish Rural Community', p.72.

41 See rests of rent where James Grant of Gelloway can be found accounting for the estate rentals to the laird, NRS, Estate Accounts, GD248/10/16 No Folio numbers.

42 Grant Court Book 2, p. 1.

several aspects of the two roles overlapped.[43] The outlying baronies of the regality, such as those at Mulben, Knockando, and Glenurquhart, had their own chamberlains who operated independently of the principal Strathspey chamberlain. These men were called upon to render their accounts yearly and drew a salary from the laird.[44] The importance of the office of chamberlain is indicated by the salary that office holders commanded. Alexander Grant of Lethendrie, brother to bailie John Grant of Dalrachney (again emphasising the close connection between the two offices and the patronage that was available to family members), was appointed chamberlain in 1710 and remained so until the death of Brigadier Alexander Grant of Grant in 1719. The estate accounts record that he was drawing a yearly salary of £200 sc., a substantial sum.[45]

The rents ingathered by the chamberlain were composed of three elements by the mid-seventeenth century in Strathspey: cash, victual, and in kind. In Strathspey, the important trade in cattle and the early introduction of written tacks had led to a predominance of cash rents. This was a common feature of rentals across pastoral areas of north east Scotland, where a persistent shortage of grain made payment in victual difficult.[46] Cash rentals were desirable as they meant that the laird did not have to market and sell the surplus produce collected as rent. Pastoral produce was often easily marketable and brought cash to upland districts. Nonetheless, grain was still a very important commodity, and in addition many customs were still paid in kind.[47] A judicial rental of Strathspey taken by the regality court in 1720 gives an idea of the sums which might be paid each year by an average tenant. For instance, William Dow in Croftmore in Abernethy parish paid 'twentie merks, a year old wedder, two hens and a firlot of malted bear, and nine merks grassum'[48] for his eighteen-year tack of half a sten part of the Davoch of Riemore.[49]

The logistics involved in ingathering such a variety of goods were complicated. For example, the grain ingathered at the mains of Castle Grant in 1716 alone amounted to 468 bolls and a firlot of oats, along with sixty bolls of bear.[50]

43 M H B Sanderson, *Scottish Rural Society in the Sixteenth Century* (Edinburgh, 1982), pp. 24–27.

44 NRS, Estate Accounts, GD248/10/16.

45 NRS, Estate Accounts, GD248/11/7, fo.7.

46 I K Whyte, 'Agriculture in Aberdeenshire in the Seventeenth and Eighteenth Centuries: Continuity and Change', in D Stevenson (ed.), *From Lairds to Louns: Country and Burgh Life in Aberdeen, 1600–1800* (Aberdeen, 1986.), p. 23.

47 Sanderson, *Scottish Rural Society in the Sixteenth Century*, p. 28.

48 "Grassum", a sum of money paid or promised by a tenant to his landlord at the grant or renewal of his lease, *DSL*.

49 NRS, Miscellaneous rentals and minutes of the Regality Court of Grant, GD248/136/8.

50 Ibid.

Large amounts of grain were required to feed the household, horses and livestock, and to pay wages and debts. Subtenants made payment to their tacksman. Tacksmen and tenants were required to make payment of their rents either directly to the laird, or his chamberlain by taking or driving their rent personally to the corrals and granaries at Castle Grant or Culnakyle. The court books also mention collectors who were appointed to uplift rents on behalf of the chamberlain, and who presumably toured the outlying davochs collecting both cash and customs.[51] Such a system must have been costly for the laird, but at least increased the likelihood of rents being paid timeously. It also seems likely that tenants were given the opportunity to pay their rents when paying suit at the head court, which also served as a formal notice to them that rents were due.

Between the erection of the regality in October 1696 and the end of the court records in 1729, fifty-six petitions for payments of rents and debts owed to the Laird are recorded in the court records. The majority of these took the form of a petition made by the chamberlain of the regality at the Martinmas term day in November of each year giving formal notice to tenants to make payment of rents and duties. Each of these pleas for payment conforms to a standard form as in the following example from the court held at Duthil on 29 November 1705:

> The hail tennants and possessors of the parish of Duthel and lordship of Glencharnick and hail wodsetters of the said parish are decerned and ordained to mak payment of their respective duties and annuities for Martmes last 1705 and also for their customes of wedders and geiss according to their tackes within 15 days under the payn of poynding and that to the Laird of Grant thir master his chamberlanes and collectors and also ordaines payment of the ministers stipend for mart[52] 1704 in monies before the expyring of eight days in money under the payn of poynding for the double.[53]

This proclamation made in open court was in effect a final warning for tenants with debts resting due to make prompt payment to the laird or undergo process of law.[54] It was established procedure that an identical proclamation would be made at a court held within each parish within the regality in

51 Grant Court Book 2, 29/11/1705, p. 65. And see also collectors appointed for collecting taxes Grant Court Book 5, p. 136.

52 Mart is an abbreviation of Martinmas.

53 Grant Court Book 2, 29/11/1705, 17/11/1727, p. 65.

54 Davies, 'Law and Order in Stirlingshire', p.240.

close succession, calling the inhabitants of each district to make payment. For instance at Martinmas 1728, courts were held at Duthil (for Duthil parish) on 22 November, then the next day at Ballintomb (for Inverallan parish), with another court at Milltown of Castle Grant (for Cromdale parish) a further two days later, and finally a court also met at Clachaig (for Abernethy parish) on 29 November: 'the petition given in before the s[ai]d judge be the laird of Grant's chamberlain the said judge decerns and ordains the wedsetters, gentleman, tenants, possessors and others of lands, milns, fishings etc. … to make payment of their customs due at Whitsunday last'.[55] The court which met at the Martinmas term was clearly the most important of the year, it was a head court where acts of court were promulgated, economic regulations made, and rents paid. As a head court, all tenants were expected to attend its meeting. Even though customs, duties and rents were payable in two instalments each year, at Whitsun and Martinmas, the court records make clear that in practice most of the rents were only uplifted after the harvest in November with customs payable at the Whitsun term.[56]

Rents were not the only obligation owed to the laird for which his vassals fell into arrears of payment. In addition to mail or money rent and customary payments owed for the possession of their holdings, the laird's vassals owed the laird the performance of various services. One of the most labour intensive was the bringing of peats; leases stipulated the number of loads of peats each tenant was required to cut from the peat mosses and deliver to the stack yard at Castle Grant each year. Tenants were also obliged to pay the laird for the compulsory usage of estate facilities such as the mill and the ferries across the Spey. These services were widely disliked. The obligation to grind their corn only at the laird's mill, was detested in particular and avoided wherever possible.[57] The obligation was founded upon the fact that the mill of the davoch had been erected for their benefit, so they as tenants were expected to patronise it. However, any tenants grinding their corn at the mill were taxed in the form of a multure, which meant that a proportion of the grain ground was claimed by the miller or the laird himself. In Strathspey, multures had been converted to cash payments by the 1650s, emphasising once more the Grant lairds' persistent need for cash to pay for their increasingly high expenditure and mounting debts. The period from the 1650s to the 1670s was a period of economic depression and conversion of rentals and duties to cash payments offered land

55 Grant Court Book 5, p. 156.

56 For an example of duties being uplifted after Whitsun see Grant Court Book 3, 16/07/1713, p. 41.

57 Barron, *Baron Court Book of Urie*, p. xlv.

owners some protection from falling rents and a slump in the prices of agricultural produce.[58] The conversion of such payments also emphasises that cash was in circulation amongst all levels of society within Strathspey by this time, especially amongst the tacksmen.[59] Suckeners, the people thirled to a particular mill, resented the payment of multures because grain could be ground at home, for free, in hand querns. The usage of such querns was banned for people thirled to a mill: 'none shall grind anie of ther corneis upone qourneis in tyme coming except the milne be broken or tyed be storme'.[60] Suckeners were forced to pay whatever rate had been set down by the baron or regality court, placing them at the mercy of the closed-market estate economy. The sucken were also obliged to repair and maintain the mill when necessary, a duty which featured in a number of court sessions, as did cases where tenants were sued for performance of the duty or for the fine owed to the miller or tacksman of the mill.[61] However, such cases do not appear very often in the court records. This is surprising as the payment of multures was of obvious financial importance to both the laird and tacksmen of the various mills. The printed court records for the baron courts of Monymusk, Stitchill and Urie contain several references to actions for the payment of multures by the miller and laird.[62] This suggests that the Grants may have been reasonably successful in enforcing the payment of multures and thus were not required to take legal action very frequently.

4.3 Poinding

If payment of the outstanding debt was not received within due time, then the chamberlain of the regality would again petition the bailie, this time craving him to sue the debtors for payment in court and extract decreet thereupon. Such a letter survives from 1730, between the chamberlain of Strathspey and bailie John Grant of Dalrachney:

58 D Watt, 'The laberinth of thir difficulties: the Influence of Debt on the Highland Elite c.1550 – 1700', *SHR* 85:1 (2006), p.41.

59 NRS, Baron Court Extracts, GD248/76/2 fo. 55.

60 Ibid, fo. 19.

61 Ibid, fo. 59.

62 Hamilton, *Monymusk Papers*, p. 229; Barron, *Baron Court Book of Urie,* pp. 5, 10 and 15; Gunn, *Records of the Baron Court of Stitchill,* pp 16, 36–7, 44 and 112–3.

> Sir,
>
> I beg youle upon sight extract decreet against the persons underwritten and send it with a bearer my factor will sign it when he comes home this day. This night he send it south [to the Laird Sir James Grant residing in London by this time]. So despatch the bearer [directly] it will cost you due small trouble.
>
> Wm Wattson in Castle Grant for duely[63] of cropt 1720 £121
> John Grant in port for duely of Anagach cropt 1720 £40
> Isobell Grant in Rynabealach for duely of cropt 1720 £23. 5s.
> John McCnog in Culfoich for his duely of cropt 1720 £45
> Thomas Stuart their for cropt 1720 £26. 13s. 4d.
> John Grant of Glenbeg for the milnrent of Craggan whitsun 1729 £120[64]

Once the court decree had been granted and had been extracted, such as that sought by the chamberlain above, a precept of poinding was adjoined, enforceable against the debtors' property within the jurisdiction in which the decree was issued.[65] Poinding was the process by which a debtor's property might be seized, valued, and sold to realise funds to satisfy a creditor. Where the debts in question arose from rents owed the process was known as poinding of the ground.[66] Poinding was a judicial process supposed to proceed under warrant from the regality court and was usually undertaken by the parish's court officer. The officer would go alone, or sometimes accompanied by other notable estate workers such as the forester, and personally uplift and impound a tenant's goods.

Other individuals were empowered by act of the regality court to poind for debts. Most important of these was the miller, who was empowered to poind for debts at the mill.[67] In addition to the debts owed to them in their capacity as miller, millers were also empowered to poind for debts owed to other officials within the regality:

> The haill gentlemen, tenents and possessors of the lands of Cromdell and Inverallan are ordainit and decerenit to content and pay to Gilbert MacPhail law[fu]ll son to mr Gilbert Macphail minister at Cromdell pr[incipa]l schoolmaster at Cromdell two firlottis of meall out of ilk dauch of land within the said parishones and the severall millarts w[ithi]

63 "Duele", to delay or be delayed, *DSL*.
64 NRS, Papers of the Bailie of Grant, GD248/224/7, fo. 22.
65 J Erskine, *An Institute of the Law of Scotland* (Edinburgh 1773), p.514.
66 Ibid.
67 This was also the case in the Barony of Monymusk: Hamilton, *Monymusk Papers*, p. 238.

> n the said lands are ordainit and impowert to poynd the possessors of the saids lands at the severall milnes'.[68]

The payment of the schoolmasters' meal was evidently another tax evaded by the people of the regality as it was the subject of litigation in the court.[69] The school masters' difficulty in ingathering their salaries was in part due to local custom at the mill, whereby each peck[70] was divided in three parts: with one part going to the tenant, miller and laird respectively:

> The said day in respect of the complaint given in be mr Wm Grant school master at Cromdale showeing that he receives ill measur from many of the tenantes of his schooll meall and that the devisione of the pek in four partis is not customarie in this countrey but in three pairtis wherby he is at a loss by the [lack] of the fourt part when it falles to his payment tharfor the bailie ordains and allows the said compl[aine]r to cause mak ane lipie[71] or fourt pairt And ane pek of the syse of the Laird of Grants pek at Castle Grant.[72]

The power to poind tenants emphasises the status of the miller within the social hierarchy of the regality. That the millers enjoyed similar power to court officers is also found in the records of the baron court of Urie.[73] The mill was an unavoidable feature of seventeenth and eighteenth century rural life. A trip to the mill was a necessity for all inhabitants who held arable land. It was simple for the miller at the 'mill-eye' to seize victual owed by tenants in lieu of rents and for other dues.

The regality court also specifically empowered other individuals in the community to poind for debts. These included the captains of the watches who guarded the marches of Strathspey and who were given power to poind those not contributing provisions or weapons to the upkeep of the watch.[74] There is some evidence that constables and birlawmen were also appointed by act of court to poind for debts.[75] It seems that the constables were empowered to

---

68 NRS, Baron Court Extracts, GD248/76/2, fo. 56. See also: C S Romanes (ed.), *Selections from the Records of the Regality of Melrose*, Vol II (SHS, 1915) p. 127.

69 See for instance Grant Court Book 2, p. 40; Grant Court Book 3, pp. 28, 30, 32; Grant Court Book 5, p. 91.

70 "Peck", unit of measurement equivalent to 7 ¾ pints. *DSL*.

71 'Lipie', unit of measurement equivalent to a quarter of a peck. *DSL*.

72 Grant Court Book 2, 04/12/1704, p.40.

73 Barron, *Baron Court Book of Urie*, p. 29.

74 NRS, Baron Court Extracts, GD248/76/2, p. 62.

75 Grant Court Book 3, 25/11/1712, p.31.

poind for fines owed for breaching acts of the regality court. Another individual who was permitted to poind was the 'collector general' of the regality, usually an important tenant, he was responsible for overseeing the people collecting taxes and other payments to the estate.[76] It is unclear whether any of these other individuals poinded with specific warrants issued by the court against a named debtor. These men were probably only allowed to poind for minor debts. Documentary evidence suggests that poinding for small debts and customary payments could take place without a warrant.[77]

In all other instances poindings could only proceed upon decreet and warrant of the regality court. A description of a poinding from 1728 illustrates the process whereby a debtor's goods were seized, valued and sold. The defenders in this case, Malcolm McInver and Christian Fraser, had refused to pay a debt of £12 sc. owed by them to John Grant the schoolmaster of Cromdale. As a result, the bailie

> Adduced Thomas Gresich officer of the regality and desired that he should poynd the s[ai]d defenders moveable goods and gear equivalent to the tenor of the decreet who accordingly in virtue of his office proceeded and adduced two sworn and admitted assessors and having set before them some sheep belonging to the defenders … desired the said assessors estimate the said sheep to their value of the pursuers claim … and the said officer thereafter having poynded the said sheep and driving them forth of the dwelling house belonging to the defender in order to bring them to the cross of the regality in order for appreciating them at the said cross and offering the hail [to the pursuer][78]

The case shows how a double valuation of the debtor's property was necessary by two different assessors or birlawmen to get a fair price for the debtor once the officer had seized the property in question.

In the case described above, however, all did not go to plan for the unfortunate officer, as 'Elspet Fraser spouse to John Urquhart in Cottartown of Castle Grant resisted, opposed and masterfully deforced in open contempt and defiance of the said bailzie's decreet and authority and relieved by violence the said sheep'.[79] Deforcement was an occupational hazard for all officers of the

76 Grant Court Book 5, 17/11/1727, p.138.

77 NRS, Papers relating to the arbitration between Grant younger and Grant elder, GD248/22/3/32, fo. 10.

78 NRS, Papers of the Bailie of Grant, GD248/224/7, fo. 2.

79 Ibid.

law. It was by no means unusual for them to be prevented from carrying out their orders, especially in cases of poinding where a debt was disputed, and individuals wished to protect their property.[80] Women were often the court officers' undoing, it being widely believed at the time that women committing a crime stood far less chance of being prosecuted than their male counterparts.[81] Deforcement would often result in physical violence and assault on officers, who, by the nature of their role as bailiff, were widely disliked throughout the country. The resentment of court officers and other bailiffs was rooted in the nature of the duties which they were entrusted to execute.[82] Poinding was regarded as being especially shameful because of its public nature as diligence. Having a court officer come and seize property for non-payment threatened the debtors' standing and credit within the community. In this respect poinding was more than simple diligence. It was a punishment and a threat, used to coerce debtors.

Poinding was also costly and could be an even more expensive process for a debtor if costs were awarded against them. The debtor might lose his livestock or gear if he could not pay in due time and was then at the mercy of the valuation of the birlawman.[83] The intervention of Elspet Fraser on the behalf of her kinswoman proved to be costly, with expenses of £17. 8 s. being awarded against them. The break-down of costs is shown below; the extra costs incurred as a result of the deforcement and subsequent second poinding and appraisal are evident:

> The sum of ane decreet: £12
> The expenses of plea:[84] 12s
> The officers fees: 4s
> The charge of payment:[85] 2s

80 There are twelve cases of deforcement in the regality of Grant court records.

81 Whatley, *Scottish Society 1707–1830*, pp. 197–200. The Grant baron court records bear witness to another assault by a woman upon a court officer, NRS, Baron Court Extracts, GD248/76/2, fo. 62.

82 Muldrew, *Economy of Obligation*, p. 276.

83 This was a real fear as voiced in the precognitions for Mungo Grant of Mullochard's exculpation case before the High Court, NRS, Papers relating to the case of Grant of Mullochard v. Grant of Grant, GD248/22/3/49X.

84 Expense of plea refers to the cost of raising an action.

85 The charge of payment is a formal demand for payment of the amount owed to the creditor. It includes any interest and associated costs, and generally gives the debtor a certain time period within which to make payment. If the debtor does not satisfy the debt within the period specified, the creditor may then use diligence to recover what is owed.

The expenses of poynding twice: 12s
The expenses of two apprysors for two days: £1.4s
Clerks fees at poynding and deforcement: £1. 16s
The petition lybelled: 12s
Total: £17. 8s. od.[86]

This is the only indication we have for the costs involved in using the court to pursue tenants for debts, or indeed the cost of any action in the regality court of Grant.

4.4 Debt and Divisions in the Grant Family: Unwarranted Poinding 1710–1711

4.4.1 *Rental Crisis*

Despite the use of the baron and regality courts to help collect unpaid rents, and the threat of poinding hanging over many tenants' heads, rests of rents and in turn the debts of the Grant family increased steadily following the erection of the regality in 1696. The estate accounts record that difficulties did not ease as the climatic downturn continued into the first decade of the eighteenth century. For instance, in 1710 rests of rent allowed for the harvest of that year alone totalled £3,576 5s 2d.[87] This was out of a total rental of some £14,000. Many tenants were owing several years rent. The 1706 accounts show that the boatman of Cromdale had not paid any rent in five years, whilst David Blair the clerk to the court was resting three years rents for his land.[88] There was clearly little chance of ever getting payment of many such debts. Testamentary evidence shows that in common with many other leading Highland families the Grants of Freuchie had been accumulating large debts since the mid sixteenth century, largely through local credit networks.[89] Ludovick Grant of Grant had inherited huge debts from his deceased father when he succeeded to the Grant estates in 1665, and under his lairdship these debts continued to

86 NRS, Papers of the Bailie of Grant, GD248/224/7, fo. 3.

87 NRS, Estate Accounts, GD248/113/7, fo. 2.

88 NRS, Estate Accounts, GD248/10/16.

89 Watt 'The laberinth of thir difficulties', p. 30. Unfortunately, there is no direct evidence to indicate the precise nature of much of Ludovick Grant's expenditure (beyond his overzealous participation in the revolution) to offer a comparison with the work of Watt which considered Ludovick's predecessors.

grow alarmingly.[90] With nearly all of Grant's income being derived from his rental it is easy to appreciate that financial disaster was looming.[91] The management of the Grant estates, which had led to the accumulation of such debts, came in for severe criticism from the tacksmen and tenants of the estate. It also led to dispute and litigation within the family. The dramatic events which unfolded provide us with the best documentary evidence of the collection of debts and poindings in Strathspey, and of how ordinary people interacted with, and viewed the regality court. In turn a greater issue is revealed, concerning a conflict between changing types of authority: with the laird representative of traditional Highland society and clanship on the one hand, and the modern administration of the law on the other.[92]

4.4.2 *Case Study: Ludovick Grant of that Ilk v. Mungo Grant of Mullochard and Others*

A little before 10 a.m. on 15 May 1711, Ludovick Grant of Grant arrived at the caput of the regality of Grant, and his former home, at Castle Grant. His son Alexander, who was the new laird, was in London.[93] Accompanied by retainers and servants from the nearby mains, the purpose of Ludovick's visit could hardly have been more dramatic. In July of the previous year Ludovick had been forced to transfer control of the Grant estates to Alexander.[94] The disposition effecting this settlement now lay within the Grant charterhouse within the Castle. Along with his followers Ludovick's intentions were plain: to seize or destroy the offending charters and burn Castle Grant to the ground. However,

90 The testament of James Grant of Freuchie shows that he had liabilities totalling £72,000, Fraser, *Chiefs of Grant*, Vol. III, pp. 346–351. Between 1705, when the issue of Ludovick Grant's mismanagement of the estates was first raised, and 1711 Ludovick Grant paid out £37,000 as loans and in lieu of debts. His testament further illuminates his financial malaise, NRS, Edinburgh Commissary Court Register of Testaments, CC8/8/86.

91 This situation was to continue throughout the eighteenth century, with Grant debts peaking at £123,438 in the 1780s, see A Ross, 'Improvements to the Grant estates in Strathspey in the later Eighteenth century: Theory, Practice and Failure', in R W Hoyle (ed.), *Custom, Improvement and the Landscape in Early Modern Britain* (Farnham, 2011). Other revenue streams such as forestry were still negligible at this time.

92 This is an issue which has been covered extensively by Dodgshon in, R A Dodgshon, *From Chiefs to Landlords: Social and Economic Change in the Western Highlands and Islands, c. 1493–1820* (Edinburgh, 1998). The conclusions of this chapter generally accord with those of Dodgshon; however, with some distinctions which will be dealt with more fully at the conclusion of this chapter.

93 NRS, Alexander Grant of Grant's papers, GD248/22/3/34. Alexander was forced to reside in London whilst on parole as he waited to find out if he would have to return to France as a prisoner of war.

94 Fraser, *Chiefs of Grant*, Vol I, pt. II, p. 326.

upon reaching the gates he found the way barred by supporters of his son who had taken possession of the castle. Many of these men were experienced soldiers, such as Mungo Grant of Mullochard and Robert Grant of Lurg. All were armed. Enraged that his plan had been foiled, Ludovick instead sought revenge in the courts, suing his disloyal kindred for their violent possession of his family home. In their turn Mullochard and his allies sought exculpation for their actions, laying before the Justice Court the reasons which they argued warranted their taking up arms against their former chief. The primary reason for the clan's disaffection to their chief was the collection of rents and poinding of the ground.

The justiciary court minutes of the case provide the best idea of the nature and origins of the dispute embroiling Ludovick Grant, his son, his son's commissioners and the leading gentry and tenants of the area. Mungo Grant's information for the lords of justiciary lays bare the financial woes which had befallen the Grant estates:

> It appeared some years ago, that the estate of Grant was under a very considerable load of debt, which during the continuance of the panel [Ludovick Grant] and his ladies management sensibly increased, so that it was upon good grounds feared, that the affairs of the family should in a little time be past all hopes of recovery. This melancholy prospect moved the friends and relations of the family to lay the case before the panel and intreat that some alteration might be made in the management of the estate, and he was easily prevailed with in May 1710 to grant a disposition of his lands and estate in favour of Brigadier Grant his eldest son … and the son induced into possession in a very solemn manner by the fathers declaring to his vasell and tennents in ane open court, that he had made over the right of his estate to his son, whom they afterwards were to look upon as their master.[95]

As Alexander was away pursuing his career in the military, he immediately took care to appoint commissioners to run his estate in his absence.[96] However, events were about to overtake Alexander. In August 1710 Alexander set sail from the Netherlands returning home on leave; however, his ship was captured in the English Channel and he was taken prisoner. He was paroled, finally returning home to Castle Grant in November 1710. In an open court

95 NRS, High Court of Justiciary, Minutes, 1710–1711, JC7/5 p. 209.

96 Factory being registered in July 1710. NRS, Register of Deeds Minute Book, Mackenzie, RD7/3.

held on 4 November, he constituted a factor and several commissioners, drawn from prominent North East landowners, allowing Alexander's administration of the estates to begin in earnest.[97] As part of the settlement on Alexander, and in return for renouncing his liferent over the Strathspey estates, Ludovick Grant was to receive an annuity of £300 stg. for his upkeep, in addition to the fruits of the home farms at Castle Grant and at Culnakyle (his new residence in Abernethy). However, despite appearing to hand over the control of the family estates with good grace, dissatisfaction and resentment stemming from the new management of the estates led events to take an uglier turn. Struggling to service his mounting personal debts Ludovick sought funds from his son's commissioners. His requests fell on deaf ears. With his financial woes mounting, Ludovick, encouraged by his second wife Jean Houston, decided to resume management of his former estates, illegally, and without any of the administrative machinery of courts, chamberlains, and factors.[98]

In fact, the dispute between Alexander and Ludovick had been simmering for some years before the confrontation at Castle Grant. The disagreement had its basis in a settlement made in 1698, when Ludovick had granted the fee of the Grant estates to Alexander reserving the liferent of the said lands to himself.[99] In 1705 he had come north from Edinburgh to reside year-round in Strathspey. As liferenter, Ludovick had continued, legally, to uplift the rentals of the estate; however, in 1706, alarmed at the mounting debts, Alexander sought to stem his father's encumbrance of the estate with further debt. Ludovick continued to uplift some of the rentals of the estate after this point, poinding the ground for such debts where necessary. When tenants refused to pay the debts that Ludovick claimed they owed, he would poind without warrant, in defiance of both local custom and due process. A tacksman on the Grant estates, James Grant of Auchnahyle, gave evidence in a precognition recalling how Ludovick had poinded two cows which belonged to Alister Gow, the blacksmith in Clachaig. Though Auchnahyle had been present in recent courts he had heard of no relevant decreets being made:

> They [the cows] were delivered to [Ludovick] Grant but that Alister Gow redeemed his cattle by payment of a certain sume of money. … the declarant knows the goods were seized and the payment made without

97 Grant Court Book 3, p. 3. The commissioners included: William Grant of Ballindalloch, Brodie of Brodie, Captain John Grant of Easter Elchies, Joseph Brodie of Milltown.

98 Jean Houston was daughter of Sir Patrick Houston of that Ilk. The family held lands in Lanarkshire and West Lothian. Ludovick Grant was Jean Houston's third husband.

99 See disposition in Fraser, *Chief of Grants*, Vol III, pt. II, pp. 485–7.

> any decreet or order of law and declares that till of late the custom of the country was to decern the tennents in the court for what they owed the heritor, and further declares that this custom was innovat since the present Lady Grant [Jean Houston] went to Strathspey. The declarant used to be in the courts when such decreets were pronounced for rear[100] and yet that the declarant has been present at courts holden in the country of Strathspey upon Grant's lands since my Lady went there.[101]

Relying on loyal, unquestioning servants to carry out his commands, while bullying and intimidating others to comply with his wishes, from 1707 to 1711 Ludovick Grant was able to poind at least twenty-six Grant tenants without a court warrant.[102] No court officer or bailiff could refuse to answer the call of their laird and clan chief; warrant or no warrant they did as he bade them do. John Grant was one such man; officer of the regality court in the parish of Abernethy, he also gave evidence before the justiciary court. He described the poinding of Alister Gow in similar terms to Auchnahyle, 'declares he uplifted the goods and carried them to Cullnakyle without decreet or order of law and declares he used to poynd by decreet for country debts [debts in the area]'.[103] John Grant's deposition also makes clear that some of the poindings executed on behalf of Ludovick Grant were by no means small in scale, and were not intended to go unnoticed: 'uplifted from James McAlister Dow in Riemore, twenty seven head of cattle, three horses, a parell[104] of sheep, ten firlotts of meal, two calves, a parell of goats and two chists containing cloathes and five pounds scots of money'.[105] Such was the scale of the stock uplifted that McAlister was obliged to send his daughter and a stockman to tend his livestock corralled at Culnakyle. His daughter went about the milking, making butter and cheese, and sending these back to her father at Riemore, until such point as he was able to realise the cash required to redeem his stock. McAlister was evidently a farmer and tenant of some importance; however, even a tenant of his stature was not safe from the activities of the old Laird Ludovick. When

100 'Arrears'.

101 NRS, Declarations of Mullochard's witnesses against lord and lady Grant GD248/22/3/35, fo. 1.

102 NRS, List of claims against Ludovick Grant and Lady Jean Houston, GD248/22/3/60.

103 NRS, Declarations of Mullochard's witnesses against lord and lady Grant, GD248/22/3/35, fo. 2.

104 "Parcell", a flock, *DSL*.

105 In McAlister's own claim as part of the indictment against Ludovick Grant he claimed that sixty-three sheep and twenty-seven goats had been uplifted. NRS, Declarations of Mullochard's witnesses against lord and lady Grant GD248/22/3/35, fo. 2.

the regality officer was asked what the nature of McAlister's debt was, the officer was uncertain:

> Declares he does not know for what cause he brought them there save that as he was informed it was for the pryce of timber ... and declares that he uplifted the goods and cattle without any decreet or order of law other than that Duncan Grant of Lettoch made shew of reading the laird of Grant's order to him uplifting as said is, which order the declarant did not understand because he can neither read write or speak English.[106]

There is an undoubted irony to be found in Ludovick's wasted efforts in making a pretence of legitimacy. The manipulation of the regality's officer is plain to see. Officers such as John Grant were unpopular in any case by virtue of the work they undertook on behalf of the Laird; seizing their peers' property for debts they either disputed or were unable to pay cast them as pariahs.[107] Such men could hardly afford to lose the favour of those in power, regardless of the legality of the acts they were commanded to execute. In several cases the debt at least seems to have existed.[108] But in the case of James McAlister Dow the basis of his debt and the reason for the subsequent poinding appears to be have been a grudge held by Ludovick against McAlister Dow's son. Duncan Grant of Lettoch, another tacksman questioned in the precognition, believed that the son had cut the laird's woods without license and thereafter had broken the prison at Castle Grant and had fled Strathspey.[109] This could be the Alister MakAlister who was found 'guilty of firwoods' at a court in Duthell in December 1709, although without the son's name it is not possible to trace him in the records with certainty.[110] Lettoch recalled how he had gone with six or seven men to poind McAlister at Riemore; it is easy to imagine how intimidating this must have been for the people being poinded and emphasises the power of the laird in the district.

Whilst at first the ordinary people of Strathspey were clearly in no position to question the legitimacy of Ludovick's actions, upon his public renunciation of the headship of the clan in July 1710, perceptions changed. With the clan gentry moving against the laird, the people began to accept the authority of

106 Ibid.

107 Muldrew, *Economy of Obligation*, p. 276.

108 NRS, Declarations of Mullochard's witnesses against lord and lady Grant GD248/22/3/35.

109 NRS, Declarations of Mullochard's witnesses against lord and lady Grant, GD248/22/3/35, fo. 4.

110 Grant Court Book 2, 14/12/1709, p. 131.

Alexander's new commissioners rather than of the old laird. Ludovick had initially tried to make his actions appear legitimate, as, when questioned in the precognition, he had argued that it had long been customary to poind summarily in Strathspey, without decreet of the regality court, so that, by inference, he had acted legally. Whether poinding of the ground upon rents could proceed without court decreet was disputed by the institutional writers. Stair wrote that poinding of the ground upon annual rents may proceed summarily without declaring the right in a petitionary judgement.[111] However, this was qualified by later authorities such as Erskine, who wrote that summary poinding could not take place where the debts in question fell to be paid at either Whitsun or Martinmas; as was the case with the type of debts poinded for by Ludovick.[112] The long serving clerk to the regality court, David Blair, who had been clerk to the Grants' courts since at least 1690, spoke of local custom in regard to poindings, to which Ludovick was clearly paying no regard: 'he never saw any of the tenants pursuers in the recrimination convened or decerned in any court of the country for the pryce of rears but declares that the tenants were decreeted for their rents and that poyndings without tryall or sentence usually proceeded as the declarant heard only for small services and customs'.[113] The twenty-seven cows taken from McAlister Dow clearly didn't correspond to small services or customs.

After July 1710 Ludovick continued to argue that he had a right of management in the Grant estates thanks to his annuity, which he claimed entitled him to act as a manager issuing tacks and adjusting conversion rates on his son's behalf.[114] However, his actions were wholly at odds with these claims, with coercion becoming a key tactic in his struggle to exert control over the estate. The witness statements from the justiciary court case record how he took to wearing a sabre in order to intimidate the tenants and indeed the commissioners themselves.[115] Alexander Grant of Lethendrie, chamberlain to Alexander Grant of Grant was one of those Ludovick sought to intimidate:

> Alexander Grant in Lethendrie, chamberlain to young Grant, declares that the Laird of Grant [Ludovick Grant] upon severall occasions and particularly a little after mertimass last discharge the declarant to medle

111 Stair, *Institutions of the Law of Scotland*, ii, v, x, p. 436.

112 Erskine, *An Institute of the Law of Scotland*, p. 514.

113 NRS, Declarations of Mullochard's witnesses against lord and lady Grant, GD248/22/3/35, fo. 8.

114 NRS, High Court of Justiciary, Minutes, 1710–1711, JC7/5, p. 258.

115 NRS, List of claims against Ludovick Grant and Lady Jean Houston, GD248/22/3/60.

> any manner of way with the rents as chamberlain for young Grant otherwayes he would make hime repent it.[116]

In autumn 1710 the new commissioners called together the inhabitants of the regality to answer to a head court to pay their rents as was the custom. However, on the appointed day the people were forcibly prevented from attending by Ludovick's servants, every action possible was being taken to ensure no rents were uplifted, or possession poinded, other than by Ludovick himself:

> In September last the declarant as officer [Donald Roy officer for Cromdale parish] did convene the country to answer to a court holden by young Grant's factors, but he was threatened and boasted to dismiss the tenants and discharge there attendants and that accordingly he did dismiss and discharge them.[117]

It is for this reason that no court for the collection of rents in autumn 1710 is to be found in the court records. In fact, following Alexander Grant's return to the army in July 1710, the commissioners were unable to hold any courts in the face of Ludovick's threats. With the most essential part of the management of the estate, the collection of rents, unable to take place, the commissioners were useless. Alexander returned briefly in November 1710 and convened a regality court, the first since July, to formally establish the commissioners, bailies, and officers in their roles, and to make a public show of doing so. However, even after Alexander's intervention, it was not until 24 April 1711, a gap of some eight months, that the commissioners were finally able to re-establish the system of regality courts in Strathspey. Without regality courts poindings could continue to be executed without decreet or indeed without the debt even existing, leaving tenants vulnerable to arbitrary processes. In turn without the local system of courts the people of Strathspey lost their most convenient means of challenging the seizure of their goods and gaining some redress. This raises the point of why the victims of summary poindings had not simply complained to the regality court in the months before it had ceased to sit. The answer was quite simply was that Ludovick Grant was both sheriff principal of the shire and competent to sit as a bailie in the regality court. Although Ludovick seldom availed himself of his right to sit as judge in his court, it is clear that the possibility of him doing so was enough to deter the people of the regality

116 NRS, Declarations of Mullochard's witnesses against lord and lady Grant, GD248/22/3/35, fo. 1.

117 Ibid, fo. 7.

from going to court against him, as one witness put it, 'application to a judge would have only provoked the pursuer [Ludovick] to have executed his threatenings before it could have been prevented, besides that the pursuer himself was sheriff and judge ordinary of the bounds'.[118] Thus we find that there was a desire and need for courts which were capable of upholding due process, but at the same time there was an acceptance that the Grant courts in Strathspey were neither independent nor unbiased.

It was these grievances relating to poindings and a lack of courts which were the main motivations leading to the gentry and tenants garrisoning Castle Grant in May 1711, and in turn raising criminal proceedings against their former laird and master. However, the large debts of the family and the despotic manner in which Ludovick Grant had conducted himself, reveal that notions of clanship and honour also motivated the armed resistance to the former clan chief. His intimidation of his former tenants, disregard for due process and dire mismanagement of the estate, were regarded as deeply damaging to the honour and good name of the Grants and thus it was perhaps this notion of a threat to the clan, along with personal injustices that caused the men of Strathspey to act. This sentiment is clear in a letter written to 'the garrison of Castle Grant' by John Grant of Dalrachney on behalf of Alexander's commissioners, 'I would have you consider that the ruine or standing of the family depends on you and that you may expect your reward'.[119] There is also a clear sense in the charges brought by Mullochard against Ludovick Grant that Mullochard was a reluctant litigant, unwilling to take any kind of action which might bring the name of Grant into disrepute. On the other hand, he and his fellow co-defendants clearly abhorred the behaviour of their former chief, especially regarding the collection of rents and his pretentions as lord and master of Strathspey. The information on the case for the lords of justiciary show how far Ludovick Grant had fallen in the estimations of his clan:

> To this [the argument of Mullochard] the pursuers [Ludovick Grant and Lady Jean Houston] answer, that he is of an ancient and noble family and clan … as chief, superior, head of the clan, master, benefactor, Lord etc. who had maintained the dignity and reputation of the hole clan, but these are bombasts and words of vanity.[120]

118 NRS, Justice Court Minutes, JC7/5/195, p. 246.
119 NRS, Letter addressed to the garrison at Castle Grant, GD248/22/3/34, fo. 34.
120 NRS, Justice Court Minutes, JC7/5/195, p. 234.

Whilst Ludovick Grant was undoubtedly a figure of increasing unpopularity, by and large the hatred of the people was reserved for his second wife Jean Houston, regarded as a bad influence, she could not be redeemed in the eyes of the clan by ties of kinship, 'the lady who seems to be the chief actor and manager in these exactions'.[121] The resentment felt towards Houston was made worse by the fact she was a Lowlander, an incomer and her marriage to Ludovick was already her third. For the men of the clan it was undoubtedly easier to lay most of the blame for events in Strathspey at the feet of the troublesome second wife, who was upsetting established authority by undermining the role of her husband and the clan chief in a very patriarchal society.

With both Mullochard's party and Ludovick Grant remitted to pass before an assize by the lords of justiciary it was perhaps inevitable, given both sides' concerns about the good name of the clan, that an out of court settlement should have been reached. Mullochard and Dalrachney along with two commissioners, Captain John Grant of Easter Elchies and Joseph Brodie of Milntoun, paid £50 each in reparations to Ludovick, all other charges being dropped in return for the commissioners being allowed to resume full management of the estate. Meanwhile arbitration between Alexander and Ludovick resulted in an 'amicable' resolution of their dispute over the settlement of the estate. Ludovick's annuity was reduced in return for Alexander taking over liability for all of Ludovick's personal debts.[122]

4.5 Conclusion

Debt and credit were central aspects of rural life in seventeenth and eighteenth-century Strathspey. As a result, the pursuit of debt actions in the regality court, especially those made by the regality chamberlain, was a central part of the work of the court. When such litigation is taken together with actions for the collection of rentals made by the chamberlain through the court, it is clear that the forum of debt was one of the main ways that people came into contact with the regality court and the legal system.[123] As creditors, debtors, and executors, the people of Strathspey could often be brought into contact with the regality court, the witness statements in the case of Ludovick Grant v Mungo Grant of Mullochard confirm that there was a familiarity with

---

121 Ibid, p. 212.

122 NRS, Papers relating to the arbitration between Grant younger and Grant, GD248/22/3/39.

123 Muldrew, *Economy of Obligation*, p. 243.

the court and its procedures. This led to an exposure to the legal system which is much greater than in the present day. Litigation rates in recent years in England are believed to be around 25% of the rate which was found around 1600.[124] Robust statistics are not available here, but the impression given is of something similar.

The case of Ludovick Grant v. Mungo Grant of Mullochard, concerning illegal poindings, clearly demonstrates how feudal franchises continued to play a major role in the rural communities of Scotland. There was a clearly a desire for local courts capable of upholding due process and independent of the machinations of the local landowner. However, there was a risk of partiality in the franchise courts and the power of the laird or clan chief was capable of bypassing legal procedure. As a result, the people of Strathspey were forced to search for legality in the justice court. In turn, this is indicative of a wider dispute between traditional notions of chieftainship and the modern administration of the law as a jurisdiction holder.

The conflict between Mullochard and Ludovick Grant reveals how notions of clanship pervaded society and justice in Strathspey in the early years of the eighteenth century, leading to the oppression of the tenants of the Grants, but also inspiring them to retaliation and revolt, notionally for the good of the clan rather than solely for personal redress, in the face of the illegal seizure of their possessions. Clearly some landowners such as Ludovick Grant were increasingly distancing themselves from the type of patriarchal behaviour still expected by the clan gentry and tenants, instead choosing to pursue profit from the land regardless of the damage they were wreaking upon traditional bonds of kinship. This behaviour is arguably demonstrative of wider trends in Scottish society in the eighteenth century, whereby chiefs increasingly sought to increase the income they derived from their land often at the expense of the traditional paternalistic model of estate management.[125] On the other hand, Ludovick's son Alexander displayed rather more sympathy when exercising the social and political roles expected of a landowner. In addition, the gentry of the clan Grant, the majority of whom were wadsetters and thus quasi-landowners themselves, were vehement in

124 Muldrew, *Economy of Obligation*, p. 236.

125 See for instance, T M Devine, *Clanship to Crofters War: The Social Transformation of the Scottish Highlands* (Manchester, 1994), pp. 43–44; T M Devine, *The Transformation of Rural Scotland: Social Change and the Agrarian Economy, 1660–1815* (Edinburgh, 1994), pp. 47–50; Dodgshon, *From Chiefs to Landlords*, pp. 102–117. Dodgshon cites various examples of how landlords increasingly sought to increase their rental income, although none are quite as drastic as Ludovick Grant's actions.

their support of the traditional clan model in Strathspey. This suggests that it is important not to overstate the process of transition from paternalistic to commercial management of land in the Highlands in the early eighteenth century

CHAPTER 5

Criminal Jurisdiction

The criminal jurisdiction bestowed upon barons and lords of regality has become the most enduring image of heritable justice in Scotland, and the Highlands especially. The symbolic power of life and death granted to many jurisdiction holders in their charters of infeftment styled '*cum furca et fossa*' shocks and intrigues many in the present day. For others it serves to confirm their notions that the cocktail of landownership, clanship, and jurisdiction, concentrated in a small number of men, was a vehicle for corruption and oppression. Yet, for all the emphasis placed in popular culture upon the power to punish those living upon their lands, criminal justice played a relatively minor role in the workings of the court. In the regality of Grant only around a quarter of cases found in the court books relate to crime. However, whilst popular culture has overstated the power of barons and lords of regality some historians have done exactly the opposite. Ann Whetsone, for example, wrote that 'by 1700 the national courts had made substantial inroads into the rights of the Lords of Regality. Serious crimes and major civil suits disappeared from regality courts'.[1] An analysis of the court records of the regality of Grant shows rather that a middle ground should be tread.

The extent of regality courts' criminal jurisdiction has long been a point of dispute amongst both writers of the period and modern-day historians. Whilst it is uncontested that regalities were competent jurisdictions in cases of theft (both infang and outfang), slaughter, and the various quasi-criminal offences relating to acts of violence such as bloodwitt, riot and deforcement, the higher element of its jurisdiction is less clear. Like Mackenzie, Balfour, Skene and Hope all argued that the four pleas to the crown fell beyond the jurisdiction of regality courts and indeed had always done so.[2] This conclusion is supported by modern historians such as Julian Goodare.[3] Whilst regality courts theoretically enjoyed a cumulative criminal jurisdiction akin to that of the justiciary court, and in a few limited cases continued to hear the four pleas to the crown into the eighteenth century, the majority of regalities found few opportunities to put their theoretical powers into practical execution.[4]

1 Whetstone, *Scottish County Government*, p. 2.

2 Goodare, *The Government of Scotland*, p. 184.

3 Ibid, p. 184.

4 Ibid, p.185. However, according to Davies the regality of Montrose tried a case of arson as late as 1735, Davies, 'Law and Order in Stirlingshire', p. 292.

 | DOI:10.1163/9789004472549_006

Limitations upon the theoretical criminal jurisdiction of regalities came from both above and below. Hence, they were limited by the high court of justiciary in the most important criminal pleas, as well as in ones which were politically motivated. Additionally, until 1708, many important actions, found their way to the privy council. Indeed there had been concerted efforts from central government to take away the administration of justice from lords of regality and other Highland elite.[5] At the other end of the spectrum, regality courts found their criminal jurisdiction as a court of first instance for bloodwitts and petty theft limited by baron and sheriff courts, who were the de facto courts of first instance in such cases.[6]

It was these lesser crimes which made up most of the criminal workload of the court. Minor thefts, i.e. those thefts which were liable to result only in a punishment targeting the thief's means rather than his person, were common in the regality court of Grant in the years immediately preceding 1700. This was largely due to the ravages of the famine of the late 1690s; minor theft features only infrequently in the court records thereafter. Indeed, on average only one case of petty theft was brought before the court each year after this date. Violent crime played a much larger role in the day to day workings of the court and shall be considered in greater detail.

5.1 Violent Crime and the Regality Court of Grant

> The carrying of arms so much insisted on, is no qualification of violence whatsoever, for the carrying of arms in that country is full as usual as wearing cloaths.[7]

It is often said that Scotland in the seventeenth and eighteenth centuries was a violent place, especially in the Highlands.[8] Southern prejudices promoted the belief that lawlessness prevailed and adversaries were more likely to defer to fists or swords than a court of law.[9] The court records of the regality court of Grant record many instances of physical violence. Disagreements escalating

5 Goodare, *State and Society in Early Modern Scotland*, p.267.

6 Ibid p. 289.

7 NRS, Justiciary Court Records, JC7/5/195, p. 238.

8 A Kennedy, 'Crime and Punishment in Early Modern Scotland: the Secular Courts of Restoration Argyllshire, 1660–1688', *International Review of Scottish Studies*, 41 (2016), p. 9.

9 A M Kilday, 'The Barbarous North? Criminality in Early Modern Scotland', in T M Devine and J Wormald (eds.), *The Oxford Handbook of Modern Scottish History* (Oxford, 2012), p. 386.

into physical violence were a common problem in agricultural communities such as the farming townships found in Strathspey.[10] Living together in close-proximity with little privacy and having to manage and share the meagre natural resources with which nature had endowed their holdings inevitably led to conflict. In such cases it often fell to the court of the landowner to enforce internal order for the good of all concerned, reflecting the reciprocal arrangement between lord and vassal whereby each sustained the others' interests.[11]

5.1.1 *Trends in Violent Crime*

Keeping the peace was one of the fundamental roles of franchise jurisdictions. Jurisdiction holders owed a duty to both the crown and their vassals to secure peace locally. One of the greatest threats to the peace and the stability of the community was violent crime, which usurped the rules of ordered society by removing dispute resolution from the forum of the local courts and instead placed it on the level of private vengeance. In the context of Strathspey in the early modern period, riots or breaches of the peace also described as assaults, bloodings and bloodwitts were the most common type of violence to appear in the court records. There are 105 such cases from the erection of the regality to the cessation of records in 1729. The number of violent crimes appearing in the court shows no identifiable trend over time, with the number of violent crimes pursued each year remaining relatively stable. The greatest number of cases occurred in 1703 when thirteen cases appear in the records. In contrast, in the six years preceding 1703 only two violent crimes were recorded in the court record. The low number of cases from 1697–1702 fits with the general drop off in all business, apart from theft, during this period.

236 people who were involved in cases of violence in the regality court have been identified in the court records. Some patterns emerge from examination of the parties to violent crime. Unsurprisingly, the majority of aggressors and victims in assault cases were male and came from the tenant/subtenant class.[12] It is imperfect to group together the wide range of people included within the tenant/subtenant class. Unfortunately, the court records often give little detail of the status of individuals within this section of society. In altercations affecting this social group most disputes occurred between people living within the

10 Brown, *Bloodfeud in Scotland*, p. 58.

11 Mitchison, *Lordship to Patronage*, p. 5.

12 With a lack of information about most litigants, I have grouped those people identified as residing 'in' a place as falling within the tenant/subtenant class. This is opposed to those people identified as being 'of' a place and thus falling within the gentleman class of tacksman/wadsetter/feuar. Servants are always denoted as being 'servant of X'.

same, or neighbouring townships, reflecting the tensions inherent in cooperative farming life. Such tensions were clearly at the basis of a riot brought before a court at Boat of Cromdale in August 1708, when a dispute between Donald Stewart in Craigbeg and William Strasor in the neighbouring township of Auchnarrow erupted into violence over communal grazings.[13] The initial dispute and resolution in court all took place within two miles. It was clearly recognised that peace within the community could be best obtained through settlements negotiated locally by parties who were closely connected to the case.[14]

Gentlemen rarely feature as aggressors or victims in the Grant court books, appearing only ten times. However, of these there are several cases of significance. In contrast, other contemporary court records show that gentry were frequently implicated in violence. For instance, a disproportionately large number of gentlemen from Strathspey were indicted in the northern circuit of the justiciary court.[15] An underlying reason for this trend is that the wadsetters and tacksmen had traditionally provided many of the clan's soldiers.[16] In the early years of the eighteenth century these gentlemen found a new martial outlet in the independent companies policing the Highlands, especially in Colonel William Grant of Ballindalloch's company of Grants, in which several of the regality's gentlemen served alongside ordinary tenants.[17] These men had ready access to arms and a licence to commit certain acts of violence. Kilday has studied this trend and attributes the number of violent acts committed by soldiers to large amounts of time spent unoccupied between duties whilst armed.[18] Of the gentry in Strathspey, the kin of John Grant of Dalrachney were particularly violent. Indicted several times before the justice court they were also indicted before the regality court of Grant. Two of the family, George and David Grant, were imprisoned in Castle Grant in November 1723 for threatening Robert Grant of Kinchurdie.[19] Both David and George had both been convicted of attempted murder only three years previously and had since had further

13 Grant Court Book 2, 14-16/03/1708, pp. 111–112.
14 Brown, *Bloodfeud in Scotland*, p. 56.
15 See later in this chapter.
16 P Simpson, *The Independent Highland Companies* (Glasgow, 1996), p. 10.
17 See for instance, NRS, The Knock notebook, RH2/8/96. The notebook reveals that Patrick Grant of Tullochgorum, George Grant of Clurie, Patrick Grant of Glenlochy, John Grant of Glenbeg, Ludovick Grant of Badeniden and Lewis Grant of Auchterblair served amongst others along with a member of the Dalrachney family.
18 Kilday, 'The Barbarous North?', p. 394.
19 Grant Court Book 4, 07/11/1723, p. 88.

appearances before the justice court.[20] They were required to grant letters of lawburrows to the effect that Kinchurdie and his brothers, who included Lewis Grant of Auchterblair (another soldier, bailie and wadsetter), would remain unharmed in future.

Ten years previously in March 1713 another member of the Dalrachney family, Alexander Grant of Lethendrie (chamberlain of the regality) had been before the regality court as the pursuer in an action for riot and assault regarding an altercation between him and Robert Grant of Lurg.[21] The defenders and witnesses were cited to appear a further six times before the court. Resolution was finally reached after the case was submitted to arbitration under the laird, Alexander Grant of Grant. The continuation of this case over two years suggests that negotiation was ongoing behind the scenes.[22] The fines and very large cautionary bonds imposed (offering specific protection to each party's brothers rather than the generic 'their wives and children their goods and gear shall be harmless and skaithless' found in most letters of lawburrows) reflect both the importance of the parties and also that this case brought their wider kin groups into conflict. Such a dispute between cadet branches of the family whilst not unheard of, was nonetheless unusual, and would have threatened internal order and stability within the regality and clan.[23] This case also demonstrates the power of the laird in the resolution of disputes; the authority of the regality court, embodied in a gentleman-bailie, was in itself insufficient to force the parties (both of high office and status in the regality) to reach settlement and final resolution was only reached by the intervention of the men's patriarchal clan chief and laird. There was a confidence in the personal justice of the laird to which the gentry were happier to submit than justice handed out by one of their peers.[24]

In a small number of cases members of the gentry were the victims of violence committed by their social inferiors. For instance, in July 1704 three men in the parish of Cromdale attacked and wounded John Grant of Tullochgorum.[25] The perpetrators, two of whom were soldiers, were called before the regality court to render assythement of £50 each to Tullochgorum.[26] Whilst the severity

20 NRS, Minutes of the Northern Circuit of the High Court of Justiciary, JC11/4, pp.133–140; NRS Minutes of the Northern Circuit of the High Court of Justiciary, JC11/5 pp. 50 and 52.

21 Grant Court Book 3, p.38. Lurg was also a bailie of the regality court.

22 M Wasser, 'Violence and the central criminal courts in Scotland, 1603–1638', (Unpublished Ph.D. thesis Columbia University, 1995), p. 202.

23 For instance, there was a serious dispute between Robert Grant of Auchterblair and Duncan Grant of Mullochard in 1675. See Fraser, *Chiefs of Grant*, Vol. III, pt. II, p. 455.

24 Brown, *Bloodfeud in Scotland*, p. 44.

25 Grant Court Book 2, 04/12/1704, p. 42.

26 Ibid.

of the injuries suffered by Tullochgorum are not made clear by the records, it is evident from the size of the assythement that the case was regarded as being particularly serious. The attack upon Tullochgorum, who was both a bailie and a wadsetter, was probably viewed as an attack upon authority and social order within Strathspey.[27]

The other major social group that features in violent disputes in the court records was the large class of agricultural and domestic servants. However, in only three cases were the servants the victims of an assault at the hands of their master. This is probably attributable to a judicial reluctance to intervene in domestic matters such as the disciplining of servants, and the actual number of such incidences would have been likely to have been much greater.[28] In nearly all assault cases concerning servants, the aggressor was a tenant within the same township as the servant's own master, again showing that most disputes were between neighbours.

5.1.2 *Gendered Differences in Violence*

Several patterns emerge when we consider women's relationship to violent crime in the regality of Grant. Firstly, women were proportionally more likely to be victims of violent crime. Of these cases few were domestic assaults. This is easily explained by the degree of licence which was allowed for the 'reasonable' chastisement of women by their spouses during this period. Despite this, some indictments were brought by wives against their husbands. Patrick Macmanir in Dell was 'unlawed in ten pounds for beating and striking of Nell Grant in Braes of Lurg his spouse prove be the pursuers oath'.[29] In this case the parties appear to have been separated which may explain why this case of domestic abuse came to be before the court. Most assaults on women were committed by male neighbours. In such cases, an action was brought by the wife with the concurrence of her spouse. Some unmarried women in service were also able to access justice, as several cases against chastising masters prove. For instance, at a court in Milntoun in 1712 'Duncan Nairn in Lagan unlawed in 5 lib for beatting of Barbara Grant his hyre woman'.[30] It is notable that such people, occupying perhaps in the most vulnerable position in society, were able to access legal

27 See, also the case involving an attack on Ranald MacDonald of Gellovie in Laggan Kirk in July 1715, Grant Court Book 3, pp. 88–90. This case is also interesting as evidence of a Jacobite tacksman choosing to submit his case to the laird of Grant's court at the height of Jacobite unrest.

28 J R Ruff, *Violence in Early Modern Europe 1500–1800* (Cambridge, 2001), p. 134.

29 Grant Court Book 2, 17/06/1707, p. 87.

30 Grant Court Book 3, 23/11/1712, p. 29.

redress through the local courts. This is important evidence of how all levels of society in Strathspey used the regality court. It is likely that unmarried women were encouraged or helped to raise actions by family members, as in a case from November 1716, when Issobell Grant's father petitioned the regality court:

> The said day anent ane delatione given to the said bailie ag[ains]t Thomas Grant in Tulchine ffor waylaying of Issobell Grant dochter to John Grant in Callendar betwix Knockandow and Tulchane in the hillway and ffor offering to force her and therby did hurt and abuse her to the effusion of her blood and bruiseing of her bodie therefor the said bailie oblidges the said Thomas to undergo the lawe for the cause forsaid.[31]

This is the only case of sexual assault in the court records. Issobell's case was perhaps typical of many such assaults during the period. Study of the north east assizes in England during this period has shown that 43% of reported rapists assaulted their victims whilst they were traversing remote fields or moorland.[32] Issobell fell victim on just such a remote moorland. Thomas Grant's cautioner was obliged to present him at a future court under the pain of 500 merks, a very substantial sum reflecting that this was no ordinary assault. However, there are several possible reasons why the case was not prosecuted as a rape, or attempted rape, and why no other sexual assaults are found in the records. The first is that rape was very difficult to prove and thus prosecution for assault offered a greater chance of success.[33] Secondly, in an age where great importance was attached to the virtue of women, there was little to be gained by women or their family from reporting sexual assaults.[34]

Women were also aggressors in cases of assault brought before the regality court. Kilday's study of the justiciary court records for Lowland Scotland has recognised women's overlooked role as perpetrators of violent crimes.[35] In the regality of Grant the involvement of women in assaults is much lower than the figures cited by Kilday yet still worthy of note. Assaults committed by women were often directed against other women or were carried out in conjunction

---

31 Grant Court book 3, 20/11/1716, p. 97.

32 Ruff, *Violence in Early Modern Europe*, p. 141; for Scottish examples taking place on highways see, B P Levack, 'The Prosecution of Sexual Crimes in Early Eighteenth-Century Scotland', *SHR* 89:2 (2010), p. 189.

33 Ibid, p. 188.

34 J Kelly, "A most inhuman and barbarous piece of villainy' An Exploration of the Crime of Rape in Eighteenth-Century Ireland', *Eighteenth Century Ireland/Iris an dá chutúr*, 10 (1995), pp. 78–107, p. 79.

35 A M Kilday, *Women and Violent Crime in Enlightenment Scotland* (Woodbridge, 2007), p. 82.

with a co-assailant, often their husband. This is another trend also recognised by Kilday.[36] There are only two cases of a man pursuing a woman for assault in the court records.[37] This may simply reflect that men were less likely to be the victim of women's violence.

5.1.3 *Types of Violence*

a) Violent Threats and Caution

Within the pages of the court books there is to be found a wide spectrum of violent acts committed by inhabitants of the regality. The range of violent disputes reveals much about tensions within the community. At the more benign end of this spectrum came verbal threats such as that made at a court at Milntoun of Castle Grant in 1724: 'Daniel Reid Servitor to the laird of Grant threatened in face of court to doo bodily harm to John Adam mer[chan]t in Grantown ordained both the said parties to enter prison untill they secure the peace to one another for the future'.[38] Two years later Isobel Happy was subjected to threats, as a result she petitioned the court, 'Ag[ain]st Christian Bain spouse to McLuieban in Cromdall and Janet and Elspet Bains her sisters anent threatening to murder her and upbraiding[39] her the said Isobbell Happy'.[40] Such threats were usually defused by the practice of requiring potential aggressors to find surety for their future conduct. Violent transgressors were usually forbidden to leave court or imprisoned until caution was secured. Cautioners faced large penalties if the bond of caution was not observed, this was one of the few available means of guarding against the possibility of future violence between the parties.[41] Harrison has written that caution and lawburrows were essential preventative measures in rural areas that lacked the predecessors to policing present in the early-modern burghs.[42] Caution was also a mechanism by which the acts of an individual could be made the concern of the wider community.[43] Those inhabitants of the regality who became cautioners showed a deep commitment to the community and the common weal; by inference they were regarded as good neighbours. The practice of rendering

36 Ibid, pp. 94–5.

37 Kilday, 'Women and Crime in South-West Scotland', p. 88.

38 Grant Court Book 5, 31/01/1724, p. 18.

39 "Upbraiding", physically or verbally abusing or assaulting. *DSL*.

40 Grant Court Book 5, 28/06/1726, p. 116.

41 There are several people who rendered caution who then went onto reoffend; however, the system of caution appears to have been reasonably effective and the only practicable means of keeping the peace available to the court.

42 J G Harrison, '"Policing" the Stirling area, 1660–1706', *Scottish Archives*, 7 (2001), p. 18.

43 Falconer, *Crime and Community in Reformation Scotland*, p. 61.

caution also reflects how reliant the justice system was on the inhabitants of the community to regulate the behaviour of those people who wished to be a part of it.

Court records denote that there were separate 'caution books' attached to the regality court in which the names of cautioners were recorded.[44] In the majority of cases the cautioner came from a township within two miles of the one where the cautionee lived, clear indication that they were kinsmen or close acquaintances. However, in only 15% of examples did the cautioner come from the same township as the cautionee. This suggests that the notion of the community stretched further than the individual townships or davoch to embrace a cluster of neighbouring townships. Alternatively, this may also suggest that too close a neighbour might not be an appropriate choice as a cautioner. 40% of the men who stood as cautioners were gentry. Tacksmen and wadsetters were considered to have a degree of responsibility for the conduct of their sub-tenants.[45] As sub-tenants were usually tied to a particular tacksman and would follow him should he move to new lands at the expiry of his tack, there was a relationship of mutual dependency between to the two parties.[46] However, there are only two examples in the Grant court books of a tacksman standing caution for his own sub-tenants.[47] They were more likely to be found standing caution for residents on lands neighbouring their own. It seems that the gentry class had a wider responsibility to the well-being of the community and were expected to lead their social subordinates by example. Undoubtedly in many cases a substantial tenant or gentleman was required to act as a cautioner as they were the only people able to realise the sum set against the panel's future conduct. If a gentleman was willing to stand caution for a panel it was also undoubtedly good for the reputation of the panel if an esteemed member of the community was willing to vouch for his future good conduct. Some wadsetters appear multiple times in the court records as cautioners. One such man was Robert Grant of Dallachaple. Dallachaple was a procurator who often had cause to be present in the regality court upon legal business. This might be the reason for his frequent appearances as a cautioner.

When it was feared that tensions between individuals might escalate into further violence, parties could register letters of lawburrows in an effort to maintain the peace. Lawburrows were not often granted by the court, with

44 Grant Court Book 4, 07/11/1723, p. 88.

45 Taylor, *The Wild Black Region*, pp. 19–21.

46 Ibid, p. 28.

47 Donald Grant of Tullochgiban, Grant Court Book 2, 30/01/1710, p. 137; John Grant younger of Gelloway, Grant Court Book 3, 05/07/1715, p. 85.

only twelve recorded prior to 1729. Kilday has written that letters of lawburrows were popular by virtue of their speed, inexpensiveness and the fact that no evidential burden had to be discharged before letters were granted.[48] In the regality court records it appears that lawburrows were usually sought after violence had already taken place, in anticipation of further quarrel between the two parties. Parties to lawburrows had a certain amount of time in which to compear with their cautioner in court. Failure to compear in court in order to grant letters of lawburrows resulted in a fine and in extreme cases being declared an outlaw.[49] The court record from 18 February 1695 gives some idea of the pressures that the regality court might exert in extreme cases, to force a person to grant letters of lawburrows:

> The said day James Grant of Acherneck hath herby enacted bound and obliest himselff to find securitie and lawburrowes to Lachlane Grant in Pluscarden and by ane sub[sequen]t bond be himselff and his cau[tione]r to be given and delyvered to James Grant of Gelloway bailie ag[ains]t the last of Febr[uar]y instant bade the failie of ffyve hundreth merks or else to compear befor the comissionars of justiciarie at Elgin upone the eight of march nixt yeiris.[50]

Perpetrators of violent crime were given a small amount of time to find a cautioner before further action was taken. By threatening to refer Grant of Achernack to the commissioners of justiciary in Elgin, the bailie reveals several things. Firstly, it suggests that appearing before the commissioners was regarded as a more serious prospect than an appearance before the regality court and was thus a good way to ensure that Achernack found a cautioner. It is also rare evidence of the links between the regality of Grant and the central courts and can be taken as evidence that the two jurisdictions were cooperating and that the regality authorities regarded a commission of justiciary as a superior jurisdiction.

b) Violent Disputes

Not all cautionary actions were effective in preventing disputes from escalating. Physical assaults were much more likely to be the subject of litigation than threats alone. The level of description of violent crimes in the court books

48 Kilday, 'Woman and Crime in Enlightenment Scotland', p. 94.
49 Grant Court Book 1, 16/02/1695, p. 55.
50 Grant Court Book 1, 18/02/1695, p. 56.

varies greatly. However, occasionallythe court records paint a vivid picture of the events which unfolded:

> The said day John Fraser in Deshar is absolved from the claim at the instances of Gregor Grant and Donald Hay [sur]gianis ffor their curing of Turner who was woundit by the said John and employed by him for that effect in respect that the said John under silence of night wes coming from his neighbours house with ane sword in his hand and goeing towards his house he was [illeg] assaulted be the said Turner, Alexander Stuart and Wiliam Voir in Desher with disigne of purpois to offright him and rub ane affront[51] upon him and not knowing whither they were men or Ghostis he strak at them with the sword and it hapened the said Turner to be wounded in the bellie.[52]

Two points are emphasised by the case of John Frazer: firstly, it reinforces the observation that disputes were predominantly the result of fraught relationships within geographically close-knit communities, where competition, close-proximity, and a lack of privacy bred conflict. Disputes over grazing rights and boundaries, the impounding of livestock and other acts which were of great significance in rural communities were antagonising. A further good example of this came in August 1708 when a fight broke out between the people in the neighbouring townships of Craigbeg and Achnarrow. The court chastised the men involved for trying to resolve a boundary dispute with violence rather than referring the argument to a perambulation undertaken by the regality court.[53]

Secondly, the case involving John Frazer shows that the use of weapons in disputes was widespread and could lead to the rapid escalation of a disagreement. It was customary to wear arms in Strathspey. Mungo Grant of Mullochard alluded to this in a statement made to the justiciary court in 1712 when he said that 'the carrying of arms so much insisted on, is no qualification of violence whatsoever, for the carrying of arms in that country [Strathspey] is full as usual as wearing cloaths'.[54] Contemporary writers such as Sir George Mackenzie of Rosehaugh also testified to the customary nature of carrying arms in the Highlands in the late seventeenth century.[55] This practice undoubtedly eased the transition from verbal disagreement to bloodshed. In a society where every

51 To attach shame, contempt or humiliation, DSL.
52 Grant Court Book 2, 23/02/1703, p. 2.
53 Grant Court Book 2, 4/03/1708, p. 111–112.
54 NRS, Minutes of the High Court of Justiciary, JC7/5/195, p. 238.
55 Mackenzie, *The Laws and Customs of Scotland*, p. 316.

man carried at least a dirk, it was all too easy to lash out when tempers frayed with serious consequences. Whilst the carrying of firearms was prohibited by statute, it was lawful to carry swords and blades until the disarming act of 1716.[56] However, the effectiveness of this statute was doubtful, as the affray between James Blair and Donald Grant in 1725 shows:

> The which day anent the information given be James Blair in Dellifure ag[ains]t Donald Grant lawful eldest son to John Grant in Biananach mentioning that he was lesed and mutilated in his right hand by the said Donald Grant armed with a sword and other unlawful wapons and in respect the said judge judges it proper until further probation of the said alleged lesia be held and that the said James Blair is dangerously wounded in his right hand as appears therefor ordains both parties to secure the peace as accords in law to prevent further danger … [subscribing an act of caution] At command of the said James Blair who cannot wryte in respect of the wounds he has in his right hand and forearm his hand touching the pen Alexander Cumine [clerk] doe subscribe for him.[57]

In the case of James Blair, the injuries to his right hand were especially serious given his position as procurator fiscal and writer within the regality. Blair was still seeking assythement for his injuries a year later when he twice again appeared in court:

> craving assythement for loss of health by ane blood and ryot committed by the defender upon the pursuer to his great loss and prejudice and anent the claim given in be Robert Cumine in Auchcroisk surgean for performing the cure upon the said pursuer viz of one large wound and nyne small wound all in the hands. The said judge decerned and hereby decerens the said defender to make payment to the said James Blair of ane hundred pounds scotis money as assythement for all damage sustained be him throw the said ryot and bloodwitt and forty pounds scotis

56 The following were exempt from full disarmament: the peerage; officers of the law; and crucially for our study, commoners with a yearly income exceeding £400, or who were qualified to vote. Crucially this meant that the wadsetters in Strathspey could retain their arms. (See: An act for the more effectual securing the peace of the Highlands in Scotland 1716, 1 Geo.I. st. 2. c.54.) This exemption was also included in the more effective disarmament act of 1725.

57 Grant Court Book 5, 13/04/1725, pp. 48–9.

> money to the said surgean for his pains, attendance and medicaments in performing the said cure.[58]

It is unclear if James Blair was successful in gaining payment of the assythement he claimed was due. Donald Grant was one of several individuals who appeared several times in the regality court accused of assault.[59] Violence went through all social classes; James Blair the fiscal himself had previously been indicted for brawling in 1724.[60]

5.1.4 *Process*

A number of court appearances in 1724 allow us to understand the process used by the court in relation to violent crime. These concern John Adam, a merchant, who held a tack of one third of old Grantown and had seven citations relating to violent crime before the regality court of Grant. Whilst no direct evidence from the regality of Grant survives as to how cases of riot and bloodwitt were instigated, evidence from other contemporaneous court records show that prosecutions for assaults and riots were usually initiated by a private libel of complaint.[61] These letters or libels gave details of the alleged crime and the remedy sought, usually being both punishment and assythement. These papers were then served upon the defender by a regality officer. Private prosecution was the norm during our period of study, with the prosecution of violent crime still being regarded as the interest of the victim rather than the public. However, in many cases one of the regality's procurators fiscal would lend his concurrence to the prosecution in question. The fiscal was joined to the action to represent the laird's interest in the case and ensure that the laird received the fines that he was due. In addition, the concurrence of the fiscal probably served to lend authority or maybe even legal expertise to the pursuer's cause.[62]

The process of raising a prosecution can be seen in the main action involving John Adam. John Adam was in debt to Gregor Burgess, a tenant who held tacks of land in both the multiple tenant farms of Achnagall (now Achnagallin) and Auchnahannet. In June 1724, after citation before the court to make payment, Adam violently assaulted Burgess.[63] Burgess accordingly made a libel

58 Grant Court Book 5, 27/01/1726, p. 82 and 25/02/1726, p. 86.

59 Grant Court Book 5, 02/06/1729, p. 164 and 28/07/1729, p. 172.

60 Grant Court Book 5, 26/07/1724, p. 31.

61 Davies, 'Law and Order in Stirlingshire', p. 254 and p. 388.

62 Wasser, 'Violence in the Central Criminal Courts', p. 106.

63 In 1719 Adam was resident in Achnagall and thus had been a neighbour of Burgess, who had even stood cautioner for Adam in both 1719 and 1724 when Adam was required to

of complaint which was read out in court: 'The which day Gregor Burgess in Auchnagall with concur[ren]se of the proc[urato]r fiscall complains that John Adam merch[an]t in Grantown for wrestling, beating and blooding of him and craves that he may be fyned according to law'.[64] Adam was called three times at the court house door but failed to appear. He was given seven days to compear and present a cautioner, whilst another man was admonished for failing to present Adam at court as required.[65] Adam again failed to compear a week later, and it was not until a month after his initial citation that he finally appeared in court. When Adam appeared before the bailie he refused to answer to the libel on oath, as the bailie requested. He was thus fined £10, whilst the case then went to probation.[66] It appears that many cases stopped at this point, with defenders simply admitting the libel against them, with the pursuer's version of events being attested under oath usually sufficient proof to satisfy the court. In cases of bloodwitts, probation was by witnesses who could attest to the libel by deposition. Probation might also require visual proof that the alledged 'skaith' or blood had actually occurred in addition to eyewitness testimony:

> The said day Thomas Walsone and Duncan Nairn in Curr are ilk ane of thame unlawed in fiftie pounds scotis for ther pleying beatting wounding and blooding of one another provine in court by reasone Nairnes wound wes seine to the whole court and Donald Makalaster servant to Curr deponed he knew Nairn to have bled Walsone.[67]

In the Adam case, the defender instead chose to protest against the punishment imposed by the bailie, arguing that the pursuer's information was 'fell' and offered his own version of events.[68] Adam then went on to offer surety of £50 that his version of events was true:

---

render lawburrows: Grant Court Book 4, 24/07/1719, p. 9; Grant Court Book 5, 31/01/1724, p. 18. Burgess' kinsman John was a soldier in William Grant's company and was very active in the regality court. It is possible that John Adam also served in this company; a 'John Grantoune' is mentioned in the same paymaster's account as Burgess; NRS, The Knock notebook, RH2/8/96.

64 Grant Court Book 5, 26/06/1724, p. 25.

65 Grant Court Book 5. 26/06/1724, p. 26.

66 Ibid, 27/07/1724, p. 28.

67 Grant Court book 2, 12/06/1705, p. 49.

68 "Fell", malicious, cruel. *DSL*.

> The which day John Adam mer[chan]d in Grantown defender of the ryot within pursued compeared and granted his bill payable to the Laird of Grant for fifty pound Scots in satisfaction of any thing that could be laid to his charge thereanent. Therefore John Grant of Burnsyde Bailzie assoilized and absolves the said John Adam from all further actions thereanent.[69]

Whilst John Adam succeeded in this instance in having the case against him dismissed, it was only a matter of weeks before he was again called against the court for further fighting.[70] Somewhat unusually, Adam was required to find two cautioners as opposed to the usual one, perhaps reflecting his recidivism.

5.1.5 *Punishment*

Assaults and riots, regardless of their severity, were always punished with a fine by the regality court. The level of the fine levied was clearly dependent upon the seriousness of the crime committed; however, recidivism, the ability of the panel to meet the expense of the fine, and the status of the victim were also considerations taken into account by the bailie and reflected in the fine.[71] Fines ranged in size from that handed down to Patrick Grant in Badiniden who was, 'unlawed in 40s. for striking of Donald Roy taylor in Bellamor', clearly a very minor case, but also reflecting that Patrick Grant may have been a man of small financial means.[72] At the other end of the scale, serious riots, where blood had been let, regularly resulted in fines of £50 for the inhabitants of the regality. This was the largest fine with which a baron court could punish perpetrators of violent crime. In addition, aggressors might be expected to render assythement to their victim in way of compensation for the injury:

> The said day anent the ryot comittit be John Dunbar in Tomnak and upone Robert Ross in Dellachaple wounded him in the heid with a trie or patle of ane pleugh. Both parties examined the said Robert haveing deponed that John Dunbar was the first aggressor and threw the said Robert to the ground and the said Johne did strike him one the heid and cutte his heid and because it with ane patle[73] to the great effusion of his blood and that he was eight days [before] he could doe work and imployed ane

69 Grant Court Book 5, 27/07/1724, p. 29.

70 Grant Court Book 5, 26/09/1724, p. 34.

71 Falconer, *Crime and Community in Reformation Scotland*, p. 120.

72 Grant Court Book 2, 09/03/1704, p. 23.

73 'Pattle', a plough-staff, DSL.

> chirargian [surgeon] to cure his heid … unlaws the said John Dunbar in thrertie pounds to the fiscall and dicerns 5 lib Scotis of assythement.[74]

Davies has suggested that it was ordinary practice in many cases for assythement to be included as part of the fine and only later divided, explaining why it is not often mentioned in court judgements.[75] If the injuries suffered by the victim had been serious enough to warrant medical attention, then the costs of treatment might also be sued for: 'The said day Alaster Mcalkynach in Tullochcrome being pursued at the instance of Gellovie for an assythement of fourtie merkes debaited by him for medicaments and surgeon fies in curing of a wound given by the said Mcalkynack to the said Gellovie'.[76]

The use of a weapon was clearly accepted by the court as being a more serious offence than an assault without weapons and thus resulted in a larger fine. Such principles are clearly visible in a case from 1716:

> The said day Ewan Cattenach in Tulloch and Jon Makalaster there are convict of pley ryot and bloodweit with the said Ewan for striking of the said Jon with ane Scot spaid and the said John by wounding of the said Ewan in the hand with ane drawne dirk proven be famous witnesses and therefore Ewan is unlawed in ten pounds and John Makalister in fiftie pounds and arrests them both in court till they pay or secur for ther fyn.[77]

5.2 Serious Crime and the Regality Court of Grant

> Duncan Grant of Mullochard bailie decernes and adjudges the said Donald Forbes to be taken from the court and keiped under guard. And by the said guard to be brought at one of the cloak in the efternoon of this day the 7th instant of De[cembe]r to the gallowes above Duthell and upon the said gallowes betwixt the said one of the cloak and three hours in the efternoon to be hanged by the neck by the hand of the hangman till he be dead and this is given for doome.[78]

---

74 Grant Court Book 3, 19/11/1712, p.27.

75 Davies, 'Law and Order in Stirlingshire', p. 255.

76 Ibid, p. 90.

77 Grant Court Book 3, 14/06/1716, p. 93.

78 Grant Court Book 2, 06/12/1703, p. 17.

In October 1703 Donald Forbes was found guilty by an assize of stealing from four Grant vassals including Patrick Grant younger of Tullochgorum. Whilst awaiting sentencing Forbes escaped from the prison at Castle Grant and went on the run, fleeing south to Badenoch. The fugitive was re-captured several days later in Mackintosh of Borlum's pigsty with a bag of stolen money. He would be, on 7 December 1703, the last known man to be hanged by the regality court of Grant.[79] Forbes' death was not only the last known example of the use of capital punishment by the court, but also marked the beginning of the decline of the court's exercise of its jurisdiction in serious crimes. The disappearance of capital punishment from the records of many franchise courts around this time or even earlier, has been taken at face value by many as evidence or an indicator of the courts general decline.[80] However, the court books of the regality of Grant show that the courts were certainly not 'losing their grip' in civil causes and violent crime; thus, the steady decrease in the prosecution of more serious or capital crimes, rather than being an indicator of a system of justice in decline generally, is a puzzling anomaly. This section of the chapter will consider the prosecution of serious crime by the regality of Grant, compared with the northern circuit of the justiciary court, sitting in Inverness.

Crimes demanding corporal punishments, such as theft of livestock and slaughter, justified more serious retributive penalties largely because they threatened the social order. These offences are immediately recognisable in the court records, as the trial for capital crimes proceeded before an assize.[81] In theory, serious crime within the regality should have been handled by the regality's own justice court. Each regality had a statutory requirement to hold two such courts annually.[82] This arrangement mirrored the provisions for the justice ayres. However, it is doubtful that this edict was ever effective.[83] Given that the regular holding of ayres met with only limited success prior to 1708, it is unlikely that lords of regality were any more fastidious in holding their own justice courts as prescribed by statute.[84] Indeed, the amount of business

79 Forbes' execution was originally scheduled for 10 am on 8 December; however, the execution was brought forward so that he was executed immediately after his sentencing. This was presumably to prevent him from trying to escape once more.

80 B Lenman and G Parker, 'Crime and control in Scotland, 1500–1800', *History Today*, 30:1 (Jan. 1980), pp. 13–17, p, 13.

81 Davies, 'Law and Order in Stirlingshire', p. 259.

82 *RPS*, 1440/8/3.

83 Mackenzie wrote that the act had long been in desuetude at the time he wrote his *Observations*. See, G Mackenzie, *Observations on the Acts of Parliament*, (Edinburgh, 1688), p. 34.

84 W C Dickinson, "The High Court of Justiciary", in The Stair Society, *An Introduction to Scottish Legal History* (Edinburgh, 1958), p. 408.

probably did not justify convening regular justice courts. Justice courts are first recorded on the Grant estates in 1580, but were most frequently convened on their lands in the 1660s and 1670s.[85] During this period the Grants received privy council commissions to hold justice courts in order to apprehend robbers and caterans passing through their lands.[86] The last recorded justice court held in Strathspey was in 1675 and it is clear from the records of the regality of Grant that no courts specifically designated as justice courts were held during the regality era in Strathspey.[87] Instead, serious crime, as and when it arose, was simply dealt with by the court in the course of its ordinary business.

Patterns in the prosecution of serious crime in the regality court fall neatly into two separate periods: prior to 1703 and thereafter. The five years following the ratification of the Grant's charter, in October 1696, until 1703, were easily the busiest for the regality court in terms of the prosecution of serious crime. However, this increase in business had little to do with the erection of the laird of Grant's jurisdictions into a regality, as the enhanced jurisdiction had little tangible impact on the work of the court. It was very much a case of continuity, perhaps best highlighted by the regality clerk's failure to make any mention of the new regality whatsoever until 1700.[88] Instead, any inhabitants of the regality indicted on serious criminal charges, faced trial before a court of the united baronies, lands and parishes of Strathspey, as had been the case throughout the 1690s. This was clearly a court very similar to the Strathspey justice court of old, in terms of both procedure and jurisdiction.

Thefts were the most common serious crime prosecuted in the regality court. These were predominantly of livestock, as had also been the case during the restoration period. However, the volume of thefts dealt with by the court in 1696 to 1701 was dramatically higher than during the restoration period.[89] The ratification of Grant's charter of regality on 12 October 1696 coincided with the height of the nationwide famine, known as 'King William's ill years', which afflicted Scotland during the 1690s. Across Scotland there was a marked increase in theft, largely motivated by hunger, as the famine worsened.[90] Many

85 NRS, Court Pages, GD248/37/1; For restoration era courts see: NRS, Baron Court Extracts, GD248/76/2.

86 NRS, Privy Council Acta, PC1/39, p.439 and p. 529 and PC1/40/47, p. 165.

87 NRS, Baron Court Extracts, GD248/76/2, fo. 128.

88 Grant Court Book 1, p. 149.

89 Twenty-five people were indicted for capital thefts between October 1696 and January 1701, with only fourteen indicted between January 1662 and October 1675 (the period during which the record of Strathspey justice courts is complete).

90 Cullen, *Famine in Scotland*, pp. 81, 161 and 162. And P Hopkins, *Glencoe and the end of the Highland War* (Edinburgh, 1998), p. 439.

people in Strathspey had suffered serious financial hardship as a result of the activity of both Hanoverian and Jacobite troops in the warfare of 1689–90 and had not yet recovered by the onset of the famine in 1695. Estate rentals for the years 1695 to 1702 show steadily increasing arrears of rent and an increasing number of holdings left waste (nearly ¼ of Glenchernick parish by 1702).[91] These economic hardships are clearly reflected in the number of thefts committed: with thirty-seven people being indicted for thefts in Strathspey from 12 October 1696 to January 1701, of whom twenty-five appeared on capital charges.[92] The court records allude to the desperation of many of those accused of thefts, with many references to how thieves had stolen food or livestock for their own immediate consumption. For instance, a witness deposition against Gavin Roy, a shepherd accused of the theft of wedder hogs recalls:

> The said pannalls compeired and denyed the lyball and the compleaners aduced James Bayn herd to Ludovick Grant in Kirktoune as ane witness who compeired and confessed he saw the said Gavin kill the sheip lybelled … and confessed he took fyr from his mothers house and made fyr betwixt them and roasted and eat some of ane hog.[93]

Besides theft of livestock, the inhabitants of the regality took to stealing other food stuffs. Thus, the court book records a complaint by John Frazer in Achnahannet against John Barron, son of Donald Barron in Abernethy, 'for braking his house and stealing his cheise'.[94] Unable to find caution, and 'notour' as a thief, Jon Barron was hanged at Ballintomb.[95] Clearly hunger did not incline the bailie of the regality, James Grant of Gelloway, to greater clemency, the theft of foodstuffs being especially serious in time of famine. In August 1698 Jannet Kween discovered this to her cost, when she was scourged for stealing cabbage from her neighbour.[96] This was the final period where corporal and capital punishments were handed down with some regularity by the laird of Grant's court, with eight inhabitants of the regality sentenced to death between October 1696 and January 1701.

---

91 NRS, Estate Rentals, GD248/108/16.

92 There is a direct parallel with 1674 which was a year of severe food shortages. Following the shortages two menwere tried and executed by the Grants' baron court for theft. NRS, Baron Court Extracts, GD248/76/2, fo.128. Devine, *Clearance and Improvement*, p. 31.

93 Grant Court Book 1, 23/07/1696, p. 92.

94 Ibid 17/08/1698, p. 128.

95 "Notour", notorious, *DSL*.

96 Grant Court Book 1, 17/08/1698, p. 133.

Whilst 1697 saw better growing conditions in most of Scotland, this was insufficient to compensate for the cumulative effect of the harvest failures of 1695 and 1696.[97] As a result, the situation faced by many in society remained, or became even more, desperate. Thefts of livestock and foodstuffs continued and in response there was a spate of 'executions', with three men hanged, one man lugged, another three men scourged, and four banished from the bounds of the regality in 1697 alone. In this year, the bailie and laird must have been trying by fear and example to impose order on a society which the court books record as being beset by theft and disruption. The southern division of the Highland commission had used similar methods in the early 1680s, whereby targeted executions advertised in the most striking and impressive way possible, to would-be criminals and law-abiding persons alike, that justice was being done.[98] Corporal punishments were also preferred where the criminals were impoverished, as it was believed that heavy punitive damages were no solution in such cases, leading instead to greater impoverishment and further crime.[99]

The timing of this purge of incorrigible criminality in the first full year of the regality, appears like a conscious exercise of power; however, there is no specific evidence that this is the case. Historians have asserted that Ludovick Grant of Grant was a harsh and corrupt judge, especially in his role as sheriff of Inverness.[100] Rather, his actions seem to have been a response to the crime rate which had been rising throughout the 1690s.

Whilst many thefts appear in the court books, many more were settled out of court. Where the burden of proving a crime was beset by evidential difficulties, it was often better financially to settle out of court rather than risk the expense of litigation without securing a conviction.[101] It is clear that this happened in the regality of Grant. In August 1698 two tenants pursued a thief in order to retrieve goods stolen from them. They had their goods returned but failed to hand the thief over to the authorities. In response the court legislated to try to stop the practice:

97 Cullen, *Famine in Scotland*, pp. 41–2.
98 Kennedy, *Governing Gaeldom*, p. 240.
99 Hopkins, *Glencoe and the end of the Highland war*, p. 441.
100 Kennedy, *Governing Gaeldom*, p. 240. This is based on NRS, Anecdotes, GD248/30/3/10, this manuscript account draws on a family memoir penned in the 1760s which eulogises the exploits of former Grant chiefs including Ludovick's actions as a judge.
101 Lenman and Parker, 'Crime and Control', pp. 14–15.

> The said day it is statut and ordained that all persons within the countrey apprehending theaves with the fang or without fang upone attemptes shall not ffyn[102] with them and let them go free under the failie of ane hundreth pounds totties quoties [as often as necessary]'.[103]

Witness depositions from the period also make clear that the victims of theft were likely to go in search of their stolen property and to try and take it back, rather than have recourse to the law, and it is likely that many crimes were dealt with in this way.[104]

Relative to theft was the issue of banditry. Bandits and caterans had plagued Strathspey throughout the seventeenth century; however, following the restoration bands of caterans began to operate on a much larger scale than had previously been seen.[105] These men and their depredations quickly became the primary cause of disorder in the eastern Highlands.[106] Whilst this problem was acute, it was subordinate to the threat that the Stuart monarchy saw in the conventiclers, meaning little action was taken by central authority besides the issuing of commissions to prominent landowners in the north east.[107] The Grants of Freuchie received sixteen judicial commissions from the privy council as the Grants became one of the key government agents in the Highlands, their franchise courts playing an important role in supporting the government's attempt to suppress thefts in the Highlands.[108] For instance, in December 1664 the Grants received a commission for their bailies to act as sheriffs for the purpose of apprehending caterans and robbers passing through Strathspey.[109] Judicial commissions allowed central government to assert visibly its claim that it had direct control over justice throughout the whole of Scotland. At the same time, these commissions also reveal central government's reliance on local power and kin networks to uphold law and order in the localities.[110]

The Williamite administration perceived Highland disorders as a threat to national stability.[111] The Grant family and their heritable jurisdictions were again called upon to support the central government's preoccupation with the

102 "Fine", to compound with a person. *DSL*.
103 Grant Court Book 1, 17/08/1698, p. 130.
104 See, Stuart (ed.), 'Process against the Egyptians at Banff 1700', p. 185.
105 Pittock, *The Myth of the Jacobite Clans: The Jacobite Army in 1745*, p. 32.
106 Stevenson, *Alasdair MacColla and the Highland Problem*, p. 282.
107 Ibid, p. 284.
108 Ibid.
109 NRS, Privy Council Acta, PC1/39, p. 435.
110 Kennedy, *Governing Gaeldom*, p. 193–195.
111 Stevenson, *Alasdair MacColla and the Highland Problem*, p. 297.

'Highland problem', and such cases dealing with theft and banditry demonstrate how franchise courts were involved in curbing the lawlessness which was described at the time as being endemic in the Highlands.[112] Their effectiveness in tackling the perennial issues of banditry and theft is difficult to judge. Cases such as that pursued against Margaret Bayn in December 1700 give us some indication of the approach adopted by the laird of Grant's court. In May 1696 the court of Strathspey found Margaret Bayn and her father Patrick guilty of stealing sheep.[113] Margaret was banished from the regality; however, in February 1699, she is known to have returned to Strathspey, as two men in Tulloch were fined for 'for recepting of Margaret Bayn banished formerlie for theft'.[114] Two years later she was again found in Strathspey, imprisoned and brought before a regality court held by Alexander Grant of Grant at Castle Grant on 13 January 1701:

> Being called and brought from the prisone at Castle Grant as she who was apprehendit within Strathspey for several delinquencies especiallie for hunting with the Halkit Steir[115] and glendey[116] broken men and keithren.[117] And therefore having inccured the certification for not observing the tenor of the said banishment is ordained be the said judge to be brought to the regalitie cross at Grantoune tewmorrew the 14 instant and bound thereto her bodie maid bear from the belt upward and scourged by the hangman with threatie strippes and one of her ears cutt off and then banishes her out of Strathspey for ever and her recepters to pay ten lib toties quoties.[118]

112 A Kennedy, 'Managing the Early-Modern Periphery: Highland Policy and the Highland Judicial Commission, c. 1692–c. 1705', *SHR* 96:1 (2017), p. 37.

113 Grant Court Book 1, 20/05/1696, p.75.

114 Ibid, 15/02/1699, p. 139.

115 The Halkit Steir (speckled calf) alias Donald Macdonald, was one of the most infamous caterans of the restoration era. He plagued the Highlands but was captured by the laird of Freuchie at the behest of the committee of estates in October 1660 and imprisoned at Castle Grant. From Castle Grant he was conveyed to Aberdeen by an armed guard of Freuchie's tenants and thence to Edinburgh. Fearing the vengeance of Macdonald's kinsmen, Freuchie petitioned for the release of the Halkit Steir under caution, which was granted. Macdonald then reverted to his cateran ways. See NRS, Baron Court Extracts, GD248/76/2, fo. 22, and Kennedy, *Governing Gaeldom*, p. 84.

116 "Glender", applied to one who has fallen into immoral habits. *DSL*.

117 "Kithan", a rascal, a blackguard, the devil. *DSL*.

118 Grant Court Book 1, 13/01/1701, p. 160.

The case of Margaret Bayn questions the efficacy of the Grants' tactics when tackling theft and banditry. Exclusion from the community was the main mechanism available to tackle thievery and was more commonly used to punish women than men. Yet the consequences of banishment for the individual are clearly demonstrated by Margaret's keeping company with 'glendey broken men'; the banished were likely to augment the ranks of broken men who were the main source of banditti in the Highland region. Social stability was further endangered by those who ignored the terms of their banishment and returned to their community. This was presumably possible only if they were able to rely on friends or were able to coerce people into harbouring them. The regality of Grant's increased use of corporal punishments during the 1690s might be explained by the inefficacy of banishment in improving social stability in the region.

The most serious crime in the Grant court books is the slaughter of Francis Grant younger of Moyness, a cousin of Ludovick Grant of Grant, in July 1700. After a lengthy evidence-taking process, which unfortunately is only alluded to in the court records, the three perpetrators, Duncan Dun Donalich and John Breaks Cameron elder and younger, who appear to have been vassals of Grant, were found guilty of, 'art and part of slaughter and theft and intercommuning with thiefs and robbers' at a regality court presided over by Alexander Grant of Grant at Castle Grant on 3 December 1700. Both Breaks along with Donalich were sentenced to be hanged and their goods and gear escheat.[119] The men were imprisoned below Castle Grant awaiting their execution; however, a bizarre series of events ensued. Three women connected to the prisoners, Katherine Innes, Agnes Cumming, and Margaret Maclean, succeeded in secretly conveying whisky to them just prior to their execution. Break younger and Donalich embarked upon a suicidal whisky drinking session in the pit beneath Castle Grant and died before reaching the gallows:

> These Women accused and indicted at the instance of the procurator fiscall for their contriving to bring such quantity of aquavitae to the said Donalich and Break that were sentenced to be hanged wherby the said condemned persons might die by the said aquavitae being in prison at Castle Grant ... the said aquavitae was three pynte and ane mutchkin[120] was conveyed to the prison by these women and given to the said

119 Grant Court Book 1, pp. 153–157.

120 "Mutchkin", equivalent to ¼ of a Scots pint. *DSL*.

> prisoners to have. They drank till Donalich died immediately and Break died throw the stress of going to the gallows.[121]

A month passed, during which time the bailie made consultation with 'the best known of the lawers of this natione', to ascertain the nature of the women's crime and determine their punishment. The lawyers replied that the women 'could not be reached for their lives upon that crime since it was no tym in the adjournales of such natur and as to poysoneing they could not be touched and that upon confession ane arbitrarie punishment might be inflicted with banishment'. The three women were accordingly sentenced to be scourged with 'thirty stripes' of the hangman's cords at the regality cross. Innes and Maclean, who were unable to find security, were then banished from the regality; Cumming was permitted to remain. It has been shown that homicide levels in Scotland were lower than other comparable societies in the early eighteenth century.[122] Hence it is to be understood that any such occurrence in Strathspey must have been extremely rare, though the regality of Grant was evidently still capable of dealing with such cases when they arose.

The moveable goods belonging to Donalich and the Breaks were escheated. Several court cases ensued resulting in part of the escheat being granted to a creditor of one of the criminals, with Alexander Grant of Grant presumably taking the remainder. In connection with the execution of Break elder, another inhabitant of the regality sought to prove his honesty, and distance himself from the deceased, by declaring at the regality cross that a mare that he had acquired from him had been purchased lawfully.[123]

Following the execution of Donald Forbes in December 1703, no further corporal punishments are recorded in sentences passed by the court, and only one further assize is recorded, convened to try a thief in 1721.[124] There were no banishments between 1701 and 1720. However, a further five people were thereafter banished by the regality court before the end of the records in 1729.[125] This modest reversion to the use of banishment reflects an increase of crime in the court books during the 1720s after two decades during which social stability

121 Grant Court Book 1, 13/01/1701, p. 158–9. Break senior appears to have been executed according his sentence.

122 WWJ Knox, 'Homicide in Eighteenth-Century Scotland: Numbers and Theories', *SHR* 94:1 (2015), pp. 48–73, p. 55.

123 Grant Court Book 5, 04/12/1700, p. 157.

124 Grant Court Book 4, 18/07/1721, p. 66.

125 The kirk session records of Abernethy reveal that the regality of Grant continued to regularly impose banishments until 1748. See: HA, Kirk Session of Abernethy Minutes, CH2/1054, p. 368.

must have improved. Whilst no serious crimes were recorded in the court records during 1704 to 1720, the number of courts on average increased year by year from eight in 1697 to 1703, to an average of fourteen from 1704 to 1720. The main question arising is whether this reduction in criminal business, greatly down from the 1690s, reflects a return to normality, after the disasters of the 1690s, or was instead due to the regality jurisdiction decreasing in importance. Comparison with the surviving seventeenth century Strathspey court records suggests that the level of crime from 1704 to 1720 was probably more typical and that the 1690s were exceptional in this respect. Changes to the criminal justice system in Scotland following union also impinged upon the criminal jurisdiction of the regalities.

5.3 The Northern Circuit of the Justiciary Court and the Regality of Grant

Intervention by central government in the Highlands increased following union, primarily in the form of the new system of circuit courts introduced in 1708. Of the relationship between the circuit courts and regalities from 1708–1748, Cairns has speculated:

> the regalities, depending on the level of justice granted to them, could exclude it, but regular circuit courts after 1708 seem to have taken at least some of the business of the lords of regality, since they or their bailies had to turn up in person to repledge the accused.[126]

It is unclear whether the justice court had its workload curtailed by the active prosecution of crime in regality courts, or whether the reverse was true and regalities found the justiciary court encroaching upon its criminal jurisdiction. Examination of the records of the northern circuit of the justiciary court when it was sitting in Inverness, allows a direct comparison to be made with surviving records of the regality of Grant between 1708 and 1729. Thereafter, until the abolition of the regality in 1748, it is possible, by reference to surnames and place names denoting a connection to the regality of Grant, to evaluate whether cases that fell within its jurisdiction were being taken to the justiciary court.

126 J W Cairns, 'Historical Introduction', in K G C Reid and R Zimmermann (eds.), *A History of Private Law in Scotland*, Vol I (Oxford, 2000), pp. 122–123.

5.3.1 *1708–1710*

2 May 1708 saw the first circuit court to be held in Inverness for thirty-seven years. It heralded the start of a three-year purge of a backlog of cases intended to ascertain the state of criminal justice in the localities and wipe the slate clean.[127] Whilst justiciars had traditionally gone on ayre throughout Scotland since the fourteenth century, the provision of circuit courts had always been irregular, with frequent legislation on the subject proving largely ineffective in providing the Highlands with a system of circuit courts which was anything more than sporadic.[128] It was only after the union with England, that central government was provided with a means of exercising direct judicial control in the localities, and in turn alleviating the problems presented to litigants by the long distances and poor communications that they faced in taking a case to Edinburgh. Legislation now provided for three circuits in Scotland, with the northern circuit visiting Inverness, Aberdeen and Perth in May and October of each year.[129] With the addition of an October circuit the provisions of the new Act mirrored those of the Courts Act of 1672.[130]

The years from 1708 to 1710 produced the highest number of indictments; thereafter, the amount of business dealt with by the court fell away dramatically. Study has shown that 80% of the cases dealt with by the high court of justiciary in Edinburgh, and whilst on circuit in 1708, were either adultery or fornication.[131] The evidence in the records for the court held in Inverness in May 1708 supports this, with such cases dominating proceedings.[132] Inhabitants of the regality of Grant did not escape citation for sexual offences before the circuit court, and it is recorded that in 1708 four men from the regality were indicted for adultery: three from Urquhart and one from Ballintomb in Inverallan parish, with a further man from Ballachastel being indicted in 1709. There is only one recorded prosecution for adultery in the court books of the regality of Grant, coming in 1727, although civil punishments for the offence continued to be enforced by the court on behalf of the kirk session into the

127 See Davies, 'Law and Order in Stirlingshire', pp. 465–6; and B P Levack, 'The Prosecution of Sexual Crimes in Early Eighteenth-Century Scotland,' p. 182.

128 Dickinson, 'The High Court of Justiciary' p. 408; Cairns, 'Historical Introduction', p. 53. Apart from during the Cromwellian period when the Commission for the Administration of Justice successfully held regular circuits in the North, see F D Dow, *Cromwellian Scotland 1650–1661* (Edinburgh, 1979), pp. 56–7, 145, 178–9, 221–2.

129 6 Ann. C.6.

130 *RPS*, 1672/6/50.

131 Davies 'Law and Order in Stirlingshire'.

132 See NRS, Minutes of the Northern Circuit of the High Court of Justiciary, JC11/1, pp. 21–45; and Davies 'Law and Order in Stirlingshire'.

1740s, long after such offences had ceased to be prosecuted before the circuit court.[133] Such evidence hardly tells us much about encroachment by either court on the other's jurisdiction. Rather it tells us of the de facto decriminalisation in the secular courts of these offences, so that henceforth, only the kirk sessions heard such cases.[134]

The records of the regality of Grant show that indictments for minor thefts were only infrequently being brought before the court during this period, with three such cases being heard by the regality court in 1708 to 1710.[135] These were probably of insufficient severity to be taken to the justice court, the jurisdiction of which was supposedly limited to serious crime and cases of special importance.[136] The hearing of such minor cases would have been seen as a transgression upon the jurisdiction of sheriff and regality courts alike. Over the same period, four cases of theft, in which eight inhabitants of the regality were indicted, appeared before the Justice court in Inverness. Initially, it appears that the justiciary court was to an extent encroaching upon the jurisdiction of the regality.

Of these four cases, one was dismissed and another found not proven. The third was against Duncan McGregor in Abernethy, indicted for stealing livestock from a Grant tenant in Abernethy, although McGregor was captured and incarcerated in Forres. McGregor subsequently broke the tollbooth at Forres and was charged with that offence as well, although he would later claim that he found the prison door open and simply walked free.[137] As McGregor resided in the regality, the crimes of which he stood accused fell within the regality's jurisdiction. However, as McGregor had also committed crimes elsewhere, and was captured outside the regality, it seems appropriate that he was tried by a court with a wider geographical jurisdiction. This is a pattern repeated in other cases, whereby crimes perpetrated by inhabitants of the regality outside the bounds of the regality, were left to be tried by the justiciary court with no attempt being made to repledge them. The fourth theft case of 1708 also conforms to this pattern. A group of soldiers were accused of public violence, theft, robbery, hamesucken and oppression, whilst quartering on a house near

133 Grant Court Book 5, 16/11/1727, p. 132.

134 Levack','The Prosecution of Sexual Crimes in Early Eighteenth-Century Scotland', p. 173. For evidence of continuing prosecution of sexual offences in Strathspey see generally: HA, Cromdale, Inverallan and Advie Kirk Session Minute Book, CH2/983/1.

135 Grant Court Book 1, pp. 113, 125, 131.

136 Wasser, 'Violence and the central criminal courts', p. 98.

137 NRS, Minutes of the Northern Circuit of the High Court of Justiciary, JC11/2, No pagination. 02/10/1710.

Ballindalloch. Amongst their number were James and George Grants, brothers of John Grant of Dalrachney, along with two other important gentlemen of Strathspey who also acted as bailie deputes: Mungo Grant of Mullochard and Robert Grant of Easter Duthil. They all escaped the hangman after being acquitted by an assize.[138]

The profiles of these eight individuals indicted for thefts in 1708–10 can tell us much about justice and society at the time. Six of those indicted were gentry. There are several possible reasons for this. Firstly, that the justiciary court was seen by some of the gentlemen of the regality as a vehicle for seeking retribution against other gentry within the regality. They may have believed that the chances of success were greater by pursuing these disagreements away from the regality court. Alternatively, it could be that, as the regality was trying men of lesser social standing, the circuit court was viewed as a more appropriate jurisdiction for trying gentlemen.[139]

There is also evidence of defenders showing preference for the justiciary court. On 5 October 1710, John Grant in Lettoch and Donald Grant in Easter Lethendrie, who were being pursued in the regality court for theft, succeeded in having their case advocated to the justiciary court. The causes for raising an action of advocation included a partial court and a state of enmity between the judge and the defender.[140] As a result, questions about how people perceived the quality of justice done by the regality court naturally arise. In a similar study it was argued that advocations were part of a wider trend, whereby the central courts exerted pressure upon the heritable jurisdictions in the localities.[141] However, in our case the defenders were prolific litigants in the regality court, appearing both as pursuers and defenders in their own right, and also as procurators on behalf of others.[142] Such knowledge of the law and the workings of the court suggest that these men may have been manipulating the system to their own advantage, by having their case transferred away from the regality court where, regardless of bias, the chance of conviction was

138 NRS, Minutes of the Northern Circuit of the High Court of Justiciary, JC11/2, 02/10/1710.

139 In Mackenzie's treatise, *The laws and Customes of Scotland*, he writes that theft and other crimes perpetrated by the those of higher social standing were to be perceived as more serious crimes than if they had been committed by ordinary Scots. See Mackenzie, *The Laws and Customes of Scotland*, p. 67.

140 Davies, 'Law and Order in Stirlingshire', p. 437.

141 Ibid, p. 451–2.

142 John Grant appears in the court records on six occasions; Grant Court Book 1, p134; Grant Court Book 2, pp 119. 125 and Grant Court Book 3, pp 68, 104. Whilst Donald Grant is recorded in court four times; Grant Court Book 2, pp 15, 138; Grant Court Book 3, p.81; and Grant Court Book 4, p. 14.

undoubtedly greater. That it was possible to achieve this outcome could alternatively be taken as evidence of central authority's changing attitude towards the heritable jurisdictions, with opportunities to bring more cases under central control being seized upon. Whilst these two men are often mentioned in the court records, there is no evidence of a process of theft being pursued against them in the regality court records, and equally the process drops from the records of the circuit court as well. Both men were found in the regality court after 1710, with John Grant pursuing a debt in January 1715.[143] Thus, we have an example of two local men who were adept at using the legal system at both a local and a national level as it suited their needs: even as defenders it was possible to pick and choose in which jurisdiction their best chances of success lay. This suggests that the central courts were reactive when seeking to take business away from the local courts with the impetus for greater intervention sometimes coming from people in the localities themselves.

5.3.2 *1711–1747*

In 1711 the circuit court was reduced to a single circuit in the spring, as there was simply insufficient business coming before it to necessitate a second circuit.[144] For instance, when the commissioners of justiciary visited Inverness in May 1714, one man was put to the horn but no other business is recorded.[145] No court at all was recorded there in May 1719. In the regality court only five thefts appear in the records in the ten years from 1710 to 1719. Thereafter, indictments for theft before the regality court increased dramatically in the decade 1720 to 1729. Clearly the regality of Grant was not losing business to the circuit court during this period, although the incomplete nature of the records after 1729 make it difficult to say whether there was a decline in the workload of the court after this point. The lack of cases appearing before the circuit in Inverness certainly suggests that this was not the case.

Following the changes of 1711 it was not until 1720 that business with links to the regality of Grant next appeared before the commissioners of justiciary in Inverness, when, the brothers of John Grant of Dalrachney once again found themselves before the circuit court.[146] James, Lewis and David Grant, along with two other men, were indicted, and subsequently convicted, for the attempted murder of James Stewart, a servant of James Grant of Rothiemurchus, whom

143 Grant Court Book 2, 31/01/1706, p. 68; Donald, by then tenant of Conedge, was called as a witness in 1719, Grant Court Book 4, 15/08/1719, p. 14.

144 10 Ann. C.33.

145 NRS, Minutes of the Northern Circuit of the High Court of Justiciary, JC11/3, no pagination.

146 NRS, Minutes of the Northern Circuit of the High Court of Justiciary, JC11/4, p. 133–40.

they brutally assaulted in the Dell of Rothiemurchus.[147] Rothiemurchus lies within the regality of Huntly, just beyond the southern boundary of the regality of Grant. The Dalrachney brothers had first confronted Stewart at the nearby market, before following him to the Dell. There David drew his broad sword, dealing Stewart two deep blows to the head, one to the shoulder and a further wound to the arm. To the horror of onlookers, George too drew his sword but was restrained by his wife. The attackers withdrew, leaving Stewart bathed in blood and dangerously wounded. The doctor who attended Stewart revealed to the court that so serious was the attack, he was bed bound for five weeks afterwards.[148] This case tells us two things about the relationship between regalities and the justiciary court. Firstly, it questions whether the regality of Grant was still attempting to repledge inhabitants of the regality from higher courts. Regalities had a right to repledge from the justice court only where the process had been begun in the regality court. If the process had begun in the justice court then the bailies had a right to sit alongside the justices in the court and share in the profits of justice.[149] The Grant estate accounts suggest that attempts at repledging were made as late as 1719, 'to John Allan, Alves for his pains with the witnesses for coming to Dunphaill from Forres to instrument him anent repledging Fraser who was carried to the prison of Forres from the country'.[150] It is not clear from which jurisdiction Fraser was being repledged. The Grants had continued to attempt to exercise their right to repledge, albeit unsuccessfully, in the sheriff court until at least 1700.[151] No such attempt was made in this case despite the panels' brother being a bailie of both the regality of Grant and Huntly; there is no evidence that he tried to sit with the justices either. It might be inferred that the regality had abandoned an important element.

Following the attack, James Grant of Rothiemurchus delivered the injured Stewart to the bailie of the regality of Huntly for his own safety.[152] This bailie was presumably John Gordon of Glenbuchat, bailie principal of the regality of Huntly (although James Grant of Rotheimurchus was himself also a bailie

---

147 James Stewart in Knock of Kincardine (situated within the bounds of the regality of Grant) was a relative of the famous bard and Jacobite officer John Roy Stewart from Knock of Kincardine; Forsyth, *In the Shadow of Cairngorm*, p. 129–30.

148 NRS, Minutes of the Northern Circuit of the High Court of Justiciary, JC11/4, p. 138.

149 *RPS*, 1587/7/18.

150 NRS, Estate Accounts, GD248/113/7, fo. 9.

151 See Stuart (ed.), 'Process against the Egyptians at Banff', p. 175.

152 No record of the incident survives in the Huntly court books for Badenoch.

depute of that regality).[153] Conceivably Rothiemurchus might even have given Stewart up to John Grant of Dalrachney, as he too was a bailie of the regality of Huntly, being appointed to this role in 1715. No record of this case survives in the regality of Huntly court records. This is significant, as it supports the argument that certain regalities had willingly ceded superiority in jurisdiction to the justiciary court in serious crime and were working with the justice court. The action taken in this case reflects legislation from 1710, whereby bailies of regality (along with other 'inferior judges') became points of contact for the handing up of information to form the basis of indictments in the circuit courts, emphasising the new working relationship between the justice court and regalities.[154] Furthermore, there was arguably little financial incentive for jurisdiction holders or their bailies to pursue serious crimes in their own courts. This is because lords of regality were entitled to the escheat of any inhabitants of their regality who were convicted before the justice court, although whether this practice was followed is unclear.[155]

By the 1720s it appears that attitudes towards jurisdiction were changing in Scotland. We find that in cases where the crime took place in a different jurisdiction to where the parties were resident, it had become appropriate for a court with a nationwide jurisdiction to hear the case. This also enabled greater scope for the effective enforcement of sentences throughout Scotland, unlike in the franchise courts. Whilst the court books of the regality of Grant show that the regality continued to exercise its jurisdiction in serious crime, it was now confined to doing so only where it had exclusive competence. Where issues of jurisdictional overlap arose, the justice court had become the appropriate jurisdiction to hear such cases.

Of the twenty-one people from the regality who were indicted in the justiciary court from 1710 to 1748, ten were gentlemen, thereby continuing the pattern established in the years 1708 to 1710, whereby a disproportionate number of those indicted were gentlemen. Amongst these men another two other bailies of the regality, Robert Grant of Lurg and John Grant in Balmakaan of Urquhart, were indicted. John Grant in Balmakaan was indicted twice in four years, along with his officer and forester in Urquhart.[156] Of these men only Dalrachney's

153 Glenbuchat was another famous supporter of the Jacobite cause, but whom during this period was acting as a government agent. He fell victim to a similar assault in 1724, when, implementing rent increases in Badenoch, he was attacked in his own home by eight Macpherson tacksmen and left for dead.

154 8 Ann. C 16.

155 Mackenzie, *The Laws and Customes of Scotland*, p. 410.

156 NRS, Minutes of the Northern Circuit of the High Court of Justiciary, JC11/7, p. 178.

brothers George and David (along with an accomplice) were found guilty, and even then, only received nominal fines of £15 and £30 stg. respectively. The chances of successful prosecution in the circuit court, especially of gentlemen, were very small. Nonetheless, aggrieved parties were using the justiciary court to seek redress away from the supposed biases and power networks of the local courts, where the gentry often held sway. This is supported by many similar cases in the records of the circuit court concerning officials from other regality, baron and burgh courts across the north, with claims of wrongful imprisonment and oppression being common. One such example concerned the bailie depute of the regality of Coupar Angus. At a time when the bearing of arms in Perthshire and Angus was banned, he unlawfully incited inhabitants of the regality to provide him with an armed guard at Coupar Angus market. He aggravated this offence further by summarily imprisoning anyone refusing to join his guard. For this the bailie was fined £100, imprisoned for one month in Perth tolbooth and disqualified from presiding over the regality court of Coupar Angus for the space of a year.[157]

5.3.3 *After Abolition, 1748–1753*

The disenfranchisement of heritable jurisdiction holders of their criminal jurisdiction on 25 March 1748, should inevitably have led to a transfer of business to the circuit court. The Heritable Jurisdictions Act enhanced the powers of the circuit courts in anticipation of the new demands to be placed upon them as a result of this disenfranchisement: the number of circuits annually was again increased to two, with the court sitting for six days each at Inverness, Perth, and Aberdeen.

The first circuit court to be held under the new regime was held in Inverness on 2 May 1748. However, the new regulations governing the circuit courts appeared to have caught-out the sheriffs and justices of the peace in the shires attending the court at Inverness. The porteous rolls were empty, and the justices of the peace had failed to hand in their reports.[158] The court sat for the statutory term of six days before moving on to Aberdeen. Nonetheless, after this shaky start, over the next four years a modest number of cases that would formerly have fallen within the jurisdiction of the regality of Grant were brought before the circuit court. For instance, on 28 October 1749 two cases relating to rioting and assault within Strathspey were before the commissioners of justiciary.[159] The two cases were clearly retaliatory actions, in which the Strathspey

157 NRS, Minutes of the Northern Circuit of the High Court of Justiciary, JC11/5.

158 NRS, Minutes of the Northern Circuit of the High Court of Justiciary, JC11/13, p. 1.

159 Ibid, p. 115.

gentry were again the primary actors. Both actions were dismissed and appear to have been nothing more than an attempt to play out local squabbles in court. Of the other cases originating from regality, Alexander Fraser miller at the mill of Muckerach was banished from Scotland for assaulting Alexander Grant, tacksman of the milltown of Muckerach over a disputed tack of the mill there in 1750.[160] In the same year a case of parricide was dismissed, whilst a resident of the barony of Urquhart was hanged for theft in 1751.[161]

Whilst the overall amount of business handled by the circuit court undoubtedly increased after 1748, there was no great influx of cases from the Grant lands in the first five years following the abolition of heritable jurisdictions. However, even this small number of cases marked an increase on the dearth seen prior to 1748. The modest number of cases originating from Grant lands could suggest a transfer of business from the regality court to the circuit court. However, the most noticeable link with the regality of Grant compared to the years prior to 1748, are the large number of gentlemen residing within the bounds of the former regality called to serve as assizors. Only three Grants from the regality appear in the records as assizors prior to 1748, whereas in the five years after this date fourteen are recorded. This suggests a greater connection between the court and society in Strathspey than there had been previously.

5.4 Conclusion

The court records left by the regality suggest that we should tread a middle ground when assessing the criminal jurisdiction of the court. On the one hand, it was not as extensive as popular culture would have us believe. On the other hand, contrary to the assertions of historians such as Ann Whetstone, serious crime continued to come before the regality court.[162]

In light of this evidence, what exactly in practice was the criminal jurisdiction of the regality of Grant? For whilst the charter erecting the regality endowed Ludovick Grant of Grant and his successors with the jurisdiction to entertain all pleas bar treason alone, in practice, especially after 1700, it was more restricted. In fact, there was little practical difference between the former baronies of Strathspey and the new regality in terms of criminal jurisdiction.

160 NRS, Minutes of the Northern Circuit of the High Court of Justiciary, JC11/15, p. 4.

161 NRS, Minutes of the Northern Circuit of the High Court of Justiciary, JC11/15, p. 14; NRS, Minutes of the Northern Circuit of the High Court of Justiciary, JC11/16, no pagination, 2/5/1752.

162 Whetstone, *Scottish County Government*, p. 2.

It might be more accurate to characterise the criminal powers of the court as being largely akin to a private shrieval jurisdiction. Nonetheless, the volume of criminal cases being brought before the court emphasises the usefulness and vitality of the court during a period when, according to most historians, the opposite should have been true.

The serious crimes dealt with by the regality court were typical of the region and the period. Theft, slaughter and banditry are all resonant of the Highland problem that so occupied central government during this time and which also vexed the regality court. There was a peak in the number of criminal cases during the latter 1690s. This can be attributed to the effects of the famine experienced during these years and the Grants' attempts to restore order to a society clearly in disarray. During the final five years of the seventeenth century the regality court of Grant sentenced seven people to death, with a further eighteen handed corporal punishments. The last recorded hanging ordered by the regality took place in 1703, after which the criminal jurisdiction of the court was almost entirely restricted to assaults and minor thefts. This is surely a reflection upon the social dislocation of the 1690s, rather than the regality court declining in importance after this point.

Assaults made up a large proportion of the court's criminal business thereafter; the prosecution of violent offenders is one of the best examples of the effectiveness of a local jurisdiction such as the regality of Grant. The court's handling of such disputes demonstrates the usefulness of local justice administered by local people. Furthermore, through the widespread use of caution in connection to violent crime, maintaining the peace became the business of the wider community and promoted social solidarity across class divides. Quantitative analysis of the Grant court books reveals that rates of commission and prosecution of crime were consistent with other jurisdictions and regions of Scotland. For instance, the records from the regality of Falkirk show twenty-five such cases for the period 1696 to 1701, but only fifteen for the five years 1710 to 1715.[163] By comparison the regality of Grant determined only seven cases of violent crime from 1696 to 1701 and seventeen for the period 1710 to 1715. Violent crime and lawburrows made up roughly 10% of the overall work of the regality of Falkirk whilst for the regality of Grant the figure was slightly higher at 14%.[164]

Finally, the system of circuit courts introduced in 1708 can be dismissed as a factor leading to a reduction in the number of criminal cases coming before

163 Davies, 'Law and Order in Stirlingshire', p.273.

164 This is probably explained by the much larger amount of debt in the Falkirk court books: Hunter, *Court Books of the Barony and Regality of Falkirk and Callendar*.

the court. Very few cases originating in Strathspey were ever tried in the circuit courts; indeed, very few cases were tried before the justices in Inverness at all. It simply appears that after 1708, most criminal cases in the regality continued to pass through the regality court, the circuit court being of limited importance until the changes of 1748. However, the circuit court quickly became a means for disgruntled litigants to bypass local power networks when it suited them, especially amongst the gentry. The numerous complaints found in the circuit court records describing injustices and oppressions committed in other heritable jurisdictions across the north, suggest a greater dissatisfaction with heritable justice than is evident in the Grant records and would be worth further investigation.[165]

165 For instance: NRS, Minutes of the Northern Circuit of the High Court of Justiciary, JC11/1 pp. 21, 23 and 93.

CHAPTER 6

Economic and Social Control

Feudal courts, such as the regality court of Grant, performed many functions which would be alien in the modern court system. Of this Mitchison has written: 'In the eighteenth century much of what we would call government in both England and Scotland was done by the courts'.[1] This was true of the regality court of Grant, under the auspices of which, landowner, gentry and church were able to exercise many of the functions which we associate with modern day government. The laird, gentry of the regality and kirk all used the regality court to help exert social, economic and religious control over the inhabitants of Strathspey.

Economic management was one of the main concerns of the court: only through regulations emanating from feudal courts was it possible for estates to facilitate a limited market economy which enabled the area to be effectively self-sufficient in goods and services.[2] With the erection of the regality came the right to hold fairs and markets. By encouraging trade at these events, coupled with control of trades and prices, landowners such as the Grants could try to extract the maximum economic value from their estates prior to the growth of the national market economy and improvements in forestry and agriculture. Several historians have addressed economic control in early-modern Scotland. Evidence in the regality of Grant court books corroborates much of this research.[3] However, this study will fill a gap in the scholarship by providing an insight into the organisation of the rural economy in a regality. This study will also show how regality courts were able to enact economic measures in response to times of crisis, such as those experienced in the 1690s.

Social control was largely the concern of the kirk. However, the kirk's programme of social control was reliant upon the legitimacy and authority of the regality court to lend further authority to the kirk sessions and uphold their judgements. In many respects social and religious control in early modern Scotland has received much more attention from social historians than economic history during the same period. Scholars such as Bardgett, Todd, Parker,

1 Mitchison, 'The Government and the Highlands, 1707 – 1745', p. 25.

2 Whyte, *Agriculture and Society in Seventeenth Century Scotland*, p. 36; Davidson, 'The Scottish path to capitalist agriculture', p. 231.

3 A Gibson and T C Smout, *Prices, Food and Wages in Scotland, 1550–1780* (Cambridge, 1995); Symms, 'Social Control in a Sixteenth Century Burgh'; Cullen, *Famine in Scotland*.

 | DOI:10.1163/9789004472549_007

Mitchison, Leneman, Cornell and Davies have all covered the work of kirk sessions in detail.[4] However, the relationship between kirk sessions, and courts of barony and regality around the beginning of the eighteenth century is still largely unexplored, an omission that will be addressed here.

6.1 Economic Control

Some of the main advantages to be gained from the erection of lands into a regality were economic. The creation of a burgh of regality, with the right to hold markets and fairs, represented an important source of private income for landowners.[5] The charter erecting the regality of Grant permitted Ludovick Grant and his successors to hold thrice yearly fairs at the Castletoun of Freuchie, in addition to a weekly market there. It reads: 'Grantown is created a free burgh of regality with the usual trading rights for the burgesses and inhabitants. There is to be a market every Friday and three free markets annually, for three days, on the last Tuesday of April, penultimate day of August and [details missing of third]'.[6] However, in 1693, a year prior to the granting of the regality, Ludovick Grant had obtained an act of parliament in his favour allowing him to hold fairs and markets on his lands.[7] Within Strathspey these were Grantoune fair, held on the last Tuesday of April at Ballachastel, along with another fair there called the Castle fair on the third Tuesday of August. He was also permitted to hold an annual free fair at the kirk of Duthil on the first Tuesday of June called Bettie's fair, whilst at Abernethy there was to be a fair called Katherin's fair on the 16 November. Along with these fairs a weekly market was held on Fridays at Ballachastel. At these fairs and markets Ludovick Grant was empowered to uplift the 'hail tolls, customes, emoluments, profits and dueties'.[8] This

4 F D Bardgett, 'The Monifieth Kirk Register', *Records of the Scottish Church History Society*, 23 (1987–9), 175–195; M Todd, *The Culture of Protestantism in Early Modern Scotland* (London, 2002); G Parker, "The Kirk By Law Established and the Taming of Scotland: St Andrews, 1559–1600" in G Parker, *Empire, War and Faith in Early Modern Europe* (London, 2003); R M Mitchison and L Leneman, *Girls in Trouble*; Cornell, 'Gender, Sex and Social Control'; Davies, 'Law and Order in Stirlingshire'.

5 W M Mackenzie, *The Scottish Burghs* (Edinburgh, 1949), pp. 80–2; I D. Whyte, *Scotland before the Industrial Revolution: An Economic and Social History, c.1050–c.1750* (Harlow, 1995), pp. 183–4.

6 RPS, 1696/9/192 [translation of original].

7 This grant in 1693 was one of sixteen grants of markets and fairs made to develop local trade and ease convenience for those distant from burghs; Mackenzie, *The Scottish Burghs*, p. 94.

8 NRS, Charter in favour of Ludovick Grant, GD248/6/280.

act of parliament in favour of Ludovick Grant appears to have anticipated the erection of his regality; the subsequent erection of his lands into a regality did little to enhance further trade on his lands through the creation of market centres. These grants can be considered as part of a nation-wide movement to create new trading centres in the seventeenth century.[9] These fairs and markets allowed the lord of regality to have a monopoly of domestic trade within the bounds of the jurisdiction. However, there is no mention of these fairs or markets within the court records. Instead, economic control as exercised by the regality court effectively covered two areas: controlling food supplies; and the regulation of employment of tradesmen and servants.[10]

6.1.1 *Food Supplies*

The regality of Grant, as with most other landed estates within Scotland, was probably largely self-sufficient in terms of food.[11] In order to assure the supply of food upon which the people of Strathspey depended, it was thought to be necessary to control prices whilst also upholding trading and manufacturing standards, and protecting the Grants' own monopoly and trading privileges.[12] These controls were essential features of government throughout early modern Europe and Strathspey was no different, where they were exercised by the regality court. Evidence from the regality court books shows that the court imposed controls upon the pricing and origin of foodstuffs including livestock, barley, malted bear, beer and whisky.

Ale, beer, and whisky were very important food stuffs, being safer to consume than many water supplies, while also providing an important source of calories.[13] As a result, most larger townships had their ale or whisky houses and brewers. The court set down strict maximum prices for these drinks in line with acts of parliament of the time.[14] The prices that brewers were permitted to charge consumers reflected current grain prices. This can be seen in an extract from a head court held on 19 November 1663 at Ballintomb. The court enacted that 'no brewster shall tak thereafter so long as the malt is cheap but fourteen penies for the ail and sixteen penies for the beir under the pain of five

9 Whyte, *Agriculture and Society*, p. 183 – 192.

10 The regulation of wages and prices would continue in Scotland until circa 1800. Devine, *The Scottish Clearances*, p. 119.

11 Mitchison, 'The Government and the Highlands, 1707 – 1745', p. 25.

12 Symms, 'Social Control in a Sixteenth Century Burgh', p. 109.

13 Ibid, p. 122. F.M. McNeill, *The Scots Cellar* (Edinburgh, 1973), p. 2.

14 Gibson and Smout, *Prices, Food and Wages in Scotland*, pp. 39–41.

libs toties quoties'.[15] Maximum pricing protected consumers and prevented unrest and resistance to the brewing monopoly within the regality. The distilling of whisky was also regulated by the court but the distillers of the regality had more discretion in pricing:

> The four bailies of Strathspey have with the consent of the gentlemen of the countrey statut and ordained that the bre[wer]s within the said four parishes shall buy the malt of the four parishes ... and pay therefore eight merks each boll and sell ther ale at 16d. per pint. And that none of them shall presume to buy or import malt out of any plaice without the said parishes ... and oblidges the brewer to buy and the seller to sell at the said pryce of eight merk per boll and not bellow ... statutes that noe aquavitae be imported to the four parishes and ordains the brewers to brew aquavitae of the country malt and serve the four parishes at reasonable raites of sufficient stuff.[16]

Such price controls also had the benefit of stopping people from reverting to home brewing and ruining the monopoly of the brewers and the laird.

Brewers swore in court to abide by the pricing and standards laid down in the acts of court and acts of Parliament governing their trade. After swearing to uphold the acts, they were entitled to enjoy the privileges afforded to brewers within the regality. Any brewers found contravening these regulations were liable to be fined. For instance, at Old Toun of Abernethy on 16 May 1664, seven brewers from the parish of Abernethy were fined £5 each for breaching the 'act anent ail and beir'.[17] An individual brewer was unlikely to be successful in flouting the rules, whilst continuing to attract custom, if meanwhile his competitors offered the lower, statutory price. However, as this court at Abernethy shows, it appears that there were many brewers breaking the rules. It is possible that the brewers were acting in solidarity perhaps as a cartel within the parish, all selling for higher than statute prices. A year later in 1665 the court extracts record that, at a court appropriately held in the malt kiln of Ballachastel, all the brewers of the parishes of Cromdale and Inverallan were fined for charging in excess of 16 pence per Scotch pint.[18] Combinations of tradesmen were an

15 NRS, Baron Court Extracts, GD248/76/2, fo. 130. The same can be seen in: Romanes, *Selections of Records from the Regality of Melrose* Vol. II, p. 35.

16 Grant Court Book 2, 22/7/1703, p. 13.

17 NRS, Baron Court Extracts, GD248/76/2, fo. 78.

18 Ibid, fo. 68.

occasional feature of life in the Scottish burghs, and this is a feature of life in Strathspey we will encounter again when discussing other trades.[19]

Birlawmen were responsible for upholding the economic acts of the regality court, and thus checking that the brewers were not breaking the acts of the regality court.[20] This would have entailed periodically visiting the alehouses of the district to check pricing and perhaps also the quality of brewers' produce.[21] In royal burghs there were dedicated ale-tasters to test the quality of ale and beer brewed. It appears that similar testers were also sometimes appointed in Strathspey, there is only one mention of such a role in the court records.[22]

Brewers within Strathspey were only permitted to purchase grain for malting and brewing from within Strathspey itself, thus helping the preserve the self-sufficiency of the region and providing a regular market for the victual produced by the laird's tenants:

> ordains all the brewers of the said parish to buy their meal and malt within Strathspey so long as they can … and whoever does so on the contrar and brings their malt and meall from murray without Strathspey shall lose the price of ane boll of malt of unlaw.[23]

The controls on brewing imposed by the regality court mirrored legislation of the Scottish parliament.[24] Fears that imported foodstuffs from outside the realm would be to the prejudice of domestic produce were both national and local concerns.[25] Only when there was a dearth in the local supply were imports permitted.

As agents of the laird, brewers were men of greater status than many rural tradesmen and craftsmen. However, the survival of place names such as 'brewer's croft' tell us that these men were not able to rely solely on the income of their trade and that they depended upon agriculture as a by-occupation. Indeed, with most brewing taking place in spring and autumn, its seasonal nature left time for agriculture during the summer months when warmer temperatures caused problems for cooling, fermentation, and storage of ale.[26]

---

19 Gibson and Smout, *Prices, Food and Wages in Scotland*, p. 46.
20 Grant Court Book 2, 15/11/1705, p. 57.
21 Symms, 'Social Control in a Sixteenth Century Burgh', pp.119–121.
22 NRS, Baron Court Extracts, GD248/76/2, 20/05/1663, fo. 56.
23 Grant Court Book 2, 30/5/1703, p. 10.
24 See for instance, *RPS*, 1669/10/52.
25 Cullen, *Famine in Scotland*, p. 65–71.
26 P Sambrook, *Country-house brewing in England, 1500–1900* (London, 1996), p. 155.

In addition to controls on alcohol itself, the court also placed strict controls upon the malting of bear to be made into alcohol. Acts of court instructed tenants where to take their bear to be malted, and brewers from which kilns to buy the malt for brewing.[27] Individuals tried to avoid taking their bear for malting at official malt kilns, just as they also tried to avoid buying liquor from the brewers of the regality by home brewing. However, it appears that the brewers themselves were some of the worst culprits in trying to avoid using official estate facilities. The court records show that several brewers tried to avoid buying malt from the maltmen of the regality by using their own kilns. For this act they faced fines of up to £40:

> The said day in respect of ane former act that the brewars of Cromdale sould buy their malt out of the malt kilne of Castle Grant and have contraveined Alexander Steward at the boat of Cromdale and James roy Lawsone in Port present and excused for byganes But James Gilenach also absent being guiltie in buyeing of strangers malt and Thomas Forsyth in Cromdale absent and declared as guiltie they ar both unlawed in 20 lib ilk ane unless they frie themselves upon oath for byganes.
>
> The said day David Dunbar in Cromdale and Alaster Makindlay Roy in Culquoich unlawed in fourtie lib ilk ane for making of malt in their owne kilns in contraventione of the former act and prohibits them in tyme comeing from so doeing under the failie of twentie pounds toties quoties and lykwayes decernes ilk person that brewes at faires that are not constant brewers shall pay ilk ane of them ane sten of brew tallow or four pounds scotis therfor to my Lardie Grant.[28]

Clearly inhabitants of the regality were not content to home-brew solely for their own needs but also tried to turn a profit by selling their produce to thirsty fairgoers, thus impinging upon the trading privileges of the brewers.

Acts of court relating to pricing of foodstuffs appear to have been publicly proclaimed from time-to-time but with no regularity, perhaps often enough to prevent the acts from falling into desuetude and so people could not pretend ignorance. Such ordinances become less frequent over the course of the court records. The baron court extracts from the restoration era show that acts relating to brewing and malting were much more frequent during this period than later. The disappearance of such ordinances from later records may suggest

27 Grant Court Book 5, 18/12/1723, p. 7.

28 Grant Court Book 2, 01/11/1707, p. 92.

an opening up of markets to the Grants' tenants, or that few new acts of court were promulgated, with existing acts of court simply being reiterated and re-publicised but not recorded within the records.

6.1.2 *Regulation of Employment*

a) The Problem of 'Loose' Servants

The regality court placed more emphasis on controlling labour than it did on controlling food supplies. Between 1693 and 1728, the regulation of labour is mentioned ninety times in the court books: this includes acts of court setting down wages and other terms of employment for weavers, tailors, malanders and agricultural and domestic servants; along with individuals fined for breaching the regulations imposed by the regality court. This was a continuation of the practice of the Grants' baron courts during the restoration years when such regulations and fines are mentioned on fifteen occasions.[29]

The most common subject of legislation was agricultural labour. In an agricultural society such as Strathspey, there were obvious problems with seasonal surpluses and shortages in the supply of servants to work on the land. Shortages were especially keen around harvest time, whilst during winter many men were short of work and might turn to by-employments such as weaving. For many men and women who earned a living as agricultural and domestic servants, their only opportunity to participate in the market economy was through the sale of their labour to the highest bidder when demand for their services was highest in the late summer and autumn. It was common for servants to engage with masters for terms of six months to two years at one of the hiring fairs held at the terms of Whitsunday or Martinmas. A passage from the regality of Grant court books shows why this was problematic for employers and the gentry of the regality:

> Anent the representation given in be the gentlemen, tennents and labourers of the ground of Strathspey in the Regality of Grant making mention that to sustain great loss and damage anent the act of court made in relation to servant their being to serve their masters from Whitsunday to Whitsunday whereby servants being loose at the term of Whitsunday yearly they continue waiff and not of service all the summer tyme of fell purpose and design of extracting extravagant wages for days service during the summer tyme and for serving masters to gile them when in straits the haill half year free for serving sometyme in harvest to their

29 See NRS, Baron Court Extracts, GD248/76/2.

> great loss and damage if not present for remeid thereof it is statute and ordained that all servants of whatsoever rank may engage with masters from Martinmas to Martinmas hereafter that none may have opportunity of being loose in the summer tyme.[30]

Petitions from gentry and tenants and resultant legislation in the regality court reflected national concerns which had led to an Act of Parliament in 1621.[31] This act stipulated that servants could only leave their master at Whitsunday if they could show they were entering the service of another master and were not trying to remain as free agents. If the servant could not show this, then they were forced to continue in the service of their present master. Clearly such provisions were concerned not only with protecting economic interests but also exerting control over the lower ranks.

Prompted by complaints from the landholding classes of gentry, tenants and sub-tenants, the court made frequent incursions upon the liberty of servants during the spring and summer months when the seasonal shortages of labour came to be felt.For instance in May 1662 it enacted that 'everie hyreman w[i]t[hi]n the said parishines sall take thameselfis to masters within three days under the pain of ten libs scottis monie and ther fies of the preceding year is ordained to be arrestit until they fie themselffis'.[32] The next year in May 1663 the court went even further encouraging men who were short of labourers to seize servants and press them into service:

> Lykwayes it is statut and ordained that everie hyrman meikle and little and hird and hyrwoman shall bind themselffis to maisters w[i]t[hi]n eight dayes efter Whitsunday nixt and whosoever shall not tye themselffis to maisters before the said day, it sall be leisame[33] to anie man who wants servants to apprehend thame and to mak use of thame to their owne service upon suche competent fieis as the gentleman of the countrey shall think expedient.[34]

The time when servants were expected to have found a master varied from year to year, for instance the date set in 1664 was 24 April, some way before the term of Whitsunday.[35] This act of court clearly reflects the 1621 legislation, showing

30 Grant Court Book 5, 20/07/1727, p. 121.

31 *RPS*, 1621/6/33.

32 NRS, Baron Court Extracts, GD248/76/2, fo. 27.

33 "Leisame", morally or legally permissible. *DSL*.

34 NRS, Baron Court Extracts, GD248/76/2, fo. 56.

35 Ibid, fo. 67.

that officials in the court had access to the acts of the Scottish parliament and used them to frame their own legislation.[36]

Such ordinances continue in later years; however, they are much less frequent than during the restoration period, with references to 'loose servants' coming in 1693, 1727 and 1728 only. In fact, in 1706 the part of the 'Servants Act' (as the act of court of the regality court was referred to) requiring servants to serve for terms of twelve months was repealed, thus allowing servants to tie themselves to a master from Martinmas to Whitsun once more.[37] This may suggest that for twenty years from 1706 to 1727, seasonal labour shortages were not such a problem as they had been in previous years allowing restrictions to be lifted. During this period, no new acts of court concerning the duration of service of servants were issued by the court. However, existing legislation may have been repeated from time to time but not recorded. Further acts of court were produced in 1727 and 1728, perhaps as a result of poor harvests around this time.[38]

Better opportunities for employment elsewhere, particularly in the Lowlands, and the effects of poor harvests could explain why tenants in Strathspey sometimes struggled to employ tied servants.[39] Servants could command much higher wages in coastal parishes and in the Laich of Moray. Study of wages in Aberdeenshire and Renfrewshire in the 1690s has shown that servants' wages were lowest in the upland parishes of these counties by a considerable margin.[40] By moving as little as twenty miles nearer to the coast or county town, servants could expect an increase in wages of 100%.[41] Such a difference in wages must have been a drain on labour in Highland areas such as Strathspey.[42] A further reason for a shortage of servants in long term farm-service was the potential to earn much more as a day-labourer. If a servant could get regular employment on a daily rate, they could earn much more than a tied servant.[43] This was perhaps the main incentive for remaining 'loose';

36 This is true of other areas legislated upon by the court such as poaching.

37 Grant Court Book 2, 05/06/1706, p. 76.

38 T M Devine, *Clearance and Improvement: land, power and people in Scotland, 1700–1900* (Edinburgh, 2006), p. 31.

39 Devine estimates that each household across the central Highlands would send one person to the Lowlands to work the harvest each year: Devine, *Clanship to Crofters' War*, p. 136.

40 Gibson and Smout, *Prices, food and wages in Scotland*, pp. 293–4.

41 Ibid.

42 These figures should be treated with caution as it is uncertain how much payments in kind, and infiltration of the cash economy into Lowland areas skews the figures.

43 Ibid, pp. 283–6.

however, these labourers lacked the security of a tied position. Perhaps because of these factors, the minister of Duthil parish was still complaining about idle and unemployed servants in his parish when writing for the OSA in the 1790s.[44]

b) Wages

In the period from 1696 to 1708, the regality court of Grant intensively policed strict wage caps on the labouring classes and trades. No mention of wage controls can be found in the earlier court records for Strathspey. The first act of court setting out the maximum wages for malanders and labourers comes only at Candlemas 1696:

> anent the compleant given in be the gentleman and tenantes of the countrey ag[ains]t cottars greassmen[45] and comone worthies for dayes wages for ther exactioune of exorbitant wages for ilk dayes work as they shall be imloyed. Tharfor with the consent of the haill people present at court it is statute enacted and ordained be the said bailie that noe man give or any workman receive for his wages a day mor than 2 shillings of mo[ne]y or ane hadish[46] of meall.[47]

The emergence of wage controls in Strathspey coincided with the harvest failures and famine of the late 1690s. With the population of some Highland parishes believed to have reduced by as much as 20% of their pre-famine levels, it seems that Strathspey experienced labour shortages as a result of the famine, with farm servants also seeking to exploit greater wage-earning opportunities elsewhere as a result of widespread shortages of agricultural labourers.[48] Wage labourers' attempts to secure higher wages also reflect the dramatic rise in meal prices owing to the dearth which meant that prices greatly outstripped wages.[49] It seems that the wage controls were a direct response to the repercussions of the famine. In this respect there are clear parallels with fourteenth century England and the English government's response to the plague of 1349. The acute labour shortages experienced because of the black death led to huge

44 Sinclair, *The Statistical Account of Scotland*, Vol. IV, Duthil Parish, p. 312.
45 "Greasman", tenant of a house with pasture but no tenanted land. *DSL*.
46 "Hadish", ¼ of a peck. *DSL*.
47 Grant Court Book 1, 13/02/1696, p. 66.
48 Cullen, *Famine in Scotland*, pp 51: the factor to the Earl of Mar said of Corgarff (a township just a handful of miles from the eastern march of the regality of Grant and twenty-five miles from Castle Grant) that this once 'populous place … is farr from tht now, as all othyr Countries in the hylands ar, by reason of the late famine & dearth'; and pp. 157–160.
49 Cullen, *Famine in Scotland*, pp. 55 and 104.

wage increases being claimed by the remaining workforce. Landowners petitioned parliament for a wage cap, with it being statute in 1351 that servants were to labour for no more than their pre-1349 wage, their masters being restricted in turn as to the wages they could pay.[50] The later Cambridge Statute of 1388 tightened controls further, for instance, by restricting the movement of servants, as was also the case in the regality of Grant some three hundred years later.[51] Another parallel can be found in 1760s Badenoch. In 1769 the lairds and tacksmen there combined to issue an edict protecting their economic interests by restricting the seasonal migration of labourers and policing wages. Similar action was taken by the landed elite in Strathdearn and Lairg, suggesting a region-wide issue and response.[52]

The repercussions of the famine continued to be felt in Strathspey up to a decade after famine conditions had eased, with references to wage controls occurring most frequently in the years 1703 to 1708. For instance, in 1703 the issue of malanders' wages was revisited by the regality court. At the instance of the gentlemen of Strathspey new restrictions were imposed:

> In presence of the four bailies of Strathspey being conveined for ordereing of the Laird of Grant his effairs for the tyme and for regulating some missorders concerning wages given to malanders within the four parishes. They have with consent of the haill gentlemen present statute voted and ordained that the wage of evrie malender man for ane days work be two hadashes of meale and ordains that the malander shall be obliged to accept of meall onlie and prohibits any to give money to malenders for ther wages for any days work above the pryce of the countrey and oblidges the mallender to accept of no ill wher the imployer cannot pay the pryce and lykewayes oblidges the malender to serve the first imployer of him for his dayes work … and whosoever malander or imployer does in the contrair therof and shall give more then the wages in manner forsaid shall earn the payn [illegible] fourtie shilling Scotis the malander and 2 pounds the imployer and this not to extend to the work of malander whereto they are bound to ther master for 2 dayes of the weak which shall receive as formerlie.[53]

50 J Cannon, 'Labourers, Statute of' in, *The Oxford Companion to British History* (Oxford, 2009).

51 12 Rich. 2, c.7.

52 Taylor, *Wild Black Region*, pp. 134–5.

53 Grant Court Book 2, 22/07/1703, p. 12.

It is unclear why the court decided to prohibit payment to malanders in cash. Though there may have been greater shortage of specie than usual, a more likely explanation is that with falling grain prices it was more attractive to pay labourers in kind, so as to offer labourers lower real wages.[54] Whilst this act of court shows that the meal payments to malanders had increased by 100% in the seven years since 1696, day wages in Strathspey seem to have been significantly lower than other rural areas north of the Tay, where summer day wages were traditionally 4–5 shillings a day in summer and a shilling less in winter. This is also attested to in the correspondence of Edmund Burt, an agent of the British government who was based in Inverness in the late 1720s.[55] The result was that these areas exerted a pull on the labour force to the detriment of poorer rural areas, so exacerbating the labour shortages.[56]

Like the regality court's response to the problem of 'loose servants' discussed above, wage controls were another way to combat servants extracting 'extortionate' wages for their services. However, employers continued to pay both day labourers and tied servants more than was statute, so that it is clear that the controls were ineffective. Inhabitants of the regality were called individually before the bailie, they then had to plead whether they were guilty or 'free' of the penal statutes, and state what wages they were receiving, perhaps even providing evidence of such by producing discharges from their masters.

For instance, at a court held at Duthil in April 1705 inhabitants of that parish were examined by the court over illicit wood cutting, poaching and for taking wages above the rate set down in the acts of court. Four servants were unlawed in the following terms, 'James Makgivon servant to William Glass in getting eleven merkes of fie and wes confiscat being exorbitant ag[ains]t the act of court'.[57] At the Martinmas court held at Duthil in the same year a further eight servants were fined along with one master.[58] Fees above the permitted rate were much in evidence the following year with a further eight labourers and three masters fined by the court: 'John Stewart in Aviemore is unlawed in 20 merkes for giving of 10 merkes of fee to Donald Barron his servant and confiscats the servants fee payable at Wit 1707 for seiking such fee he being but ane common ordinar hyrman to whom ther is allowed but 8 merkes'.[59] No breaches

54 L R Poos, *A Rural Society after the Black Death: Essex 1350- 1525* (Cambridge, 1991), p. 223.

55 Gibson and Smout, *Prices, food and wages in Scotland*, p. 279; A Simmons (ed.), *Burt's Letters from the North of Scotland* (Edinburgh, 1998), p. 133.

56 Whatley, *Scottish Society 1707–1830*,' pp. 22–3.

57 Grant Court Book 2, 18/04/1705, p.47.

58 Ibid, 29/11/1705, pp. 63–4.

59 Grant Court Book 2, 09/12/1706, p. 82.

of the act were recorded in 1707; however, in 1708 a further sixteen labourers and servants, in addition to one master, were reprimanded by the court; the master in this case, Donald Grant of Tullochgriban, was further admonished for paying his grieves their fee upfront rather than at the end of their term.[60] The court records also suggest that masters attempted to subvert the wage cap by supplementing their servants' fees by giving them grazing for livestock or providing them with shoes.[61] It was common to include such customary payments in the wage of labourers. Most farm servants received payment of their fee in two parts: their fee and 'bounteth'.[62] The bounteth was food, lodgings, clothing and perhaps grazing rights; however, the regality court seems to have evaluated an equivalent monetary payment and included the footwear as part of payment thus putting a servant above the maximum wage.[63]

There is an irony that whilst masters of servants were the original instigators of wage controls, many of them breached the wage caps they themselves had sought. There are several possible reasons for this. Firstly, that shortages in seasonal labour were so acute, and wages in Strathspey so low compared to other regions, that employers were forced to pay above the statute maximum wage in order to be sure of securing the services of agricultural labour. Secondly, employers may have paid higher wages for valued service by faithful servants. Thirdly, an inadvertent consequence of forcing people to work for a traditional, artificial rate of pay was that the quality of their workmanship suffered.[64]

Whilst the acts of court regulating the wages of malanders were re-enacted at Martinmas 1712, it appears that controls were less rigorously enforced thereafter, suggesting that labour supplies had regularised as the effects of the famine receded or that market forces had taken over.[65]

c) Other Trades

Other rural workers, besides the brewer and servants, were regulated by the regality court. Of these craftsmen the most important were the weavers.

---

60 Ibid, 08/01/1708, pp. 103 and 105.

61 Ibid, 04/12/1704, p. 58.

62 "Bountith", what is given to servants in addition to their wages. *DSL*.

63 J Findlay, *All Manner of People; The History of the Justices of the Peace in Scotland* (Edinburgh, 2000), p. 43. And Gibson and Smout, *Prices, food and wages in Scotland*, p. 286.

64 R C Palmer, *English Law in the Age of the Black Death, 1348–1381: A Transformation of Governance and Law* (North Carolina, 1993), p. 199.

65 Grant Court Book 3, 25/11/1712, p. 31.

Weaving was the principal rural industry in the north east of Scotland.[66] The weavers of Strathspey were instrumental in providing woollen cloth and plaid for the domestic market within the regality.[67] Most weavers were drawn from the sub-tenant/cottar social group.[68] Thus, their ability to supplement their income from agriculture with by-employment was all important to their economic survival within the community.[69] The origins of present day Grantown-on-Spey were founded upon the optimistic belief that this domestic cottage industry could provide the basis for production on a large commercial scale capable of supporting a growing town and hundreds of families. This vision for the textile industry in Strathspey, like many of Sir James Grant of Grant's improving schemes, ultimately failed.[70] However, the textile industry left its mark on the regality court books.

In Strathspey, textile production was probably organised under a system whereby weavers supplied their own raw materials and sold their produce at markets and fairs, as was the case in other parts of Scotland.[71] Like brewers, weavers had to be licensed by the court to weave within the regality. In return for enjoying the privileges of selling cloth at the fairs and markets within the regality, weavers had to swear before the court that they would pursue their trade in accordance with the acts of court governing the textiles trade.[72] Unfortunately, none of the details of these acts have been passed down to us. However, it is likely that they mirrored the numerous acts of the Scottish Parliament with regards to ensuring the sizing and quality of the plaids produced.[73] This was the case in the baron court of Stitchill, where weavers were

66 R E Tyson, 'The Rise and Fall of Manufacturing in Rural Aberdeenshire' in J S Smith and D Stevenson (eds.), *Fermfolk and Fisherfolk: Rural Life in Northern Scotland in the Eighteenth and Nineteenth Centuries* (Aberdeen, 1989), p. 64.

67 Incredibly, some examples of cloth and clothing produced in seventeenth century Strathspey survive in the collections of the National Museums of Scotland. The textiles were found on a skeleton dating from circa 1650, preserved in a peatbog on Dava Moor three miles north of Castle Grant. https://www.nms.ac.uk/explore-our-collections/collection-search-results/?item_id=19627.

68 R M Mitchison, *The Old Poor Law in Scotland; The Experience of Poverty 1574–1845* (Edinburgh, 2008), p. 94; Whyte, *Scotland before the Industrial Revolution: An Economic and Social History*, p. 165.

69 Tyson, 'Manufacturing in Rural Aberdeenshire', pp. 69–70.

70 J S Smith, "Background to Planned Village Formation", in J S Smith and D Stevenson (eds.), *Fermfolk and Fisherfolk: Rural Life in Northern Scotland in the Eighteenth and Nineteenth Centuries* (Aberdeen, 1989), p. 7.

71 Gibson and Smout, *Prices, food and wages in Scotland*, p. 295.

72 Grant Court Book 2, 31/01/1706, p. 68.

73 *RPS*, 1693/4/105. This was also the case in the Regality of Melrose: Romanes, *Selections from the records of the regality of Melrose*, Vol II, p. 177.

fined for keeping insufficient weights, measures and not weaving conform to the standards set down by the acts of parliament.[74]

The court records reveal that, as with fees taken by tied servants, weavers were examined at head courts, being called to compear before the bailie and answer as to whether they had upheld the acts of court and swore to abide by them in future.[75] The procedure was carried out individually for each parish within the regality. As a result, we have lists of the weavers weaving in each parish. For instance, at Martinmas 1716 there were fourteen weavers enacted to weave within the parish of Abernethy and twelve in the parish of Inverallan.[76] All the weavers listed were men. Once admitted to weave, weavers were expected to practise that trade, and faced 'unlaw' if they failed to do so:

> The said day the bailie fynes and unlaws the haill wyvers of the parish of Duthell in 5 lib Scotis Ilk ane of them for transgressing of the actis of the court anent tradesmen and unlaws [blank] Makerwane wyver in Tullochcribane in ten pounds for not exerciseing his traid in despyt of the actis and for slighteing the samen.[77]

This suggests that the weavers of Strathspey may have pursued their trade full-time rather than as a winter by-occupation as has often been stated.[78] The spatial distribution of men named as weavers on the lists in the court records also suggests that weaving may have provided nearly full-time occupation. Few davochs had more than one weaver named as resident, the exceptions being Ballintomb with four; Muckerack with three; Tulloch, Conedge and Congess with two a-piece. This follows a pattern with other trades such as miller, maltman, and brewer whereby there was one for each, or perhaps two davochs at most. The population of these smaller self-contained units was perhaps large enough to sustain a weaver, especially when coupled with the opportunity to sell to a much wider market at fairs and markets.

Weavers and other tradesmen were required to petition the court for access to the trades, their communities, and privileges, as was the case in the urban burghs of royalty and barony. Cromdale was a burgh of barony from 1609 to 1694, and upon the erection of the regality in 1694 Grantown became a burgh of regality. Although these burghs in themselves were hardly larger than the

---

74 Gunn, *Records of the Baron Court of Stitchill*, pp. 50, 90, 147, 148, 120.

75 See for instance Grant Court Book 3, 22/11/1716, p. 98.

76 Ibid, pp. 98, 99 and 101.

77 Grant Court Book 2, 29/11/1705, p. 64.

78 Tyson, 'The Rise and Fall of Manufacturing in Rural Aberdeenshire', p. 69 – 70.

numerous farming townships which housed the scattered community of the regality, arguably the wider regality operated as something akin to a burgh or trading community:

> The said day the forsaids commissioners judges considered the petitione of James Grant in Milntoune of Castle Grant craving their warrand for permitting his sone Alex[ande]r Grant to bind himself prentise to ane master for learneing the weaver traid. They find the said petitioune just and reasonable in respect that he has hitherto been a servant ... and none has pitched upone him and that he is noe idler.[79]

The notion of apprenticeship was meant to protect crafts in the wider trading community from a dilution of standards and from outside competition by regulating entry to the craft.[80] In this example, local knowledge of the personality and good character of a potential apprentice were considered precisely to ensure standards within the weaving community. This suggests that the weavers of the regality acted like a trade incorporation although the court controlled entry to their numbers rather than the weavers themselves.

6.1.3 *The Relationship between the Regality Court and the Justices of the Peace*

Many of the administrative duties of the office of justice of the peace overlapped with the economic and administrative regulations set down by the regality court of Grant. One such duty was the determination of wages paid to labourers and farm servants. This was decided by quarter sessions of the J.P.s, a duty set out in a statute of 1617.[81] The justices could hand down punishments for those not paying the fixed rate of wages decided at the quarter sessions, and also enforce the timeous payment of wages owed to servants.[82] In addition they were instructed to put the statutes governing the weaving trade into execution, whilst they were also responsible for the quality and pricing of foodstuffs such as ale.[83] Thus it can be appreciated that the role of J.P.s was somewhat negated by the existence of cognate local jurisdictions such as the regality of Grant.

---

79 Grant Court Book 3, 19/11/1712, p. 27.
80 Symm, 'Social Control in a Sixteenth Century Burgh', p. 296.
81 *RPS*, 1617/5/22.
82 Findlay, *All Manner of People*, p. 33.
83 Ibid, pp. 34 and 78.

No records of the J.P.s of the shires of Elgin, Inverness and Banff survive contemporaneous with the records left by the regality court of Grant; however, the above analysis of the economic governance of the regality seems to reinforce opinions that, until the Union, the contribution of J.P.s to rural governance in the late seventeenth and early eighteenth centuries was minimal.[84] One could go as far as to say that in regions which tended to a strong political entity, such as a feudal lordship with powers of jurisdiction, J.P.s were superfluous. Not only in economic matters, but also when it came to other roles such as enforcing statutes on poaching and woodlands, along with the building of roads,[85] heritable jurisdictions and local power structures left little, if any, scope for landowners to act in their capacity as justices.

So much is true up until 1708. From this point, economic regulation in the regality court of Grant becomes much less important in the court record. In 1707 the powers of the J.P.s in Scotland were greatly enhanced, bringing them almost in line with the powers afforded to their English counterparts.[86] It was hoped at the time that the enhanced powers given to J.P.s might act as a counterbalance to the powers of heritable jurisdiction holders.[87] It has been claimed that by 1725, the J.P.s had not only attained equal status with the English office but had superseded the role of the barons and their courts largely due to their work in connection with the newly revamped circuit courts.[88] If the J.P.s' new-found political status and power in criminal processes was also true of economic regulation, it is possible that the reduction in economic governance found in the regality court was partially thanks to increasing regulation by the J.P.s. Certainly, following abolition of the regality in 1748, the J.P.s assumed many of the functions of the regality court. These duties included enacting regulations for tradesmen and servants in Strathspey.[89] Besides the lairds of Grant, there were a considerable number of J.P.s named within the regality.[90] An appointment as a J.P. was valued for the status it conferred, but

84 C A Malcolm (ed.), *Minutes of the Justices of the Peace in the Shire of Lanarkshire, 1707–1725* (Edinburgh, 1931), pp.xxiv-xxvi.

85 See Grant Court Book 1, 26/02/1696, p. 76, Petition from the tenants and possessors of the Braes of Glenchernick for the building of a bridge upon the river Dulnain. This was granted with the court then laying down the stipulations regarding construction, such as the wages to be paid to masons.

86 8 Ann, C16.

87 E K Carmichael, 'Jacobitism in the Scottish Commission of the Peace, 1707–1760', *SHR* 58:1, (1979), p. 58.

88 Davies, 'Law and Order in Stirlingshire', pp. 456–7 and 469.

89 NRS, The Baron Court of Strathspey, GD248/372/1.

90 As many as twenty in 1704, six of whom acted as bailie of the regality court at some time.

also as it was remunerated.[91] There were more opportunities for the gentlemen of Strathspey to participate in the legal system through the J.P. courts than in the franchise courts where offices were traditionally awarded to certain kinsmen. However, the commission of the peace was severely hampered by personnel shortages.[92] The shortage of suitably qualified individuals was particularly acute in the northern shires, a situation which would continue after 1748, placing a continued emphasis on franchise courts to fulfil administrative and judicial functions in the shires.[93]

6.2 Religious and Social Control

The kirk was, like the regality of Grant, concerned with many aspects of what may now be considered key elements of secular government. Legal and moral discipline was exercised through the system of kirk sessions that came to form the basic unit of church administration by the early years of the seventeenth century. Through its system of church courts and the settlement of parish ministers responsible to these courts, the church succeeded in setting up a system of government which was arguably more effective than that of the crown.[94] However, the success of church government was in part reliant upon the effectiveness of concurrent secular jurisdictions, especially local franchise courts, to help uphold and enforce the judgements of its courts. There is now greater recognition amongst historians that secular and ecclesiastical jurisdictions usually cooperated closely in the localities.[95]

In Strathspey the parishes of Cromdale, Abernethy and Duthil have all left kirk session records from the early eighteenth century.[96] The surviving records show that Cromdale session met on almost a weekly basis through the first decade of the eighteenth century, under the stewardship of the new parish minister James Chapman. The records for Duthil and Abernethy cover later decades and show that the sessions were still attempting to convene weekly meetings, although on many occasions there was little business to be dealt with. Several entries in the records of the session of Abernethy show that

91 Carmichael, 'Jacobitism in the Scottish Commission of the Peace', p. 62.
92 Ibid, pp. 59 – 61.
93 Ibid, p. 66.
94 Mitchison and Leneman, *Girls in Trouble*, p. 7.
95 Goodare, *The Government of Scotland*, p. 194.
96 HA, Cromdale Kirk Session Minutes, CH2/983; HA, Abernethy Kirk Session Minutes, CH2/1054; NRS, Duthil Kirk Session Minutes, GD248/552/1.

attempts to convene weekly meetings were frustrated not through lack of business, but rather inclement weather: 'no session by reason of the cold' being a frequent entry in the session records.[97]

These records are typical of kirk session records of the period, being largely concerned with sexual offences and sabbath breach.[98] The dominance of these issues in the daily life of the Scottish kirk was alluded to by Burt in his letters: 'in short, one would think that there was no sin, according to them, but fornication; or other virtue besides keeping the sabbath'.[99] Other issues coming under the consideration of these bodies included: irregular marriage, slander and adultery. However, the records make clear that the number of cases coming before the kirk sessions in Strathspey, in common with much of Scotland in the early eighteenth century, was noticeably declining. The reasons for this decline were several: firstly, there was a marked increase in lay piety meaning less need for prosecutions; secondly, government and ruling society was becoming more secular, placing less emphasis on the kirk sessions to impose social control;[100] thirdly, the kirk sessions lost the right to impose civil penalties of excommunication in 1690,[101] which was coupled with a change in policy in the civil courts, where there was a greater reluctance to prosecute moral offences.[102] We find no cases concerning the kirk in the baron court extracts of the 1660s, they only begin to appear after 1700 in the regality court records. Whilst these cases are relatively few, those that do appear reveal much about society at the time and the relationship between regality court and kirk.[103]

6.2.1 *People*

The kirk sessions and franchise courts enjoyed very close ties, primarily owing to the crossover in personnel and common interests between these courts.[104] Sessions included a civil magistrate required to put any civil disciplinary

97 HA, Abernethy Kirk Session Minutes, CH2/1054, 06/01/1740.

98 Davies, 'Law and Order in Stirlingshire', p. 83; J McCallum, *Reforming the Scottish Parish. The Reformation in Fife, 1560–1640* (Farnham, 2010), pp. 42–72.

99 Simmons (ed.), *Burt's Letters*, p. 107.

100 Mitchison and Leneman, *Girls in Trouble*, pp. 30–31.

101 *RPS*, 1690/4/119. All acts enjoining civil pains upon sentences of excommunication rescinded.

102 Mitchison and Leneman, *Girls in Trouble*, pp. 30–37; and see Levack, 'The Prosecution of Sexual Crimes in Early Eighteenth-Century Scotland'.

103 Cornell discovered extensive cooperation between kirk sessions and franchise courts in east Lothian in the first half of the seventeenth century. Cornell, 'Gender and Social Control in East Lothian', pp. 71–78.

104 Davies, 'Law and Order in Stirlingshire', p. 139.

measures laid down into execution and to put extra pressure on recalcitrant members of the congregation. In Strathspey the civil magistrates were all bailies of the regality court of Grant. For instance, on 14 December 1702, Alexander Grant of Grant attended Cromdale kirk session 'as civil judge to give his concurrence'.[105] A year later Cromdale kirk session had Patrick Grant of Tullochgorum, bailie of Inverallan, attending as bailiff.[106] Around 1720 John Grant of Dalrachney was to be found sitting on the Duthil session, often referred to simply as 'the bailie'.[107] It can be appreciated how having the backing of such powerful local figures in the community helped to enforce Presbyterian discipline within their parishes. The authority lent by these figures in the local community must have greatly reinforced the kirk sessions' legitimacy.

Besides the heritors and civil judge, several of the elders who made up the body of the kirk session in each parish had roles within the court. The position of these men further emphasises the close working relationship between regality court and kirk session. The elders represented a cross section of society from heritor, to tacksman and tenant. It was these latter two social groups who dominated the sessions. When choosing new potential elders, the men of the session were enjoined to seek out men of 'great prudence, gravity and interest in the parish'.[108] The expectation that elders should have an 'interest' in the moral and economic prosperity of the parish effectively ruled out the lower elements of society, cottars, and servants, from being ordained, in much the same way that these men were excluded from participation in the legal system through office holding or sitting as part of an assize.[109] The elders were the point of contact between the session and the wider community, with each settlement within the parish usually having an elder appointed from among its residents.[110] The davoch from which the elder was drawn composed his 'beat', like that of a modern-day policeman; he was expected to keep watch over this area.[111] In the parish of Cromdale, Inverallan and Advie men ordained as elders included: William Grant of Delay, bailie; David Blair of Easter Lethendrie, regality clerk; William Grant of Dallachaple, bailie and procurator; and David Cuthbert, bailie substitute. Whilst in the parish of Duthil in the 1720s, Alexander

105 HA, Cromdale Kirk Session Minutes, CH2/983/1, 14/12/1702, p.1.
106 Ibid, 05/09/1703, p. 14.
107 NRS, Duthil Kirk Session Minutes, GD248/552/1, p. 138.
108 A Mutch, *Religion and National Identity: Governing Scottish Presbyterianism in the Eighteenth Century* (Edinburgh, 2016), p. 86.
109 Ibid. and Cornell, 'Gender and Social Control in East Lothian', p. 59.
110 Ibid, p. 8.
111 Davies, 'Law and Order in Stirlingshire', p. 138.

Cummine in Duthil, regality clerk, and bailie John Grant of Dalrachney were elders with connections to the regality court. Cornell has emphasised that this sharing of personnel is symptomatic not only of links between jurisdictions but also of the finite pool of people available to fulfil such roles.[112]

Another court official with links to both kirk and regality was the court officer. The kirk sessions in Strathspey had their own kirk officers to summon defenders and witnesses to compear before the sessions. However, alongside the kirk officer the sessions also made use of the regality court's officers to undertake arrestment of both goods and persons:

> The Session appoints Donald Grant ground officer to repair to Glenlochy and apprehend the persons of John Stuart and Janet Cummine servants to James Grant in Glenlochy for their contumacy: according to his order from the Baillie of the Regality of Grant.[113]

For their services to the kirk sessions the regality court officers were remunerated out of fine money ingathered by the session:

> The Session considering that the present ground officer Donald Grant is useful to them in summoning and taking in persons that are contumacious to discipline have allowed him the penalty imposed upon William Fraser soldier [equating to £10 sc.][114]

6.2.2 *Kirk Session Business and the Regality Court of Grant*

The type of cases that the regality court and kirk sessions were cooperating over fall into three broad categories: the typical work of the sessions such as sexual offences and sabbath breach; slander and disrespecting church authority; funding the kirk, its buildings and ministers.

The main forms of discipline utilised by kirk sessions to punish wayward members of the congregation were rebukes and public repentance.[115] The public nature of these punishments was very important for enforcing social control, clearly encouraging and in turn discouraging certain social acts, by invoking a sense of guilt in both the offender and the public who had to witness their shaming.[116] A public rebuke or repentance also rehabilitated the offender in

112 Cornell, 'Gender and Social Control in East Lothian', p. 77.

113 HA, Abernethy Kirk Session Minutes, CH2/1054, 24/05/1741, p. 138.

114 HA, Abernethy Kirk Session Minutes, CH2/1054, p. 145.

115 Davies, 'Law and Order in Stirlingshire', p. 123.

116 Ibid, p. 125.

the eyes of the church allowing them to resume their place in the community. However, the success of these forms of punishment was wholly dependent upon the cooperation of the offender. Whilst most offenders admitted their guilt and appeared for rebuke, there was a minority who resisted the authority of the church.[117] The kirk had its own mechanisms for dealing with such people; offenders were given three chances to appear before the session when summoned to answer for their conduct. If they failed to compear after the third summonses, they were referred to the presbytery. The presbytery might impose a civil penalty or refer the case back to the kirk session. However, once these options were exhausted, or a person was thought beyond redemption, the links between the kirk and regality court became all important.[118] The regality court was used in two ways: firstly (and sometimes alongside the presbytery) as an advisory body, who might also talk with and put extra pressure upon an offender; secondly to put into execution a civil penalty imposed upon an offender by the kirk.

There are numerous references in the session records to occasions when the session decided to refer a case to the civil magistrate, demonstrating one of the main links between the jurisdictions. For instance, between May 1739 and March 1748 (from when the records of Abernethy kirk session commence until the abolition of the regality court), the kirk session of Abernethy referred thirty people from the session to the bailie of the regality of Grant. Most people were referred for failing to compear before the session or congregation; however, there were exceptions such as: John and Neil Grant in Muckerack referred for refusing to swear the oath when called as witnesses; a case of slander; and the case of Donald McCrave and Isobell McIntire who disputed paternity.[119] In some instances the elders and minister simply wished to obtain legal advice. For instance, in 1703 the kirk session of Cromdale spent months deliberating over the irregular marriage of one John Grant nicknamed 'the hirer'. In August 1703 they finally managed to get 'the hirer' to compear; however, the session were unclear with how to proceed with the case and subsequently decided that: 'the session thinks fit to refer further tryal in this affair until the laird of Grant younger came home and appoints the said John Grant to answer when called'.[120] None of these overtures to the regality judge resulted in a case in the regality court books. Hence there was evidently more cooperation between

117 Mitchison and Leneman, *Girls in Trouble*, p. 106.

118 Ibid, p. 116.

119 HA, Abernethy Kirk Session Minutes, CH2/1054, pp. 233, 368 and 265.

120 HA, Cromdale Kirk Session Minutes, CH2/983/1, 01/08/1703, p. 11.

the jurisdictions going on behind the scenes than is evident from the court books alone.

In serious cases where the offender refused to submit to the discipline of the kirk session and would not give way to pressure from the bailie or presbytery, the imposition of a civil penalty in purse or person was sought by the kirk. In such instances the case was referred to the regality court. Beyond referring individual cases to the bailie, the session could go further and request that the bailie convene a regality court to deal with offenders specifically for this purpose. Powerless in the face of widespread contumacy in their parish in August 1747, the kirk session of Abernethy decided:

> None of the delinquents compeared at this meeting. The session taking their contumacy and stubbornness under consideration do appoint the minister to speak to the Baillie of the Regality of Grant, in order that he may hold a court in this parish that all the delinquents thereof may be decerned to pay their penalties according to law.[121]

As in the regality court, amercement was the primary punishment imposed. However, in extreme cases, where the session believed an offender was beyond redemption, the punishment of banishment might be sought by the kirk session and imposed by the regality court. The best example of the referral of a woman, regarded as being beyond redemption, to the attentions of the bailies of the regality of Grant came in November 1727:

> Anent the representation given in be Wm Grant minister of Abernethy and the session of the said parish making mention that Elspet Stuart in Cottotown of Culnakyle adulteress continues contumacious to discipline in so far as she makes no evidence of repentance for her said fall in adultery and craving in that respect and because she is still ane idler and out of service that she be banished the Regality of Grant in Abernethy … the said judge statutes and ordains the said Elspet Stuart to banish herself furth of Abernethy against Monday next until she find caution for that effect.[122]

Eight months previously at a meeting of the presbytery of Abernethy, Gregor Grant of Gartenmore, tacksman of Gartenmore, Dell and Riemore, had

---

121 HA, Abernethy Kirk Session Records, CH2/1054, 05/08/1747, p. 356.

122 Grant Court Book 5, 16/11/1727, p. 132.

admitted to adultery with Elspet Stuart.[123] They had been remitted to the session to undergo discipline; however, Elspet Stuart refused to appear before the congregation and showed no penitence, eventually causing the session of Abernethy to petition the regality court for her banishment and thus physical expulsion from the community.[124] Given that Gregor Grant of Gartenmore held the most extensive wadset lands in the parish, one can speculate whether there was a desire to remove Elspet in order avoid any further embarrassment to this cadet branch of the clan Grant.

The people being convened for contravening social and moral mores before the session were drawn from all ranks. In May 1703 Isobel Grant, spouse to James Rose in Glenbeg, was compearing to answer to charges of antenuptial fornication.[125] Whilst before the session she was also accused of fornication with Ludovick Grant of Grant, which she subsequently confessed to at a meeting of the session a week later.[126] Given the delicate nature of dealing with the parish's only heritor, and that the fall in fornication had taken place several years ago, the session of Cromdale sought advice from the presbytery of Abernethy. A month later the advice of the Presbytery arrived:

> The presbyterie advises anent the laird of Grant's case that in regard he now lives in Edinburgh and that there is long time since his fall in fornication with the said Elspet Grant he therefore may be delayed till he live in this parioch and then that he be dealed with as access may be had.[127]

A degree of caution when dealing with landowners was common to the approach of most sessions, apart from during the covenanting period.[128] Cases such as Cromdale kirk session's attempts to discipline the laird of Grant, show the difficulty that the kirk had in imposing its authority if it did not have the support of the local landowner.[129]

In February 1705 one of the laird's sons, George Grant of Grant, was also delated to the Cromdale kirk session, being accused of fathering Janet Brodack's

123 HA, Presbytery of Abernethy Minutes, CH2/437/1, 29/03/1727, p. 161.

124 This case is also demonstrative of the two-way judicial relationship between session and presbytery. It was usual for adultery cases to be remitted as a matter of routine to the next sitting of the presbytery. After consideration there, the case was often sent back to the session for judgement. Cornell, 'Gender and Social Control in East Lothian', p. 70.

125 HA, Cromdale Kirk Session Minutes, CH2/983/1, 16/05/1703, p. 7.

126 Ibid.

127 HA, Cromdale Kirk Session Minutes, CH2/983/1, 20/06/1703, p. 9.

128 Davies, 'Law and Order in Stirlingshire', p. 127.

129 Mitchison and Leneman, *Girls in Trouble*, pp. 117–118.

child. The parish minister was sent to talk with the laird's son; however, George Grant denied fathering the child, retorting that 'Janet was known to be a lewd person'.[130] Yet, after two months of pressure by the session, George Grant eventually made a partial confession and agreed to submit to discipline.[131] Men such as George Grant of Grant were obviously keen to avoid appearing in public and degrading themselves in front of men of lower social status. This made it very difficult for the kirk to get such men to appear and be disciplined. George Grant was no exception and took his leave of Strathspey soon after in August 1705, confessing all to the minister before doing so, and entreating John Grant in Dreggie to present his illegitimate child for baptism in his absence.[132]

The kirk session of Abernethy continued to seek the banishment of transgressors by the regality court up until January 1748, only two months prior to the regality of Grant's abolition.[133] Fifteen women were banished from the parish of Abernethy in the 1740s upon petition from the minister of Abernethy to the bailie of the regality of Grant, ten of whom were banished in February 1740 alone.[134] These women were described as 'being strangers who came from other countries to this parish and now have fallen in whoredom with country men here'.[135] There were clearly several elements which led to the punishment of banishment being imposed. The first was the moral laxity of the women in the eyes of the church and an unwillingness to repent with sincerity. Secondly, the women were seemingly being viewed as quasi-vagabonds: master-less and out to corrupt the vulnerable menfolk of Abernethy parish. A further four women, banished forth of the parish in January 1748, were banished for being unable or unwilling to name men who would own their illegitimate children despite numerous appearances before the kirk session. In this case banishment again emphasises that the unrepentant nature of the women in question was the primary justification for their expulsion from the community.

These women were all guilty of fornication, the most common offence appearing in the kirk session records for Strathspey. It appears that the kirk session was reasonably successful in gaining the compliance and repentance of offenders without having to refer the offenders to the civil jurisdiction, as only two fines for fornication and a sole case of ante-nuptial fornication

130 HA, Cromdale Kirk Session Minutes, CH2/983/1, 15/04/1705, p. 30.
131 Ibid, 24/06/1705, p. 38.
132 HA, Cromdale Kirk Session Minutes, CH2/983/1, 05/08/1705, p. 42.
133 HA, Abernethy Kirk Session Minutes, CH2/1054, 17/01/1748, p. 368.
134 Ten in February 1740, one in April 1743, and four in January 1748; HA, Abernethy Kirk Session Minutes, CH2/1054, 24/02/1740, pp. 74, 145, and 368.
135 HA, Abernethy Kirk Session Minutes, CH2/1054, 24/02/1740, p. 74.

appear in the regality court books.[136] All three cases appeared in 1724, with the offenders cited to make payment of fines owing to the kirk session of Cromdale.[137] However, the two men guilty of fornication had no more respect for the authority of the regality court than they did for the kirk session, failing to compear before either jurisdiction, and thus incurring an extra £5 fine each, which was presumably extracted through poinding. That the kirk sessions continued to refer offenders to the regality court until just months before its abolition, suggests that the kirk was fortunate to be able to rely upon the support of the local franchise court for the enforcement of discipline. Although the kirk session records for Abernethy show several instances where offenders, referred to the bailie of the regality of Grant, continued contumacious to justice even after the intervention of the bailie, it appears to have been a generally effective partnership.

Fines ingathered were applied to kirk funds, paying officers' fees, providing alms for the poor, and the construction of bridges and other infrastructure in the parish.[138] Of the other punishments available for disciplinary purposes, the jougs were perhaps the most symbolic: an iron ring placed around the miscreant's neck outside the parish church. Donald Roy in Downan was subjected to this punishment by the regality court in 1712, for falsely claiming his uncle's betrothed was within forbidden degrees to stop their marriage, 'in respect of such false declarations he is ordained to stand in the jogs Sabath day comes eight days before the congregacione so lang as the sessione thinks fit with ane ignominious garb otherwayes to be imprisoned'.[139]

Promise of marriage held great significance in Scotland, as if it was followed by sexual intercourse it constituted an irregular, yet, valid marriage.[140] Hence a promise of marriage could be a powerful tool for unscrupulous men to manipulate women to their own ends. Proposals which were subsequently reneged upon were taken seriously by the kirk session. Just such an example can be found in the court records:

136 The Cromdale Kirk Session records show the most compeared and admitted guilt. However, the minutes of Abernethy Kirk Session in the 1730s and 1740s show that contumacy to discipline was very widespread.

137 Grant Court Book 5; 10/01/1724, p. 16; 27/07/1724, p. 27.

138 HA, Cromdale Kirk Session Minutes, CH2/983/1, 23/05/1703, p. 7.

139 Grant Court Book 3, 16/02/1712, p. 19.

140 L Leneman, *Promises, Promises: Marriage Litigation in Scotland 1698–1830* (Edinburgh, 2003), pp. x-xi.

> Wm Makoyllvor in Avielochane is decerend to pay to the session of the parish of Duthell the somme of fourtie pounds scotis for breaking of purpois of maraige with twa severall women successive efter giving up their names to the session clerk for proclaiming and accordinglie proclaimed and yet refuses to name other of these women without [Blank] Shaw in Rothiemurchis and [Blank] Stewart in Auchork.[141]

Sabbath breach was another offence commonly tried by the kirk sessions but appears only once in the records of the regality court of Grant, when in 1706 Duncan Grant in Backharne and Jon Stuart Roy in Congash were each fined £20 'for bargaineing upone the Sabath day anent excambione of possessions and dissolves the bargaine'.[142] It appears that much trading was done on the sabbath, with the session of Cromdale being moved to enact in December 1702: 'that in regard its customary to buy and sell tobaco and other commoditys upon the Sabbath day in this congregation therefore its enacted that all who buy and all who sell tobacco or any other merchandwares upon the sabbath shall pay one pound'.[143] Upholding the sabbath was treated with the utmost seriousness by the kirk. This is well demonstrated by the treatment of John Fraser in Polowick in the parish of Cromdale. He was delated to the Cromdale Session in October 1726 for fishing the Spey upon the sabbath along with his neighbour William Roy.[144] Whilst Roy submitted to discipline and made a public repentance, Fraser refused to do so and was referred to the bailie of the regality of Grant, who was exhorted to 'interpose his authority and make him [Fraser] submit to discipline'.[145] A month later in November, it was reported that Fraser had fled Strathspey and was a 'fugitive'. The flight of John Fraser demonstrates the fear that censure by the kirk could invoke in people, no doubt Fraser might have been further compelled to flee believing he faced a civil penalty for poaching in the regality court. However, Fraser's self-imposed exile was short lived as, two years later in November 1728, it was reported to the session that he had returned to the parish.[146] It was decided that the Minister would talk with him to try and convince him to repent and submit to discipline. John Fraser was not swayed by the Minister's overtures and by January

141 Grant Court Book 3, 27/11/1716, p. 100.
142 Grant Court Book 2, 18/11/06, p. 80.
143 HA, Cromdale Kirk Session Minutes, CH2/983/1, 14/12/1702, p.1.
144 William Roy Grant was eventually banished from Strathspey in 1728 for damaging woodlands.
145 HA, Cromdale Kirk Session Minutes, CH2/983/2, 23/10/1726, pp. 5–6.
146 HA, Cromdale Kirk Session Minutes, CH2/983/2, 09/11/1728, p. 27.

the session was discussing the possibility of having him excommunicated. He was once again referred to the bailie of the regality of Grant.[147] This prospect induced Fraser to flee once more, the session noting in March 1729 that he had again left Strathspey.

Drinking on the Sabbath was one of the most serious forms of Sabbath breach and was thus treated with utmost gravity by the kirk. With alcohol playing such an important role in society and with little to do upon the Sabbath, drunkenness was a problem. The kirk session of Cromdale was moved by a particularly drunken baptism:

> Wm Mcfindlay roy in Culfoichbeg, Alexander McIan Tyler in Dalifure, Thomas Kynach in Lettoch, Nile MacCharles summoned for excessive and unseasonable drinking on the sabbath day in Alexander Stuarts house at Thomas Kynack's child's baptism[148]

The result of this disturbance was a partial ban upon the sale of alcohol:

> No taverns sell any ale or liquor upon the sabbath day save what may be needful to refresh the body for the present time and that such as do drink may not be allowed to sit in the tavern above half an hour.[149]

Such a move placed the church at odds with the laird of Grant who raised revenues through the duty paid on ale sold by licensed brewers within the regality; a good example of how moral and economic concerns were difficult to separate and influenced policy within Strathspey.

Another indication of the importance of the Sabbath is that when a crime was committed upon the Sabbath it is always heavily emphasised in the court records as an aggravation of the original offence. This was undoubtedly intended to further highlight the culpability and poor character of the accused person. Committing the same crime on any other day of the week would have had no bearing on the case and received no mention in the record. Any crime committed on the Sabbath day immediately became both a civil and ecclesiastical infraction. A good example of this is the case against James Cattenach, cattle herd in Mullochard, and Donald Gow in Auchterblair, indicted before

147 HA, Cromdale Kirk Session Minutes, CH2/983/2, p. 31.

148 Both Mcfindlay Roy and Kynack were soldiers in William Grant's independent company; HA, Cromdale Kirk Session Minutes, CH2/983/1, p. 23.

149 HA, Cromdale Kirk Session Minutes, CH2/983/1, 6/8/1704, p. 23.

the court in September 1696 for stealing and killing a cow.[150] The indictment and witness statements recorded in the court books repeatedly stress that the crime took place upon the Sabbath; although this had no direct bearing upon the case itself. By committing a theft on the Sabbath, thieves also took advantage of those in the community who observed the day of rest and remained at home (apart from to attend church) thus leaving their livestock at pasture vulnerable, further aggravating their offence.

Disorderly conduct such as fighting, also became more serious if it took place upon a Sunday. There are only three such cases in the court books.[151] The court records again place emphasis that the illegal activity breached the Sabbath: 'Jon Stewart in Aviemore is unlawed in fiftie pounds Scotis for striking and blooding of Issobell Nienomes Taylor servant to Neill Grant in Aviemore and that upon the Sabath day'.[152]

Another form of disorderly conduct abhorred by the kirk and legislated against by both kirk and parliament was the lykewake. The lykewake was the practice of sitting up with the body of a deceased person whilst they lay at home prior to burial. Such occasions often became festive and even raucous as people sat up taking drink, telling stories, singing, playing music and even dancing.[153] Customs in death such as the lykewake were a relic of Catholic or even pre-Christian worship; however, they survived long after the reformation.[154] In the early years of the seventeenth century the lykewake became the target of censure from kirk session as they became aware that not only did the community ritual carry papist overtones, but it often encouraged the evils of drinking, music and debauchery so despised by the reformed church.[155] Thus, throughout the seventeenth and into the early decades of the eighteenth century the Scottish church allied itself with the civil authorities, at first to try and outlaw lykewakes altogether and later to regulate their excesses when it became clear that the lykewake had moved beyond the control of kirk and

150 Grant Court book 1, 03/10/1696, pp. 97–8.

151 Grant Court book 2; 08/12/1703, p.19; and 29/11/1705, p. 63; Grant Court Book 3, 21/07/1715, p. 88.

152 Grant Court Book 2; 29/11/1705, p. 63.

153 A Gordon, *Death is for the Living* (Edinburgh, 1984), p. 26.

154 S Livingstone, *Scottish Customs* (Edinburgh, 1996), p. 47.

155 R S Fredericks, 'Death Practices and Burial Rites in Scotland from the later Medieval Period to 1780: with Particular Reference to the Influence of Theology' (Unpublished Ph.D. thesis University of Edinburgh, 1967), p. 148.

parliament.[156] The court books of the regality of Grant show evidence of this partnership. In 1702 the kirk session of Cromdale enacted:

> That in regard there are several abuses committed at leakwakes by people passing there time there most heathenishly in dancing sporting drinking drink fiddling piping and the like therefore it's here enacted that the landlord or owners of the family where the leakwakes is pay the soume of four pounds scots that the musician pay as much and all dancers at leakwakes be fyned at discretion not exceeding three pounds scots and all this besides publick reproof.[157]

In June 1715 we have evidence of the regality court helping to enforce the kirk sessions' acts against lykewakes; the minister of Abernethy petitioned the regality court to help control the revelry at lykewakes in his parish:

> The said day anent the complaint made to the said bailly by mr William Grant min[iste]r at Abernethy against the heathenish custome of calling fidlers to likwakes and other barbarous usas … the said bailly has statute and ordained that no fidler housekeeper or any other person within the said parish be employed in fidling or dancing or any other barbarous or sinful custome or playes at the walking of dead people under the failzie of ten pounds Scots ilk person in all tyme coming … and appoints this act to be intimate from the pulpit of the Minister.[158]

The intimation and publicization of acts of the regality court by ministers during Sunday service was another visible way in which the kirk and regality cooperated. The arrangement was mutual as we find that James Chapman petitioned the court in 1708 for the acts of parliament, 'against vice and immoralitie' to be read in court, which was duly done.[159]

Many of the men accused of ecclesiastical infractions before the kirk session also committed separate civil offences and appear in the regality court records. Out of twenty-five males delated to Cromdale kirk session (almost entirely for sexual offences) between 1702 and 1705, nine also appear in the regality court records: all convicted of either assaults or stealing or damaging

156 Ibid, p. 269. The General Assembly banned lykewakes outright in 1645, followed by a ban by the Scottish Parliament a year later.

157 HA, Cromdale Kirk Session Minutes, CH2/983/1, 14/12/1702, p.1.

158 Grant Court Book 3, 15/06/1715, p. 82.

159 Grant Court Book 2, 03/11/1708, p. 115.

trees. Several of these men appeared multiple times before both jurisdictions. Among these men Charles Rose in Delliefure stands out. Charles Rose was son of David Rose in Delliefure an elder of the parish of Cromdale. Charles Rose was delated twice to the kirk session for fornication. On his first appearance his paramour Isobel Andrew admitted that she had initially named another man as her suitor on the orders of Charles Rose to cover his tracks. A year later in 1703 he had another illegitimate child this time by Christian Mclantaylor in neighbouring Culfoich. In 1704 he was fined on no less than five separate occasions by the regality court for offences of, illicit wood cutting (twice), contumacy, assaulting his servant and deforcement of a court officer. The latter offence was committed in tandem with his brother William (who also had appearances before the session) when they were being poinded. Charles Rose's conviction for deforcement is somewhat ironic given that he later found employment from the laird's grieve apprising poinded goods.[160]

6.2.3 *Slander*

> Depones he onlie heard some of his fatheres servantes and people of his famalie say that his father had spok such folish and ill words as that he would tack his excrements and put them in a dish and cast them in the min[iste]rs face when he would come to his house. [161]

This rather extraordinary passage from the regality of Grant court books shows that the religious and social thinking propagated by the ministers of the parishes within Strathspey did not always meet with the approval of parishioners. In such cases the links between civil and ecclesiastical jurisdictions in Strathspey became all important as their differing authorities were interdependent.

James Chapman, Minister of Cromdale, was the target of this anti-clerical tirade. Chapman, born in 1677, was the son of an Inverness Merchant. He was educated at King's College, Aberdeen and licensed by the Presbytery of Dalkeith in 1699, transferring to Cromdale on 25 November 1702.[162] The parish of Cromdale had been vacant for two years upon Chapman's arrival; he had revived the kirk session in the parish by December 1702 and thereafter was a prominent member of the community, featuring often in the regality court

---

160 NRS, Precognition Grant of Mullochard v. Grant of Grant, GD248/22/2/35 fo. 7.

161 Grant Court Book 2, 04/10/1707, p. 88.

162 H Scott (ed.), *Fasti Ecclesiae Scoticanae*, Vol. VI (Edinburgh, 1926), p. 358.

records from this point as an active litigant. Because he was an energetic and active parish minister, he made enemies within the parish.

In October 1707 Chapman lodged a complaint in the regality court against Allan Grant in Achnagall and John Chevis in Achroisk, contending that they 'accusit scandales […] and reproaches and scuroilous speiches lybelled ag[ains]t his lyf and conversatione and against his reputatione and ministeriall functione'.[163] For a non-criminal complaint it is evident that the case was viewed as being especially serious. Ludovick Grant of Grant, his son Alexander Grant of Grant, and David Cuthbert bailie substitute for Cromdale, all sat as judges to hear the case at Castle Grant: only important courts were held here, further emphasising the importance attached to the words spoken against the parish minister.

The slanderous words were uttered by Allan Grant during a drinking session. His drinking companions were called as witnesses. John Catenach in Lethendrie attested that 'he wes in the same companie drinking with Alane Grant and Donald Girld and heard Alane inquyre at Donald Girld if he would drink mr James Chapmanes poysone and that Alane said he would never hear him preach'.[164] James Milart in Cromdale contended that Grant had tried to induce their drinking mate Donald Girld to hear Chapman preach with offers of work: 'depones in omnibus with the other twa and adds that he offered hire to Donald Girld to drink the ministers poysone but cannot condiscend[165] upone the hyr and heard nothing of curseing'.[166]

Meanwhile it was put to Chevis by the court that he had threatened the Minister's son that he would 'stop the min[iste]rs mouth [illeg] from preaching for which Jon Chevis being called is compeared and confessed that he the said Jon Chevis said he would endeavor to stop mr James Chapmanes mouth if he would not let him alone'.[167] Chevis admitted the charges, with Chevis suggesting that he and Grant were not the only people bearing grudges against Chapman:

> John Chevis having confessed the lybell and that Chevis had given the reasone of his so expressing this that mr James Chapmane had said thinges of hurt to the said Chevis that he would lybell him for and that

163 Grant Court book 2, 04/10/1707, p. 88.
164 Grant Court Book 2, 04/10/1707, p. 89.
165 "Condiscend", could not come to agreement. *DSL*.
166 Grant Court Book 2, 04/10/1707, p. 89.
167 Ibid, p. 90.

> ther wer severall neighbours that had many thinges to say to mr James' charge for which he desyred they might be examined.[168]

Chevis was imprisoned until he paid the fine of £40; furthermore, he was required to stand in repentance before the congregation in Cromdale kirk, confessing to his rash outbursts and craving the forgiveness of Chapman. Thanks to the witness statements made against Allan Grant, he was also found guilty of the charges against him, being instructed to stand alongside Chevis before the congregation. In addition, being a man of greater wealth than Chevis, he was unlawed in £100 to be applied to the building of 'ane bell steple' for the parish church. Grant and Chevis were compelled to appear in church under pain of imprisonment. The shame of this punishment must have been hard to bear for such men, undoubtedly leading to even greater anti-clerical resentment. Alleviating their plight marginally was the bailie's final instruction that, 'mr James Chapman procur one of his bretheren to preach that Sabath day' thus saving their total humiliation before their peers.

Allan Grant in Achnagall had last appeared before the regality court only five months previously, also for slander. On this occasion he had accused a neighbour of being a witch:

> Alan Grant in Achnagall entered ane protestatione ag[ains]t Gregor Burgess there that he was ane evill neighbor and of ane evill race of people and in testimonie therof both his goodsyrs sisters were wicked and devilish the ane being brunt for ane witch and the other destroyed for crymes and that the said Allan objecting this to him the said Gregor reproched and scandalized the said Allan with this expressione that the said Allan was worse then any of these women which he protested the said Gregor to prove.[169]

Burgess then entered a counter-plea against Allan Grant: 'Gregor Burgess protested ag[ains]t the said Allane that called him a witch gyt or bratt and therefor pleaded for remeid of law'.[170] Witches' powers were commonly believed to be passed hereditarily between generations; thus, a taunt such as that made by Allan was a common starting point in witch-craft accusations.[171] A counter-plea of slander was one of the principal ways to challenge a process of witchcraft.[172]

168 Ibid.

169 Grant Court Book 2, 18/06/1706, p. 77.

170 Ibid.

171 C Larner, *Enemies of God: the witch-hunt in Scotland* (London, 1981), p. 99.

172 Ibid, p. 116.

Allan Grant's claims that Burgess' family were witches had solid foundations. In October 1661 the privy council issued a commission of justiciary to several north east landowners to catch and try two women suspected of witchcraft in Strathspey, one of whom was Mary Burgess, presumably one of Gregor's great Aunts referred to in the complaint.[173] The records do not record the fate of Mary Burgess, yet if local memory was correct it appears that she was found guilty and executed. A further two decades earlier in 1643 Katherine Burgess, also a resident in the parish of Cromdale, was found guilty by a commission of justiciary of witchcraft.[174] The taunts of Allan Grant clearly demonstrate how such events persisted in folk-memory and continued to taint relatives of the accused half a century later. David Cuthbert bailie substitute was not swayed by either man's claims and continued the case, and, failing proof of their allegations, both were fined £50. The case drops from the record.

Allan Grant and Gregor Burgess both appear multiple times in the court records. Grant especially seems to have led a turbulent existence. Two years previously John Burgess in Achnagall, presumably a kinsman of Gregor, gave evidence against Allan Grant that he shot Patrick Grant of Dalvey's doves, earning Allan Grant a £50 fine in the process.[175] Perhaps this is indicative of an enmity between the two families, both of whom were tenants in the upland davoch of Achnagall. Such neighbourhood tensions were a common cause of witchcraft accusations in Scotland.[176] Burgess' family history didn't prevent him becoming an elder of Cromdale parish in 1726 alongside the bailie who presided over the allegations of witchcraft against him twenty years earlier, David Cuthbert.

The kirk session records of Abernethy reveal that cases of slander were still being referred from the session to the regality court as late as 10 January 1748, when John Cameron, in Gartenmore, complained that 'Satirs were made upon him, and upon Donald Cameron his brother, implying curses and imprecations, which were rehearsed in William Fraser in Achtergaudach his family'. The case was referred to the bailie of the regality of Grant after investigation by the session.[177]

173 NRS, Commission for the apprehension of witches, GD248/6/1, fo. 220.

174 *RPC* 2nd S, v.7 p. 446.

175 Grant Court Book 2, 25/10/1704, p. 38.

176 Larner, Enemies of God, p. 105; A Hill, 'Decline and Survival in Scottish Witch-Hunting, 1701–1727', in J Goodare (ed.), *Scottish Witches and Witch-hunters* (London, 2013), p. 217.

177 HA, Abernethy Kirk Session Minutes, CH2/1054, pp. 366 and 368.

6.2.4 *Funding the Kirk*

As part of the reformation settlement in Scotland patrons (and heritors) gained tacks of ecclesiastical teinds. This tax levied upon the tacksmen's tenants was thenceforth incorporated into tacksmen's rentals. However, these teinds were often burdened with the minister's stipend.[178] Heritors across Scotland also became responsible for maintaining the fabric of the parish kirk, manse and school house.[179] These obligations became a bone of contention between kirk and landowners, in many respects strengthening anti-clerical feeling.[180] However, a condition inserted into Grant tacks stipulated that Grant tacksmen and tenants had to relieve the laird from the payment of public burdens such as the minister's stipend. This burden was then passed on from tenants to their own subtenants.[181] As with all taxes there was resistance to payment, and in such cases the regality court was used to help enforce payment of the minister's stipend by tenants. For instance:

> The which imediat day of Dec[embe]r within stated Auchterblair bailzie decerns each gentleman tenant lyfrenters and others to make pay[men]t to Mr Francis Grant minister of the Gospell in Duthell parish their stipends in the augmentation therof due to him.[182]

The regality court compiled 'stipend rentals' in the manner of a judicial rental, listing the amount paid by each tenant as their contribution to the stipend.[183] Stipends, taxes payable to the crown, and rents were all collected at the same time. Thus, it was easy for heritors to incorporate the collection of the stipend into the collection of their own rentals. The court could also modify the amount of stipend paid by each davoch. Payment of the stipend, as with rents, was paid both in cash and in kind, with the regality court setting conversion rates from victual and livestock to cash for the purposes of paying the minister.[184]

---

178 Bankton, *An Institute of the Law of Scotland*. By statute of 1690 the right of tithes belonged to the patron, along with the burden of the stipend they also have the right to the surplus tithes, pp. 28 and 162.

179 The burden to maintain the fabric of the church fell to heritors if there were insufficient vacant stipends for the purpose, ibid, p. 31.

180 Mutch, *Religion and National Identity*, p. 127.

181 See for instance, NRS, Tack from John Grant of Tullochgriban to his subtenants, GD248/533/2 fo. 8.

182 Grant Court Book 5, 15/12/1724, p. 42.

183 NRS, Papers of the Bailie of Grant, GD248/224/7, fos. 25 and 26.

184 Grant Court book 2, 11/05/ 1705, p. 48.

The duty upon the patron to maintain the fabric of the church buildings was, like other public burdens largely passed from the Grants onto their tenants. For instance, evidence suggests that the wadsetters and tenants of the parish were called upon to transport, materials for repairs and building by the court:

> The right honourable the Laird of Grant has granted warrand to William Grant of Dallay bailie of the parioshen of Cromdale directed to Ludovick Grant of Tulloch forrester of the woods of Abernethy for furnishing timber to the roof of the kirk of Skiradvey ther for the said bailie enacts and ordains the haill tenants of Skiradvey and Tulchen ilk ane of them for their ownparts to cut dres and transport from the said wood to the kirk of Skiradvey the haill sparr [illeg] timber and lasts for the said roof and if betwixt and the last day of this instant time under the pain of ten pund by and out over performance and also to bind set up and thatch the samen with hethor and that betwixt the last of July next under the said failzie proportionaly.[185]

The Grants as patrons also left the tenants to cover most of the costs of materials, probably only covering any shortfall that could not be raised from taxation or providing large timbers that could only be provided from estate forestry. Even on occasions when the laird himself was required to furnish stone, thatch or timber for repairs, with almost all materials being available locally, it would have cost little in theory for the Grants to discharge their duty of maintenance. For larger works it was necessary to raise revenues to fund repairs and for this purpose taxes were levied by the regality court:

> Anent the petition given in be mr James Chapman minister of the Gospell att Cromdall and Inverall anent the reparation of the min[iste]rs manse the kirks of Cromdall, Advie and Inverallan and schooll house of the said parish The said judge with consent of the ho[nourab]ld James Grant of Grant patron of the said kirks and superior of the hail lands in the said parishes decerns ordains and enacts the hail tennents of the parishes of Cromdale, Advie, Delvey and Inverallan to make payment of one penny Scots money for each pound Scots of dutie they pay for their respective possessions.[186]

185 Grant Court Book 4, May 1721, p. 56.

186 Grant Court Book 5, 10/01/1724, p. 15.

The kirk session records reveal that this system of maintaining church buildings was clearly ineffective and consequently buildings were often in a poor state of repair. An ordinance made by the kirk session of Abernethy in August 1743 that 'each Gentleman and Tennant repair the breaches or holes above his own seat, seeing it is now too late in the year to have the Church fully repaired' lays bare the parlous state of the parish kirk there.[187] With parishioners subsequently being instructed to bring heather and other materials to the kirk-yard to effect the necessary repairs to the roof.[188] However, it seems that some improvements were undertaken in the laird of Grant's local parish of Cromdale; in 1708 the court issued an ordinance reminding tenants of their duty to transport slates from Gaich to Cromdale kirk; whilst in 1729 a tax was levied upon the possessors of land in the parish to fund the construction of a new manse there.[189]

6.3 Local Governance, Conclusions

Government exercised by the regality of Grant and kirk session was the type of power experienced directly by common people throughout the Highlands.[190] Local power in the guise of bailies, elders, lairds and ministers was the familiar face of government and undoubtedly drew its legitimacy and success from this familiarity.[191] Whilst the regality of Grant self-evidently fulfilled essential elements of government such as providing courts of law and uplifting local taxes, the records of the regality of Grant make clear that social control was also at the heart of local governance in Strathspey. Mechanisms of social control were both economic and religious. For instance, tied servants were desirable because they reduced the financial burden upon farmers whilst at the same time removed the social problem of master-less men. Such cases show how economic and moral concerns were often difficult to separate. For this reason, both became the business of the two arms of local government: kirk and laird. Consideration of social control reveals several important points when considering the continuing vitality and usefulness of the regality court.

The records reveal that the court came into its own and was responsive in times of crisis. The legislation and court cases arising from the ill-years and the

187 HA, Abernethy Kirk Session Records, CH2/1054, 14/08/1743.

188 Ibid.

189 Grant Court Book 2, 03/11/1708, p. 115 and Court Book 5, 09/01/1729, p. 159.

190 Goodare, *The Government of Scotland*, p. 193.

191 Ibid, pp. 298–9.

aftermath of the crisis, are illustrative of the court at its most active being used as a tool of governance by the land-holding classes to protect their financial interests and control their subordinates by restricting wages and freedom of movement. However, at this point the grasp of the court on economic matters declined.

In contrast, the importance of the regality court in aiding the kirk to enforce social control, seems to have increased through the eighteenth century. The courts of the laird and kirk display many examples of intertwined authority and reciprocal arrangements intended to enhance the effectiveness of both jurisdictions. This cooperation between the feudal courts and kirk sessions is evidence of the effectiveness of a cross-jurisdiction approach to local government. Families like the Grants received more in return for their support of the kirk than simply fulfilling their legal obligations and sense of duty born from their faith. While the regality court was able to lend legal and secular authority to the kirk to bolster its popular support, the reverse was also the case. Thus, through acts of mutual support such as the reading of regality edicts at Sunday service, the Grants gained moral and spiritual backing for the secular policies they pursued on their estates. Furthermore, widespread adherence to religious discipline and doctrine was in the interests of jurisdiction holders as this helped to maintain peace and good neighbourhood on their lands: to the benefit of all. There were also financial incentives for the Grants to help ensure compliance through the regality court: fines uplifted by the kirk session were applied in some cases to the construction of infrastructure in the regality such as bridges thus taking the burden off the Grants' hands; the successful collection of fine money also meant more money for the poor box, which reduced the chances of those in poverty having to resort to theft to sustain themselves. In addition to the laird the bailies of the regality court had personal motives for successfully pursuing fugitives to kirk discipline: they pocketed ten percent of all fines collected on behalf of the kirk session.[192]

This system had benefits for laird, kirk, gentlemen and tenants alike, who could all benefit from working towards a peaceful, god fearing, law-abiding society. However, it must be stressed that this is not necessarily a nationwide picture of how franchise court and kirk sessions worked together, as Strathspey was a Presbyterian region with a single heritor who was traditionally also a devout adherent of Presbyterianism.

192 Grant Court Book 2, 08/12/1703, p. 17.

CHAPTER 7

The Regality Court and the Landed Estate

Woodlands, Game, Farming and Improvement

Those landowners who held rights of jurisdiction had long used courts of barony and regality to facilitate the management of their lands and its inhabitants.[1] These courts had proven to be particularly useful in protecting the landowner's forestry, fishing, and game, along with helping to enforce services owed by tenants. However, according to several historians, during the seventeenth century franchise jurisdictions were used as vital tools in engineering a shift from a traditional, customary model of managing an estate to one more commercial in orientation.[2] It is claimed that they helped land-owners to exploit the natural assets on their landed assets and were used to manages schemes for the improvement of the Scottish countryside.[3] Evidence from the regality court of Grant suggests that these claims are overstated. The records of the regality of Grant evidence a transformation, however, only in the Grants' management of their forests in Strathspey. When considering game and farming, continuity of practice is most evident.

7.1 Protecting the Laird's Woodlands and Game

7.1.1 *Woodlands and Their Management in Eighteenth-century Strathspey*

> Now, instead of the song of birds and the murmur of the deer in the thicket,
> Our ears are stunned by the crash of falling trees and the clamours of the Sassenach.[4]

1 Sanderson, *Scottish Rural Society in the Sixteenth Century*, pp. 16–18.

2 Goodare, *The Government of Scotland*, p. 182; Sanderson, *Scottish Rural Society in the Sixteenth Century*, p. 18; Whyte, *Agriculture and Society*, pp. 44–5; Mitchison, *Lordship to Patronage*, p. 81.

3 Macinnes, *Clanship, Commerce and the House of Stuart*, p. 146.

4 Translation of a satirical Gaelic verse written to lament the felling of neighbouring Glenmore forest during the same period. Forsyth, *In the Shadow of Cairngorm*, pp. 142–3.

 | DOI:10.1163/9789004472549_008

The Grant estates in Strathspey did not contain much good arable land; nor were there reserves of coal, iron or other mineral wealth; there was no sea fishing or salt pans.[5] Instead, the Grant lands abounded with timber. In the early eighteenth-century Strathspey was covered in woodlands. A count of the trees destroyed by fire in Abernethy in 1746 estimated there to be some 2,444,160 fir trees in that forest alone.[6] Similar forests covered large parts of Glenchernich in Duthil parish and Tulchan in the north of the regality.[7] It was these woods that the Grant family envisaged as ensuring their future wealth and prosperity. The construction of ships and buildings, charcoal burning, and the expanding mining industry all demanded wood: wood that could be supplied from the forests of Strathspey. In many areas of Scotland forestry had become extremely scarce by the eighteenth-century, with much of the country's demand being met from imports from the Baltic and Scandinavia.[8] With the Grant woodlands being a rare indigenous source of timber, this in theory raised the potential value of the forests of Strathspey yet further.[9] Furthermore, despite Strathspey's relatively remote location, it came to be realised that timber could be easily transported to the ports and shipyards of the Moray Firth by floating rafts of timber down the Spey. What resulted were early attempts at commercial extraction. Timber rights in Abernethy were first let in 1630 to Captain John Mason, and from this point onwards attempts at commercial extraction became a focus of the estate's activities.[10] However, despite claims that the Grant forests abounded in riches for potential investors, none of the commercial enterprises in the woods of Strathspey during our period of study proved to be commercially successful, the most notorious failure being the ill-fated 1727 foray of the York Buildings Company. This enterprise resulted in losses of some £28,000 and bankruptcy for the company.[11] In truth it was found to be impossible to compete with

---

5 Argyll used his heritable jurisdictions to promote extractive industries such as coal and salt, Macinnes, *Clanship, Commerce and the House of Stuart*, p. 146.

6 NRS, Account of damage done to Abernethy forest, GD248/24/1 fo. 23. This probably represented but a third of the trees present prior to the commencement of York Buildings Company operations fifteen years earlier. However, this number is somewhat dwarfed by the 200 million trees planted by the Grant Earls of Seafield during the nineteenth century: D Nairne, 'Notes on Highland Woods, Ancient and Modern', *Transactions of the Gaelic Society of Inverness*, 17 (1891), 170–221, p. 200.

7 The term forest here is used analogously with woodlands, rather than as meaning a hunting forest.

8 T C Smout, *A History of the Native Woodlands of Scotland, 1500–1920* (Cambridge, 1995), p. 128.

9 Smout, *Native Woodlands of Scotland*, pp. 46–7.

10 NRS, Grant Legal papers, GD248/78/4/22.

11 E Grant, *Abernethy Forest, its people and its past* (Nethy Bridge, 1994), p. 10.

foreign imports in terms of cost, transit, and most importantly of all, quality.[12] Nonetheless, there was a healthy local market for wood. By the 1770s, contracts for the extraction of timber in neighbouring Rothiemurchus were doubling the value of the rentals there, nearly all of it being sold to local buyers.[13] However, estate policy regarding woodland was at odds with the demands of the estate's tenants whose traditional agricultural and house building techniques and general day-to-day existence required the use of large amounts of timber, nearly all of which in Strathspey belonged to the laird.[14] The conflict between custom and commerce led to a greater resort to the regality court as a means of control and deterrent.

The Grants had historically had little practical control over the woodland on their estates; this lack of control was owed to the nature of the pine woods. The forests were unfenced until they were turned into a deer run in the 1860s, and livestock had customarily been allowed to graze freely amongst the birch and pine, woodlands being a key part of some township's grazings.[15] Furthermore, Highland pine woods did not require the intensive management of coppicing and fencing needed in Lowland broad leaf woods.[16] When felling took place, contracts usually spared young trees below a certain girth from the woodsman's axe and saw; these trees would form the next generation, with their seeds in turn giving rise to the natural regeneration of the pinewoods. Beyond these trees everything else was fair game for felling until the quota of trees in the contract was reached. Felled trees were dragged by oxen from where they were felled to the nearest sawmill. After sawing and dressing, the timber was distributed over land or water. Forestry operations also demanded land to house the woodsmen, build sawmills, and pasturage for horses and oxen. These factors are evident in the Grant's contract with the York Buildings Company, with the farm of Culnakyle being leased to the company for these purposes.[17] Little active management of pine woodlands took place until the later seventeenth

12 Smout, *Native Woodlands of Scotland*, p. 213. Reports from the period persistently refer to the difficulty foresters had in finding enough large trees to fulfil their contracted quota. Smout attributes this to the local habit of selectively harvesting trees before they grew to maturity as they were easier for local people to work and transport. This in turn left few trees large enough for the masts, large beams and planking wanted by outside investors.

13 Barrett, *Making of a Scottish landscape*, p. 141.

14 Dodghson, *No Stone Unturned*, p. 158.

15 Grant, *Abernethy forest*, p. 19 and Grant Court Book 1, 18/07/1695, p. 58 for mention of oxen in the fir woods.

16 Smout, *Native Woodlands of Scotland*, p. 182.

17 NRS, Contract between James Grant of Grant and the York Buildings Company, GD248/135/1/13.

century. Quite simply, the woods held little commercial value to the Grants, with much of the forests being of 'barren wood' such as birch, and Strathspey being considered too far from major markets to make commercial felling economically viable.[18] As a result of this relative lack of value, and also to prevent outgoing tenants removing couples, doors and other fittings, all tenants and their sub-tenants had a servitude or allowance to obtain free 'house timber' each year.[19] Tacks from the late seventeenth century described this right as 'freedom of cutting and transporting of timber for the use of the said lands and ground thereof out of the common woods of the country appoynted for such uses'.[20] In practice this meant that Grant vassals could only build such houses as the wood that the laird gave them allowed; however, this was expected to comprise wood for couples, cabers, pans, door frames, doors and wood for the walls.[21]

Applications for house timber were made during one summer month, probably June as was the case on other estates.[22] The sources are unclear as to whether people taking advantage of their right to house-timber were permitted to cut such wood as they needed themselves or, more probably, were expected to collect it from the foresters who selected what they considered to be suitable timber to fulfil the tenants' requirements as set out in their applications. Later, the tenants' buildings would be inspected to ensure that the wood requested had indeed been used for house repairs and had not been sold on for profit.[23] Correspondence from the 1760s (when forestry operations and management on the Grant estates were being thoroughly modernised) suggest that great liberties were taken by tenants with their house timber-leave. William Grant younger of Dallachaple, son of the baron bailie wrote 'for if you give them [the tenants] the leave to cut three or four spars for that end [house repairs], they'll under that cut a dozen'.[24] Whilst William Lorimer, tutor to Sir James Grant of Grant, was also was very critical of the people of Strathspey's right to wood, sarcastically stating that 'the people of Strathspey knowing they can get timber whenever they call'.[25]

18 Smout, *Native Woodlands of Scotland*, p. 138.

19 G A Dixon, 'William Lorrmier on Forestry in the Central Highlands in the early 1760s', *Scottish Forestry*, 29:3 (1975), pp. 195–99.

20 NRS, Tack of a Ploughgate of Tullochgriban 1673, GD248/533/5, fo. 21.

21 Dixon, 'William Lorimer on Forestry', pp. 195–99.

22 Ibid, p. 207.

23 Ibid, p. 198–9.

24 NRS, Notebook of William Lorimer, GD248/37/4.

25 Ibid, p. 197.

The laird's vassals could also purchase further timber from the estate for purposes other than house wood. Reverend John Grant (born in the parish of Duthil in 1740) writing in the OSA, describes how tenants obtained timber in Strathspey in the early years of the eighteenth century, if he is reliable here, one merk would buy a permit for a man to cut and manufacture as much wood as he could by axe and saw for a year with only modest increases in cost in the years thereafter.[26] In addition there were also public sales of estate timber each year where larger pieces of timber could be purchased by tenants.[27] The sources suggest that timber on the Grant estates sold at these roups was considerably cheaper than in neighbouring districts. Consequently, people from areas such as Deeside would travel to Strathspey to purchase cheap timber.[28]

Whilst the taking of timber for building of modest cruck houses may sound innocuous it could have destructive consequences. It was estimated that a structure of just forty-eight feet by sixteen feet (equivalent to a small house or barn) would probably require at least thirty trees in the construction of crucks, cabers, and beams [see Illustration 6].[29] Selective felling by tenants searching for house timber also led to many neighbouring trees being damaged. Such activities would clearly have hindered the Grant lairds in leasing out their forests to outside investors. Good management was especially important considering that no extensive planting schemes took place in Strathspey until the 1760s.[30] However, it appears that practices on the Grant estates in the early years of the eighteenth century lagged someway behind many nearby estates.[31]

Whilst pine woods did not require intensive management, ignorance, neglect, or corruption on the part of the estate officials could quickly lead to devastation of the woods. For instance, in well managed pine woods, tenants with wood leave were encouraged to take crooked and deformed trees, thus leaving the best for sale by the laird and perhaps even strengthening the gene pool of the wood. Through such management and supervision, the value of woodlands could be maximised. It was thus essential to employ people with knowledge of woodlands to oversee them. This job fell to foresters.

---

26 Rev John Grant is an unreliable witness, his writing on the regality court is especially sensational, although on other matters he appears to be more accurate. Interestingly he was himself the great – great – grandson of the bailie James Grant of Gelloway. Sinclair, *The Statistical Account of Scotland*, Vol. VIII, p. 133.

27 NRS, Court Book Pages, GD248/37/1.

28 Dixon, 'William Lorrmier on Forestry', p. 207.

29 Smout, *Native Woodlands of Scotland*, p. 96.

30 The first plantation was planted in 1710 a mile north of Castle Grant; however, this was only small in scale. Dixon, 'William Lorrmier on Forestry', p. 192.

31 Ibid.

ILLUSTRATION 6 A recreation of a traditional communal township at the Highland folk museum in Newtonmore. The bailes of Strathspey would have been similar in appearance to this, with walls built of turf and free stone and thatched with heather and turf
SOURCE: THE AUTHOR

The regality's foresters had several roles in performing an office which was multi-faceted. On the one hand they were game keepers; however, their main function was the day to day supervision of the laird's woods. Whilst there survives no description of their exact functions from the Grant estates during our period, there does survive a commission for a head forester in Abernethy dating from 1763.[32] This along with evidence of their work surviving from their interaction with the court allows us to build up a picture of their duties. Foresters were appointed and sworn in open court.[33] Thereafter one of their main functions was to traverse the woodlands under their charge as often as practicable. They would subsequently report on the state of the woodlands at courts and delate any people who had been unlawfully cutting or damaging the trees there, along with anyone suspected of poaching: 'The said day the forresters of the woods are examined upone oath what they know anent the

32 NRS, Head Forester's Commission, GD248/25/1/4.

33 Grant Court Book 2, 18/04/1705, p. 46.

people of ther guilt of killing of the dear roes, black cokes, heath henes or of ther guilt of cutting, felling and transporting of the woods without warrand'.[34] The foresters also occupied themselves with duties such as: felling trees for the use of the laird and for tenants; supervising licensed wood cutting within the woodlands; planting seedlings; poinding or moving on unwanted grazing livestock; preventing fires; seizing guns and axes found in the forests or moors; shooting dogs found in the forests; dackering the houses of suspected thieves for stolen wood.[35]

There were evidently differing levels of foresters in the regality. The principal foresters on the Grant estates were salaried office bearers, and as such are recorded in the rentals. Alastair Grant Mor, the celebrated champion of Richard Waitt's 1714 painting, was at that time the forester of the woods of Tulchan for which he was paid £10 for his year's work.[36]

In addition, there are references in the court records to other individuals acting as foresters who were probably cottars who received no such salary in respect of their duties, instead being remunerated from other sources such as grazing and timber rights, and perhaps even the provision of a croft. Foresters were also remunerated through fine money and rewarded for informing upon thieves.[37] The office of forester could be combined with that of court officer; for example, a John Grant worked in both roles in Abernethy in 1713 and 1714.[38] In a manner similar to other roles within the regality, it appears that one of the gentry class was appointed to the post of head forester to oversee the forests generally and the other foresters. However, the only record in the court book of this position is that Ludovick Grant of Tulloch (tacksman of a davoch nestled in the heart of Abernethy forest) who was the incumbent in the post in 1721. The court book reveals that one of his responsibilities was for the uplifting of timber, as he was instructed to allow William Grant of Delay to take timber from Abernethy for the building of a new roof on the kirk of Advie in that year. Tenants of the parish of Advie were to cut and transport wood from Abernethy which was under his ward.[39] After the regality- era had ended in Strathspey principal tenants continued to be appointed as head foresters, although the role had probably evolved somewhat in line with ever improving forestry practice. For instance, James Grant of Inveroury was appointed head or chief

34 Grant Court book 2, 16/10/1704, p. 35.
35 Smout, *Native Woodlands of Scotland*, p. 188.
36 NRS, Estate Accounts, GD248/113/7, fo. 7.
37 G A Dixon, 'Forestry in Strathspey in the 1760s', *Scottish Forestry*, 30:1 (1976), p. 40.
38 NRS, Estate Accounts, GD248/113/7, fo. 7.
39 Grant Court Book 4, 13/05/1721, p. 56.

forester for the whole woods of Strathspey in 1765.[40] His job was to oversee all general aspects of the woodland's management, including sale and overseeing all under foresters.[41]

In Glenorchy the Campbell family made the foresters themselves liable for any damage which went unreported in the forests under their watch.[42] The Grant foresters were apparently not as fastidious, and in some cases were as culpable as the people they were employed to stop. William Grant younger of Dallachaple was especially critical of sir Ludovick Grant's foresters in the 1740s and 1750s, stating that 'all your [sir James Grant of Grant] father's foresters that ever he knew were great rogues, and feared him more than the tenants feared him, probably conscious of their villainous conivance'.[43] The court books bear testimony to William Grant's accusations to an extent as they record a case of game keeper turned poacher, when in 1721 one of the foresters was brought before the court:

> James Grant in Riemore late forrester of the woods of Abernethie is fyned and unlawed in the sume of ane hundred pound Scots money for his breach of trust in the discharge of his office of forrester in as far as he is convict of concealling and keeping up from the Laird of Grant his constituent the price of a great deall of timber sold be him to the people of the country for Grants behoofe.[44]

Perhaps William Lorimer was at least partially correct when he made his stinging comparison between Abernethy and Glentannar on the Aboyne estates: 'Stealing wood in his [Lord Aboyne's] estate is as great a rarity as honesty in Abernethy'.[45]

7.1.2 *The Regality Court and the Woods*

a) Continuity and Change

Surviving court records show that the Grants were pursuing tenants for the cutting of green wood in their baron court in the early years of the seventeenth century.[46] By the 1660s when records are more complete, control of the Grant's

40 James Grant of Inveroury was a tacksman from the parish of Kirkmichael in the east of the regality.
41 Dixon, 'Forestry in Strathspey', p. 45.
42 Smout, *Native Woodlands of Scotland*, p. 189.
43 NRS, Notebook of William Lorimer, GD248/37/4.
44 Grant Court Book 4, 28/11/1721, p. 79.
45 NRS, Notebook of William Lorimer, GD248/37/4.
46 NRS, Baron Court Extracts, GD248/76/2, fo. 1.

forests was still a prominent issue in the court, but less significant than cases involving poaching and the preservation of game within the forests.[47] The woodlands cases during this time focus on the cutting of green wood, which was a statutory offence by an act of 1425.[48] The work of the court during this period also targeted tenants transporting timber out of Strathspey for sale rather than their own personal use.

Moving forward thirty years to the regality-era in Strathspey, the woodlands became much more important as their commercial value increased, with eighty-two courts dealing with the theft and destruction of timber by inhabitants of the regality from 1695 to 1729. Two peaks in the number of woodlands cases appearing in the court records are found, in 1704 to 1710 and then again in 1727, this the year that the York Buildings Company began felling operations in Abernethy forest. As with other areas of the court's work, there are evidently gaps in the material. For instance, at a court at Duthil in May 1703 all the tenants of Glenchernick were examined conform to an act of court relating to woodlands dated November 1701; yet no court record survives from this date.[49]

The regality court was used by Ludovick Grant and his successors in a much more personal way than in other areas of court business, when dealing with their forests. That lairds took a personal interest in the defence of their woodlands becomes clear in three ways: firstly, the lairds personally petitioned the court, asking it to make acts of court to protect the forests from the exploitation of tenants and to specify the penalties for breaches of the acts. For example, on 7 March 1700 Ludovick Grant petitioned the court craving:

> Ane act of court that evry heritor, gentlemen and takesmen within the said lordship shall compt for all those under them of tenants and servants that the woods shall be free of ther dammage by cutting to sell or peill any bark without libertie And in obedience W[illia]m Grant of Lurg, Robert Grant of Gartinmor, James Grant of Lettoch, James Grant of Aucherneck, Ludovick Grant of Tulloch and Johne and Alex[ande]r Grants for the tenants of Tulloch and Patrick Grant of Glenlochie doe hereby enact and engadge themselves to doe the utmost of ther endeavors to keep back their tennantes and servantes from cutting any firrwood in tyme comeing or to peill any bark And that to ther knowledge no dammage shall be done by any of the said tenantes inehabitants or servants by cutting for sale or peilling of bark and if any shall happine to transgress

47 Ibid. Fifteen court extracts dealt with woodlands compared to twenty-one with poaching.

48 *RPS*, 1425/3/11.

49 Grant Court Book 2, 21/05/1703, p. 7.

> they oblige themselves evrie ane for his own interest to delat the persone found guiltie and deliver such up to punishment under the faylie of ane hundreth lib toties quoties And shall use all meanes and paynes to get notice of the guiltide and declare the samen and further obliges themselves that ther tenantes shall not cutt and the place of deliverance of the delinquents is to be at Castle Grant.[50]

The public proclamation in open court and at places of worship of both the regality's own acts of court on woodlands and acts of parliament prohibiting the cutting of wood was an important means of warning and reminding the tenants of the estate's campaign against illegal wood cutters.[51] The proclamation of such acts was regarded as being an effective means of curbing the unlicensed cutting of wood. Proclamations were probably made in both English and Gaelic. William Lorimer advised Sir James Grant of Grant to take such steps in a letter in the 1750s: 'Mr Grant should make an act in his baron court [...] Mr Grant should publish the act of parliament against destroying the game in his estate'.[52] In total, twelve such acts of court are recorded in the Grant court books; however, it is likely that these acts were repeated at head courts a number of times each year to give them further publicity. These acts targeted: the peeling of birch bark (commonly used in tanning, but also for paper and basket weaving);[53] muirburn, where it was likely to spread and take hold in woodland; and cutting and transporting wood without a licence.

Secondly, the lairds could appear personally in court to emphasise the importance that they attached to their forests, such as at Duthil on 2 June 1720 when Sir James Grant of Grant sat alongside his bailie Dalrachney to ordain an act of court.[54] However, the most telling way the lairds of Grant took an interest in the management of their woods was in sentencing. Three cases relating to the destruction of woodlands were referred by the bailie presiding back to the laird so that he could personally determine the offenders' fates.[55] This emphasises that the forests were one of the laird's most valuable assets and any activity which damaged them was perceived as an offence targeting the laird

50 Grant Court book 1, 07/03/1700, pp. 149–150.

51 Neighbouring landowners such as Lord Aboyne went further by affixing copies of acts relating to woodlands and muir burn not only in church but also in public houses and inns. See Dixon, 'William Lorrmier on Forestry', p. 197.

52 NRS, Notes from Lorimer to James Grant of Grant, GD248/24/2, fo.1 no pagination.

53 Smout, *Native Woodlands of Scotland*, p. 91.

54 Grant Court Book 4, 02/06/1720, p. 33.

55 Grant Court book 1, 22/05/1696, p. 77, Grant Court book 2, 08/07/1710, p. 141, Grant Court book 3, 13/05/1715, p. 76.

himself. All three of these cases involved the burning of pine forest: undoubtedly the most serious woodlands-related offence to be found in the Grant court books. Whilst cutting or 'meddling' in the woods without warrant ordinarily earned the offender a hefty fine and maybe even a spell in the pit below Castle Grant, fire raising was an altogether different matter. Whilst such cases are few, they demonstrate the lengths the Grants would go to protect their property.[56] A case from 1695 reveals the ruthless response to fire-raising advocated by Ludovick Grant.

> The said day befor the said bailie the persones efter mentioned wer delated and accused at the instance of the pro[curato]r fiscall for burneing and fyring of heather adjacent to the backsyd of the Craigmor of Abernethie and adjacent to ane other plaice called Badinvadlay upone the west most syd of Neathie above the bridge. Whereby the firwoods young and old in the forsaid plaices wer destroyed and brunt to ane extraordinar woreweible [valuable] skaith.[57]

The fire had started when Alexander Gardiner, a crofter at Lettoch, had started a muir burn upon the west side of the Backharn burn. There had been no trouble until two boys aged eleven and thirteen had 'put fyr in the heather besyd the woods wherby by the impetuos and uniteruptable fyr the woods wer kendled and brunt'.[58] Two more children helped the fire to spread further into the woods, one of whom admitted that whilst 'relieving ane ox from the fyre he did cast the fyr hither and thither but not of designe to doe skaith'.[59] After hearing the witness evidence leave was allowed so that an assize could be gathered and hear evidence of the value and extent of the damage done to the woods, for which the childrens' masters and landlords were held liable. It was not until October, the fires having been set in February, that sentencing took place. This gap was clearly also to allow the laird to be consulted. In sentencing the bailie handed down a punishment 'whereby others may be terrified and feared to doe the lyk in tyme comeing because off the destructioune of the said woods'.[60] The youngest child, aged eleven, and the crofter escaped punishment. The other two boys and a girl, all aged thirteen, were sentenced to have their lugs nailed to the gallows at Ballintomb. This exemplary punishment was

---

56 I have identified eight cases.
57 Grant Court book 1, 18/07/1695, p. 57.
58 Ibid. pp. 57–8.
59 Ibid.
60 Ibid.

clearly intended to make the inhabitants of the regality take notice; however, the deterrent appeared to have little effect, as under a year later in May 1696, another group of children set fire to Abernethy forest whilst herding cattle.[61] They confessed to 'the taking out of ffyr and kendling of the heather besyd tharfor ther masters and parents are unlawed in ane 100 lib the peice besyd nealling of the luges to the gallowes except Duncan Grant his dochter whose punishment is reffered to the laird off Grant be the said bailie'.[62] The kindling of muir burn by herds during the shieling period seems to have been a recurring problem for the Grants, as another herd was imprisoned for firing the laird's woods in August 1727.[63] These occurrences were probably little more than the result of children spending long days unsupervised during the summer months; nonetheless, they had destructive consequences.

Further prosecutions for burning the woods were referred to the laird in July 1710 and in May 1715.[64] In the latter case two hire-men were imprisoned pending the laird's personal judgement, 'the said bailie decerns the saids Donald Ross and John Grant to be incarserat in the prison at Castle Grant and to be maintained upon ther masters charges untill the said laird of Grant be known how to proceed in the said matter'. Advocation of these cases to the laird illustrates both the magnitude of the crime and the personal authority of the laird.

Immediately following the incarceration of Ross and Grant (and at a subsequent court held at Duthil three days later) acts of court were promulgated in the following terms in response to the threat posed by fireraisers:

> The said day the said bailie hes enacted, estatute and ordained that no tennant, inhabitant, cotter, servant, nor malender within the parish of Abernethy and Kincardin belonging to the laird of Grant tak upon them in tyme comeing to kindle or mak any moor burn within the said bounds on hill or deall, glen or nor any woods during that tyme prohibit by the actis of parliament under the failie of ane hundreth pounds toties quoties And that evrie master of fammalie be comptable for themselves and ther household and decerns ilk toune to be lyable for any muir brun done within ther owne bounds in hill or deill or upone ther shealling, glenneing or pasturage.[65]

61 See Kennedy, *Governing Gaeldom*, p. 240. The idea of the 'monument of justice' through the severe punishment of offenders was clearly a major tactic of the Grants during the latter 1690s.

62 Grant Court Book 1, 22/05/1696, p. 77.

63 Grant Court Book 5, 19/08/1727, p. 128.

64 Grant Court Book 2, 08/07/1710, p. 141; Grant Court Book 3, 13/05/1715, p. 76.

65 Grant Court Book 3, p. 76.

However, there was no mention of the new act when the court convened at Ballintomb four days after the new enactment was first announced, showing that court regulations were applied selectively to each individual parish rather than to the regality as a whole (Inverallan parish having little woodland).[66] The kindling of muir burn between March and harvest time was prohibited by several Acts of Parliament.[67] However, despite all the above cases taking place during this forbidden time, no reference is made to these acts in the court books. The Grants were solely interested in the damage and degradation of their woodlands.

Offences other than fire-raising could also result in a serious punishment. For instance, in 1728 William Grant alias Roy was banished from the bounds of the regality, 'being convened anent peeling and destroying thirty trees of the woods of Delvey is ordained to banish himself voluntarily furth of the regality of Grant in Strathspey in all tyme coming during the laird of Grant's pleasure'.[68] Aggravating matters further was the fact that he was a recidivist, having been fined £10 for destroying the woods of neighbouring Skiradvey in February 1719.[69] The description of his banishment as being 'voluntary' suggests that he may have taken banishment as an alternative to another form of punishment as prescribed by the court.[70] William Grant's activities must have been regarded as being especially serious to warrant banishment, this being the only forestry case in the court books to garner such a punishment, most others resulting in fines. Fines of £100 sc. were the largest levied by the court, and were regularly handed down for burning the woods, cutting wood without a license and peeling bark. Additionally, offenders might be required to render damages, as in December 1727, when William Bain in Glenbeg was ordered to pay damages of £100 to the laird in addition to a fine of £50 when plough beams and other illicitly manufactured wood were found in his dwelling.[71]

66 The Grants continued to have trouble with fireraisers after the abolition of their jurisdiction. William Lorimer wrote of a case of muir burn in 1751 in the following terms showing that estate policy in advocating the exemplary punishment of fireraisers persisted, 'the punishment has been a most salutary measure, and two or three of the like nature will introduce honesty and regularity into the country[…]Tullochgriban [the factor] thinks it would have been right to have transported the fellow that raised the moor-burn- being worthless – nobody would have grumbled and it would have struck a precedent into the country people'. NRS, Notes from Lorimer to James Grant of Grant, GD248/24/2.

67 *RPS*; 1401/2/15; 1424/22; 1458/3/39; 1685/4/47.

68 Grant Court Book 5, 26/07/1728, p. 152.

69 Grant Court Book 4, 03/02/1719, p. 3.

70 See Kennedy, *Governing Gaeldom*, p. 240. Kennedy mentions that voluntary banishment was taken by thieves in 1680s who would otherwise have faced being outlawed.

71 Grant Court Book 5, 06/12/1727, p. 140.

Most fines for woodcutting were more minor and did not exceed £10. Whole davochs were sometimes brought before the court as might the heads of households for the entire regality, to be interrogated, often in conjunction with a judicial rental being undertaken.[72] Whilst in court each man was asked under oath whether he had broken any of the 'penal statutes', namely those acts of parliament relating to the protection of game, moor and woodland, or in some cases, more simply, whether they had cut the lairds woodlands. Such a court was held at Duthil on 8 January 1708 when the inhabitants of fourteen davochs in the parish of Duthil were called to compear. Only six men appeared, with twelve of the davochs having no representatives in court at all. When we consider that on average each davoch had ten subtenants in addition to the tacksman, and then a further three households of malanders it can be appreciated just how poor the attendance at this court, and others convened for the same purpose often were.[73] In this example it appears none of the contumacious tenants were fined. However, on other occasions whole parishes were fined *en masse* for illicitly cutting wood whether they appeared in court or not.[74] In spite of this, fines from woodlands were never a consistent source of income for the court, as the number of cases relating to the woods varied considerably from year to year. In this the Grants differed from other jurisdiction holders whereby nominal fines for the taking of wood effectively amounted to a means of licensing and a steady flow of income.[75] It is clear from the occasional harsh penalty handed down by the Grant courts that the situation in Strathspey was different. The Grants obviously recognised that they could not stop the unlicensed cutting of wood entirely and such cases were thereby only punished by a negligible fine, enough to account for the value of the wood lost. On the other hand, they were publicly prepared to punish cases where more serious damage was done, intending to warn and deter others from doing the like.

b) The York Buildings Company

In 1736 a court of the regality of Grant was held at which several tenants were fined for contravening the penal statutes as had been long standing practice

72 Grant Court Book 4, 08/01/1708, p. 59. This looks like it should have been an annual undertaking with tacks produced and each man questioned over his activities of the previous year.

73 Figures taken from: NRS, Estate rental of wadset lands in 1714, GD248/151/9. The number of subtenants in each of the wadset lands varied quite greatly with Mullochard having but three subtenants whilst Gartenmore had thirty subtenants. The median falls around six.

74 Grant Court Book 4, 03/02/1719, p. 3.

75 Smout, *Native Woodlands of Scotland*, pp. 134, 190.

within the court. However, alongside this are several interesting court petitions. John Grant in Auchernack of Dalvey petitioned the court for fulfilment of a contract for the floating of York Building Company timber between him and Donald and John Grant in Easter and Wester Port worth 300 merks.[76] Litigation over such a contract is not seen before in the court records and is clear evidence of the way that commercial extraction of timber was changing life in Strathspey. This transition is evident in the court records of the regality of Grant, with the court appearing to be evolving to meet the new commercial demands created by the expanding industry in timber.

The York Buildings Company originally began operations in 1675 as a water company to provide water to inhabitants of Piccadilly in London and was incorporated in 1690. In 1719 the company's patent was procured by new proprietors who proceeded to buy up several of the estates forfeited after the 1715 rebellion. The company's new management sought to diversify yet further in 1727, by buying 60,000 trees in Abernethy forest for £7000 stg., primarily with an eye to manufacturing them into masts.[77] The contract between James Grant of Grant and the company also promised the company and its employees the protection of the bailies of Strathspey and the regality court. Clearly the court was viewed as being important in preventing other persons from cutting the woods of Abernethy, stealing from the company, or targeting its workers. An act of parliament in support of the venture was passed with the navy's needs in mind.[78] However, the venture was an abject failure and by 1732 the York Buildings Company had accrued losses of £27, 913 in the five years that they had been operating in Abernethy forest. These losses probably accrued at least in part because the economic value of Abernethy forest was vastly over-represented by the Grant family's agents. Bankruptcy followed, with 30,000 trees from the contract still unfelled.[79]

Ludovick Colquhoun of Luss (later to be the 4th lord of the regality) was a creditor of the company and had all of the company's equipment at their Abernethy saw mills and forges sequestrated and delivered up to him by way of security after gaining letters of horning in a court of session case earlier that year. The keys to the buildings where the goods were housed were given to Grant of Badeniden for safe keeping; however, John Grant of Burnside,

76 NRS, Baron Court Petitions, GD248/445/2, fo. 10.

77 NRS, Contract between James Grant of Grant and the York Buildings Company, GD248/135/1/13.

78 D Murray, *The York Buildings Company: A Chapter in Scotch History* (Glasgow, 1883), pp. 57–8.

79 Grant, *Abernethy Forest*, p. 11.

who was also a creditor of the York Buildings company, 'by collusion with the keeper of the keys', was able to gain access and poind the goods there on his own behalf. The case demonstrates both how new commercial litigation was appearing before the court and how the tacksman class in the regality were becoming more enterprising and beginning to move away from the traditional clan model for finance. John Grant of Burnside was the Strathspey estate factor and was thus closely involved with the activities of the company. He had taken advantage of the ailing fortunes of the company in the manufacture of iron, which they were smelting at Abernethy after being carried over the hills from the Lecht some twenty miles distant. The diversification into iron production was no more successful for the York Buildings Company than the woodlands had been and led to them incurring large debts. Burnside bought up some of the debts and gained decreets in the court of session in 1734 and 1735.[80] He sought to enforce these decreets by poinding the goods in the custody of Badeniden throwing him into competition with Colquhoun and leading to several cases in the regality court in an attempt to stop him bringing the items to sale. Warrant was granted by the regality court to Colquhoun at two separate courts to call for deliverance of the items poinded by Burnside.[81]

The arrival of the York Buildings Company brought change for many ordinary people in Strathspey. There was well-paid work in the company's sawmills and forges, yet more work transporting ore and wood (120 horses were supposedly employed in carrying ore across the mountains from the mines at the Lecht to the forges in Abernethy), work building roads and work at felling, sawing, and blasting. It is reputed that York Building Company promissory notes circulated freely as currency within Strathspey for several years in place of actual specie, which was in perpetually short supply.[82] The frenzied activity experienced during the York Buildings Company's short tenure within the regality was not to last, but undoubtedly made an impact upon the local economy in the longer term.

The emergence of modern commercial litigation before the regality court provides a stark contrast to the recourse to the personal justice of the laird which we encountered only two decades before. Whilst this could be evidence of a creeping modernity permeating the franchise jurisdictions, and society in the Highlands in general, it is important to remember that the York Buildings Company was an external actor in the regality. Thus, there is not necessarily a contradiction between the traditional operations of the laird and litigation

80 Murray, *The York Buildings Company*, pp. 64–5.
81 NRS, Baron Court Petitions, GD248/445/2, fos. 3, 5 and 7.
82 Murray, *The York Buildings Company*, p. 59.

over the company's contract. Furthermore, it is unfortunate that the records are increasingly fragmentary after this point, so it is not possible to say whether the court experienced other aspects of renewal and continued to adapt and evolve.

7.2 Game

In the 1660s and 1670s, the records left by the baron courts of the area show that cases of poaching were more common than cases involving woodlands. Indeed, many wood-cutting cases may have been pursued with the additional intention of protecting game from being disturbed in the woods. The situation was very different half a century later, with cases concerning woodlands outnumbering those concerning poaching. This is a telling reflection upon the value of Strathspey's forests as an economic resource.

7.2.1 *Hunting, Fishing and Game in the Regality of Grant*

The job of protecting game on the Grant estates was also part of the work of the court; however, unlike forestry, the protection of game was not a commercial concern until the mid-nineteenth century, when deer runs and grouse shooting became popular. Instead, game was preserved for the pleasure and pursuit of the laird and his entourage, along with providing food for his table. Salmon fishing was perhaps the exception in this respect, as the currach fishing on the Spey was let to a tacksman and was thus a commercial operation.[83] Burt's letters attest the importance of game in the Highland diet, at least for the more affluent in society; indeed, he lamented that little else was available.[84] Game mainly consisted of red grouse (sometimes called moor grouse), black grouse (black cock), salmon (kipper and black fish when taken in spawning time), capercaillie, doves (which were detested by farmers as they ate the seed sown on their fields thereby fattening the doves for the laird's own consumption), roe deer and red deer.

No self-respecting clan chief of the seventeenth century would have pursued individual deer for his own larder.[85] This menial task instead fell to the foresters, and the provision of game for the laird's table was probably one of their main occupations.[86] Waitt's painting of the forester Alastair Mor shows

83 Grant Court Book 4, 14/11/1723, p. 94.
84 Simmons (ed.), *Burt's Letters*, p. 64.
85 D Hart-Davis, *The Monarchs of the Glen* (London, 1978), p. 33.
86 Ibid.

the forester equipped with his great hunting rifle; this was undoubtedly one of the main tools of his trade, with which he culled both game for the pot, along with vermin, and when necessary loose dogs. Whilst the laird and his entourage might indulge in the hawking or shooting of moor and wild fowl, and coursing of deer with hounds,[87] until the early years of the eighteenth century the tinchel alone was the only form of deer hunt befitting a chief of the status of the laird of Grant.[88]

Tinchels were the traditional Highland hunting matches and evidence shows that such hunting in Scotland pre-dates the Norman conquest.[89] They could be huge in scale and required hundreds of men to drive herds of deer into natural defiles where the cornered animals could be slaughtered by the laird and their guests. Vassals of the laird were required to turn out for tinchels as part of the labour services they owed to the laird.[90] John Taylor, the water poet, who toured the Highlands in 1618, including a four day stay at Castle Grant, described one such hunt on the Mar estates:

> Five or six hundred men do rise early in the morning, and they do disperse themselves divers ways, and seven or eight miles compass, they do bring or chase the deer in many herds (two, three or four hundred in a herd) to such or such a place as the Noblemen shall appoint them; then when day is come, the Lords and Gentlemen of their companies do ride or go to the said places, sometimes wading up to their middle through burns or rivers, and then they being come to the place, do lie down on the ground till these foresaid scouts, which are called Tinchels, do bring down the deer. Then after we had stayed there three hours or thereabouts, we might perceive the deer appear on the hills round about us which being followed close by the Tinchel are chased down into the valley where we lay; then all the valley on each side being waylaid with two hundred of strong Irish greyhounds, they are let loose as the occasion served upon the herd of deer so that with dogs, guns, arrows, dirks and daggers in the space of two hours fourscore fat deer were slain.[91]

87 J M Gilbert, *Hunting and Hunting reserves in Mediaeval Scotland* (Edinburgh, 1979), pp. 56–59.

88 Hart-Davis, *The Monarchs of the Glen*, p. 33.

89 Gilbert, *Hunting and Hunting reserves in Mediaeval Scotland*, p. 52.

90 See Hart-Davis, *The Monarchs of the Glen*, pp. 21–24.

91 J Taylor, *The pennyles pilgrimage or The money-lesse perambulation of John Taylor, alias the Kings Majesties water-poet. How he travailed on foot from London to Edenborough in Scotland not carrying any money to or fro* (London, 1618), pp. 51–2.

The duty to accompany the laird during his hunting was written into many tenants' tacks in Strathspey: 'the said Alexander [tacksman] obliges himself and his ser[van]ts … to accompany and convey the said Ludovick and his ser[van] ts personallie in his hostings and huntings'.[92] The regality court was used to advertise an impending hunt to those tenants who were obliged to give attendance, some of whom might have to travel upwards of fifty miles to attend the hunt.[93] The advertisements promulgated in court gave detailed instructions to inhabitants of the regality:

> The said day by ordor from the laird of Grant younger the said bailie ordaines and enactis that the haill tennantes, cottars, malenders, tradseemen and servants within the saidis landis that are fencible men shall provyde and have in readiness ag[ains]t the eight day of August nixt ilk ane of them heeighland coats, trewes and short hose of tartane of red and grene sett broad springed and also with gun, suord, pistoll and dirk and with these present themselves to ane rendevouze when called upone 48 hours advertisement within the countrey of Strathspey for the said laird of Grant or his father their hosting and hunteing and that under the failie of twentie poundes scotis ilk ane that shall faill in the promiss. And the maister to outrig ther servantes in the said coates, trewes and that out of ther fies.[94]

Even the inhabitants of Laggan, who were mainly Macdonalds, were also required to dress in the same red and green tartan as the Grants.[95] Given how onerous this service was it is unsurprising that there were issues with non-attendance and that the regality court was used to punish those who failed to furnish the laird with their attendance.[96] Inhabitants of lands which were distant from Strathspey, such as Laggan in Lochaber, were subject to smaller fines for non-attendance, perhaps in recognition of the greater difficulty they faced in attending. The final recorded Grant tinchel took place in 1706.[97] Whilst the last such hunting match known to have taken place in the Highlands was at

92 NRS, Tack of Kylintra 1675, GD248/533/5, fo. 19. The inclusion of this duty in leases was also remarked upon by Burt, *Burt's Letters*, p. 223.

93 Grant Court Book 2, 20/07/1704, p. 27.

94 Ibid, 27/07/1704, p. 28.

95 Ibid, 20/07/1704, p. 27.

96 Ibid, 16/10/1704, p. 36.

97 Ibid, p. 5.

Mar when Jacobite sympathisers gathered to discuss rebellion in 1715. As a result, such gatherings were subsequently banned.[98]

7.2.2 *Poaching Cases in the Regality Court*

The landowner alone was entitled to hunt the game on his land; however, game was inevitably targeted by other residents of the Grant estates. These poachers killed game for food; to protect their crops from the grazing of deer and doves; and in some cases, for sport or even as an act of defiance to the rule of the landowner. The laird of Grant's game was protected from poachers by various statutes, along with the regality's own acts of court.[99] The details of the regality's acts concerning poaching are unknown to us. However, the court books record that both acts of court and acts of parliament relating to game were read publicly at intervals at courts in each parish within the regality to ensure their currency amongst the people and to prevent acts of court from lapsing.[100] These acts of court were probably of long standing and were simply repeated and re-enacted at each head court. They were similar to the acts promulgated in the seventeenth century baron courts. For instance on 2 August 1669, one of Grant's baron courts enacted that 'no man in tyme coming sall kill anie roeis, black cock or ther mothers under the pain of ten punds toties quoties'.[101] Similarly, on 23 February 1660, a court at Inverallan enacted that those discovered fishing upon the Spey would be fined 40 s.[102] Such acts remained in force throughout the jurisdiction of the regality court with the fines being periodically revised.

Individuals might come before the court suspected of poaching in several different ways. The most common was when the court called together the inhabitants of parts of the regality to be questioned upon oath 'anent their guilt of the penal statutes'. The testimony of John McPhatak gives some idea of proceedings: 'Jon McPhatak gave oathe that he killed no salmond this yeir w[it]h the flie but confessit that he killed with the bail[103] for whilk he is put in the lairds will'.[104] Individuals could also be delated by the regality's foresters who also acted as game keepers. Knowledge of poachers and their activities

98 1 Geo. 1. St. 2. c. 54.

99 For killing of salmon, *RPS*, 1696/9/166. For deer and fowl, *RPS*, 1599/5/1. These are just two examples of numerous statutes tackling the issue.

100 See court held 12/06/1725, Grant Court Book 5, p. 54.

101 NRS, Baron Court Extracts, GD248/76/2, fo. 9.

102 Ibid, fo. 20.

103 "Bail", refers to the use of a torch in the method of poaching known as blazing of the water. *DSL*.

104 NRS, Baron Court Extracts, GD248/76/2, fo. 54.

also came from other estate workers and from the public. For instance, on 6 December 1725 Lewis Grant of Tulloch delated

> Alex[ande]r Fraser his serv[an]t guilty of killing dear roe in Grants forestry and acknowledged that the said roe was brought to his house was ordained to pr[esen]t his said serv[an]t and the gun he had in the forestry doing skaith. The said judge unlaws the sad Allex[and]er Fraser in fifty pound Scots for his guilt and the master in as much for recept thereof, also the serv[an]t being contumaciously absent this day is fyned in ten pounds Scots, and ordains the master to pr[esen]t his said servant and the gun at the judges house in the Ailan twixt this day and the twenty second day currant under the penalty of another fifty pounds Scots.[105]

Alexander Fraser's treatment was typical, imprisonment pending payment of a fine being the norm. There is evidence that fines from poaching were occasionally directed to the common good. Thus, in January 1715, a poacher, William Fraser, convicted of killing 'rowe buck' swore he would appear at Castle Grant to present himself before the laird for sentencing.[106] Once again, we encounter the personal justice of the laird, emphasising that poachers, when killing deer on the Grant estates, were very much committing an offence against the laird in person and could thus expect to be subject to his own personal justice. Fraser appeared at Castle Grant when summoned the next day:

> The said day compeared the said Wm Frazer and upon his former judiciall confessione for killing of rowe buck in the Laird of Grantes bounds and confest shooting at other tymes within the said bounds therefor the said bailie unlaws the said Wm Frazer in the fyn of ane hundred poundes Scotis and until he pay the sum adjudges his person to be commitit to the prison at Castle Grant to remain there upone his own expenses. And ordains the said fine to be mortified for the annualrent therof to be applyed to help the maintenance of any poor mans child within the parish of Abernethie by appoyntment of the Briggadier Laird of Grant and if out of the country by the appoyntment of Gregor Grant of Gartenmore Tulloch and Achernech.[107]

105 Grant Court Book 5, 06/12/1725, p. 76.

106 Grant Court Book 3, 15/01/1715, p.70.

107 Ibid.

By dispensing justice personally, the laird could punish severely, reinforcing his own power in the locality, whilst also saving his bailies from having to take unpopular decisions upon themselves. On the other hand, as this example shows, the laird could also use the opportunity for philanthropy thus showing himself to be a strong yet compassionate superior. Whilst there are no other instances where this practice is explicitly recorded in the Grant court books, the application of fines to the common good has been discussed in studies of other courts in early modern Scotland. Falconer has written how fines and goods escheated by the burgh court of Aberdeen in the sixteenth century were used to help maintain the physical and social structures of the burgh.[108] In England similar practice existed by virtue of the 1691 act against poachers.[109] Under the provisions of this act, a third of the fine levied upon slayers of deer went to the owner of the game, a third to the informer and the final third went to the poor of the parish. Something similar seems to have taken place, at least occasionally, in the regality of Grant.

Besides fines and imprisonment at the cost of the poacher or his master, it was common in the 1660s and 1670s for the convicted poacher to swear upon oath that he would desist from committing the same offence in the future and provide caution. For instance on 9 October 1668, it is recorded that 'the said day Alex[ande]r Grant of Delrachnie hes actit himself that he sall not kill dear nor capilkyl [capercaillie] or black cock or ther mothers or resset ane of theame in tyme coming under the pain of two hundredth libs'.[110] William Grant of Lurg undertook a similar pledge three years later in 1671 showing that poaching was not the preserve of the lower orders and that gentry could be censored by the court.[111] However, the requirement to provide caution or find a cautioner is only seen once in later poaching cases, and it seems that the practice had largely disappeared by the eighteenth century.[112] As a further disincentive to poach, convictions for poaching were irritancies for some leases on the Grant estates.[113]

Whilst gentry were to be found being prosecuted for poaching in the 1660s and 1670s the situation had changed by the early years of the eighteenth century. The records suggest that the gentry continued to be examined upon oath alongside their subtenants in relation to their guilt under the penal statutes.

---

108 Falconer, *Crime and Community in Reformation Scotland*, p. 81.

109 3 and 4, William and Mary, c.10.

110 NRS, Baron Court Extracts, GD248/76/2, fo. 80.

111 Ibid, fo. 77.

112 Grant Court Book 1, 14/02/1695, p. 52.

113 Fraser, *Chiefs of Grant*, Vol I. pt. I, p. xcv.

However, no individual prosecutions of gentry appear in the records during the regality court era. That is not to say that the gentry of the regality were not involved in poaching. Two cases from 1725 demonstrate that the gentry were having their servants go out and shoot game on their behalf, and thereby not having to run the risk of being caught doing so themselves. For instance, Gregor Grant younger of Gartenmore was fined for recepting deer which had been shot by his servant in Abernethy forest.[114] A similar case appears two years later in June 1727 when Patrick Grant, son to John Grant of Tullochgorum, was fined for poaching: 'Patrick Grant law[fu]ll son to Tullochgorm compeared and being examined anent his guilt of killing deer and roe deponed he was only guilty of killing ane roe buck for his father's use when tender, therfor amerciat in fifty pound Scots'.[115] It appears that the estate had become wise to this ruse by the 1760s as foresters were advised that principal tenants and wadsetters were to be held accountable for the actions of their subtenants, children and servants so that they could no longer escape punishment.[116]

Whilst the regality court may have been successful in censoring poaching by tacksmen in Strathspey much more trouble was experienced when trying to control the vassals of the regality in distant Badenoch. The Grants held a superiority over the lands lying alongside Loch Laggan in Badenoch some fifty miles south west of Castle Grant. The lands of Tullochcromb, Gallovie and Aberarder had been feued by the laird of Grant to MacDonald tacksmen in 1696.[117] The feuars, along with most of the inhabitants of these lands, were cadets of the MacDonalds of Keppoch, a Jacobite clan who fought against the government at Mulroy in 1688, and then in the 1689, 1715 and 1745 uprisings. In the 1689 rebellion the MacDonalds of Keppoch conducted raids against the pro-Williamite Grants in Strathspey.[118] The opposing political allegiances of superior and vassal aggravated the tension already felt by *oighreachd*[119] and *duthcas* not coinciding. This was a common cause of tension across the Highlands.[120]

---

114 Grant Court Book 5, 06/12/1725, p. 76.

115 Ibid, 22/06/1727, p. 114. There are parallels here with Windsor Forest in the 1720s whereby gentlemen caught poaching were prosecuted indirectly through their servants. See, Thompson, *Whigs and Hunters*, p. 60.

116 NRS, Court Book Pages, GD248/25/1/14.

117 C Fraser- Mackintosh, 'The depopulation of Aberarder in Badenoch', *Celtic Magazine* 2 (1877), p. 419.

118 Macinnes, *Clanship, Commerce and the House of Stuart*, p. 164.

119 The lands forming part of the patronage of a clan as opposed to the lands traditionally considered part of the clan heritage. In this case Laggan was part of the MacDonald's *duthcas* but was Grant *oighreachd*.

120 Macinnes, *Clanship, Commerce and the House of Stuart*, pp. 38- 41.

The isolated position of Loch Laggan removed from the rest of the regality and bordering the bandit country of Lochaber meant the MacDonald feuars were relatively free from the strictures of the regality and took advantage of this situation. Thus, we find that although the three feuars of Laggan, and their subtenants were called to compear at regality courts to answer to accusations of poaching, on only one occasion did they comply. These examples are especially interesting as the feuars themselves were explicitly called rather than just their subtenants as was usually the case.[121] This is perhaps not surprising given that it was a round trip of 100 miles to attend the regality court in Strathspey.[122] The Duke of Gordon owned the lands which neighboured Aberarder, Gallovie and Tullochcromb. He also had trouble with the feuars of these lands. These events culminated in an action before the high court of justiciary in 1711.[123] The Duke of Gordon accused Ronald MacDonald of Gallovie of killing some forty deer in an unpermitted drive on his lands. However, the case drops from the record. Grant troubles with the MacDonald feuars of Gallovie, Aberarder and Tullochcromb culminated in 1717. John Grant of Dalrachney wrote to Alexander Grant of Grant in the following terms, 'since the rebellion I have not charged your wassells of lagan to a court seance it should be prejudiciall to your interests let me know whether it is or not'.[124] Clearly political tensions in the region demanded that the Hanoverian Grants exercise their jurisdiction over their Jacobite vassals with the utmost caution.

7.3 Improvement and Farming

The final phase of heritable justice in Scotland coincided with the beginning of the enthusiasm for improvement. Improvement was progress, an opportunity for economic gain and the advancement of civilisation in the last bastion of the Gael. It has long been argued that courts of barony and regality were essential tools in the process of improvement, especially concerning agriculture.[125] Besides litigation and acts concerning forestry, there is virtually no

121 Grant Court Book 3, 17/07/1713, p. 42.

122 Although the Laggan feuars could be found litigating in the regality court under other pretexts, such as when MacDonald of Gallovie was assaulted in Laggan kirk in 1715.

123 NRS, Minutes of the High Court of Justiciary, JC7/5/7.

124 NRS, Grant Correspondence, GD248/170/3, fo. 39, 26/01/1717.

125 See: Goodare, *The Government of Scotland*, p. 182; Sanderson, *Scottish Rural Society in the Sixteenth Century*, p. 18; Whyte, *Agriculture and Society*, pp. 44–5; Mitchison, *Lordship to Patronage*, p. 81; Macinnes, *Clanship, Commerce and the House of Stuart*, p. 146.

evidence of this in Strathspey, where the transformation of natural and man-made landscapes was most pronounced in the period following 1762 and Sir James Grant of Grant's ambitious transformation of his estates, some fourteen years after the abolition of the regality of Grant. This may provide the explanation of why so little reference to improvement, besides trying to protect the estate's woodlands, appears in the regality court books. It is true that some early attempts at improvement were made. For instance, some tacks as early as the 1670s encouraged the tacksman to, 'win in new lands upon any part of the said lands of Kyllintra and to use all maner of husbandrie for improvement yrof'.[126] However, on such matters the courts were silent. Instead, we find more evidence of the court being used to ensure continuity suggesting that the importance of franchise courts to improvement may be less than has been claimed by some historians.

7.3.1 *Pastoral Farming*

The Grants made few attempts to regulate agriculture through acts of the regality court. This is in stark contrast to their approach to forestry. The relative lack of court material relating to agriculture is perhaps easily explained by the nature of farming in Strathspey which was reliant upon transhumance and the pasturing of cattle. Grain production did not progress beyond what was required for the payment of rentals and subsistence. Thus, any examples of agricultural regulation in the court books relate to aspects of the pastoral system of farming, such as, the shieling system, the destruction of vermin, and acts about livestock.

Transhumance was out of necessity the basis of the pastoral system across much of the Highlands, Strathspey included.[127] The low altitude pasture surrounding the townships in the valleys was limited in extent and was thus precious, being either cropped in summer or protected for winter grazing. However, there were large tracts of rough hill pasture on the hills surrounding the valleys [see Illustration 7]. Most davochs had access to hill grazing on this rough pasture. The shieling system was tailored to take advantage of these rich upland summer grazings and simultaneously preserve the home pastures. Yeld animals, goats and sheep were pastured on the uplands from sowing until harvest; however, the upland grazings were only valuable for rearing the dairy herd during late spring and early summer when the upland vegetation was at its most nutritious.[128]

126 NRS, Tack of Kylintra 1675, GD248/533/5, fo. 19.

127 L H Livingstone, 'Shieling, transhumance and changes in land use in the Scottish Highlands' (Unpublished Ph.D. thesis University of Edinburgh, 1973), p. 142.

128 Taylor, *The Wild Black Region*, pp. 60–74.

ILLUSTRATION 7 The remains of an improved shieling known as Tarsin by the Allt Bad a' Gluasaid, five miles north of Castle Grant. A hut circle is in the foreground and a fold for housing dairy cattle is visible in the middle ground. It is clear how the folding of a cattle created fertile oases in the moorland
SOURCE: THE AUTHOR

The migration to the shieling grounds, which might be as much as twenty miles distant from the township, took place following Whitsun and not later than mid-June. The precise date of the flitting was decreed by the regality or baron court:[129] 'The inhabitants of Cromdale are to send their nolt[130] and sheep to the Glens, tomorrow (Saturday) or Monday. 40s. per day that they are late'.[131] Women, adolescents and children would drive cattle and sheep to the shieling grazings.[132] If the shielings were far from the township then they would stay with the stock in bothies adjacent to the pastures. The time spent away at the shielings with the dairy herd was short; the court records suggest that mid-summer was the date usually appointed for returning from the shielings.[133] Given a departure date of mid to late May this suggests that, besides herds left to tend the yeld animals, inhabitants of the regality spent little more than a month at the shielings, a feature common of transhumance all over the Highlands.[134] The duration of the shieling period was limited by a number

129 V Gaffney, 'Summer Shealings', *SHR* 38:1 (1959), p. 27.
130 "Nolt", usually referred to cattle but could also refer to horses. *DSL*.
131 NRS, Baron Court Extracts, GD248/76/2, fo. 40.
132 Taylor, *The Wild Black Region*, p. 68.
133 NRS, Baron Court Extracts, GD248/76/2, fo. 59.
134 Livingstone, 'Sheiling, transhumance and changes in land use', p. 154.

of factors the primary one being the Strathspey folk's overwhelming reliance upon dairy products for sustenance: the people needed to be where the dairy cattle were.[135] Additionally after four to six weeks the best grazing at the shielings, the type needed to sustain dairy cattle, was spent, necessitating a return to the home pastures [see Illustration 8]. This return also coincided with the need to tathe the outfield to improve fertility for the next crop.

Tenants who failed to send their cattle or sheep to the glens or shielings as instructed by the court were fined.[136] Equally, those bringing their livestock home before the appointed time also faced fines of 40s up to £10.[137] Whilst at the shielings, women milked the dairy cows and produced milk and cheese. Meanwhile young boys were responsible for herding yeld cattle, goats, sheep and horses and keeping them away from the best grazing which was reserved for the dairy cattle.[138] There was evidently a great temptation for tenants to allow their stock to stray onto other shieling grounds and take advantage of their neighbour's pasture, especially as shielings' boundaries were notoriously unclear and were the subject of dispute in the regality court.[139] Tenants grazing neighbouring shielings could face fines or having their cattle poinded.[140] At night stock was folded to stop it from straying and to afford it protection from predators:

> The said day ordains and enacts ilk tenant to keip ther owne glenes in due tyme of yeir under failie of 5 libis and also ordains that all in the glenes shall hest[141] in inbringing their beastis to ther own proper sheallings ilk night and not wrong their neighbours shealling or particular pastur under the lyk failie.[142]

135 Ibid, p. 151.

136 NRS, Baron Court Extracts, GD248/76/2, fo. 64.

137 Ibid. and Grant Court Book 3, p. 40.

138 Livingstone, 'Sheiling, transhumance and changes in land use', p. 157.

139 Gaffney, 'Summer Shealings', p. 25. A good example is the dispute between the tenants of Connage and Over Congash in 1719: Grant Court Book 3, 15/08/1719, p. 13. Few Grant tacks specifically denoted the shieling which was pertinent to the lands set in tack. For an exception to this rule see: NRS, Tack of Gaich 1655, GD248/533/5/46 which records that Rynechkra was the shieling of Gaich. The allocation of other shielings must have been a matter of tradition.

140 NRS, Baron Court Extracts, GD248/76/2, fo. 56.

141 "Heest", to hasten. *DSL*.

142 Grant Court Book 2, 13/06/1706, p. 75.

Despite the best efforts of the court and shieling-herds, livestock often strayed or went missing. Any stray animals that had been found were taken to the regality court (or even directly to the clerk to be recorded in the court books) and declared as stray by the court so that the owner might be sought. The animal was usually entrusted to the custody of the procurator fiscal and on occasion the bailie during the interim period. May, June, and July were the months when most stray livestock were recorded in the regality court books, coinciding with summer pasturing:

> The said day the pro[curato]r fiscall brongst ane coyack[143] to the court that was strayed and taken from the catell of Robert Gow in Conndge and proclaimed the said coyack about three yeir old, black coulored and that in presence of people at the said court which quoyack wes proclaimed before at the churchis of Abernethy, Kincardine and Inverallan. The said quoyack wes comprysed at 5 lib value and delyvered to the bailie till ane owner should come within the tyme allowed by law.[144]

If a prospective claimant came forth, they had to prove that the animal was theirs by leading witnesses. The court records show that vassals would come from as far away as Aberarder on Loch Laggan to claim livestock in the regality court (a round trip of 100 miles), whilst vassals of other jurisdictions also had to compear before the regality court of Grant to retrieve livestock which had strayed into Grant bounds.[145] Stray livestock, especially pigs, could cause considerable damage to grazing land. The records suggest that there was some form of compensation system in place. In the first place this was simply 'finders' keepers' with stray animals becoming the property of the finder after a specified time. It also appears that injured parties could claim expenses from the procurator fiscal of the regality for the upkeep of the animal. Thereafter the fiscal sued the owner of the stock for damages.[146]

Livestock at the shielings and on the hill-ground was vulnerable to the depredations of both caterans and predators.[147] Whilst wolves had been virtually eradicated from the Highlands by the late seventeenth century, foxes and eagles posed a serious threat to tenants' livestock especially whilst at the shielings.[148]

143 "Quyok", a heifer. *DSL*.
144 Grant Court Book 3, 01/06/1715, p. 80.
145 Grant Court Book 5, 05/07/1728, p. 147, and, Grant Court Book 2, 10/12/1709, p. 129.
146 Grant Court Book 5, 17/05/1728, p. 145.
147 The response to the threat of caterans is discussed in the next chapter.
148 One of several traditions about the last wolf killed in Scotland relates that the final wild wolf was killed in the upper reaches of the Findhorn or Dulnain valleys in 1743, on the

ILLUSTRATION 8 The shieling grounds in summer
SOURCE: THE AUTHOR

Inhabitants of the regality made representations to the court to help reduce the losses they were suffering due to predation. In response the regality court issued two acts of court on the issue the first being recorded in 1706:

> Ilk person killing ane fox shall have twenty shilling Scotis for ilk fox young and old with the skin to be payed to thame be Alex[ande]r Grant brother of the bailie who is ordained to collect ane merk from each sten part or ane lamb therfor and also from evrie malender half ane merk which half merk is allowed to the said Alex[ande]r for collector fee.[149]

The position of collector was handed to the future chamberlain Alexander Grant later to be tacksman of Lethendrie. The subsequent act targeting foxes and eagles was promulgated in November 1727 and was announced at courts held at Milntoun of Castle Grant, Duthil, Belnaglach and Ballintomb with all the bailies of the regality and Humphrey Grant younger of Grant in attendance. The petition to the bailies bemoans that the people 'sustain continuall and dayly losses by the foxes and eagles killing their sheip' and requests that a

orders of the laird of Mackintosh. This is only a few miles from the bounds of the regality of Grant.

149 Grant Court Book 2, 09/12/1706, p. 84.

fund be created 'for encouragement and reward to those that shall be exercised in destroying the foxes and eagle to the best advantage'..[150]

Whilst the pastoral farmers of Strathspey could rear relatively few cattle themselves due to difficulty in feeding cattle through the long winters, the carrying capacity of the vast tracts of upland grazing were considerably greater than the number of cattle owned by the Strathspey folk. The result was that enterprising people from upland Strathspey began to take in 'outlandish' cattle from Lowland Moray during the summer months, to be herded alongside their own herds at a cost per head of cattle to the Lowland farmer.[151] Such cattle became known as 'gall cattle'[152] and were a key pillar supporting the local economy. Whilst the lucrative practice was widely endorsed by tenants of the Grants it came at the expense of the Grant family themselves, whose grazing was denuded whilst yielding no extra income. Thus, the estate attempted to stamp out the practice, through acts of the court:

> The said day it is statut and ordained be the Right Hono[urab]ll Laird of Grant and Lurg his bailie of the lo[rdshi]p off Abernethie statutes and ordains that noe tennant within the lordship of Abernethie nor any inhabitant shall bring in any low country beastis called gall within any of the Glennes of Glenberown, Glenlochie or to any wherever Glennes upon any pretext or reason … ordaines evrie ane having any gall nolt to dispatch them of in all heast under the failie of twentie shilling the beast.[153]

Similar bans were imposed in the neighbouring forest of Glenavon by the regality court of Huntly as the Duke of Gordon sought to protect his revenues earned by setting the upland grazings in tack; bans on gall cattle were also to be found in the borders and northern England.[154] The Grants finally banned the practice of summering gall cattle outright in 1763 as part of Sir James Grant and William Lorimer's ambitious improvement scheme for Strathspey.[155] This scheme involved depriving tenants of their traditional shieling and grazing rights as stipulated in new leases. These shieling grounds were to be the focus

150 Grant Court Book 5, p. 135–6. The two men appointed as collectors were Robert Grant of Lurg's sons, James and William, James was also a soldier in William Grant's independent company. NRS, The Knock notebook, RH2/8/96.

151 Gaffney, 'Summer Shealings', p. 24.

152 The term "gall cattle" is an anglicisation of Gaelic, translating literally as 'foreign' cattle. In this case meaning the cattle came from the Lowlands.

153 Grant Court Book 2, 17/06/1707, p. 87.

154 Gaffney, 'Summer Shealings', p. 25; Winchester, *The Harvest of the Hills*, p.78.

155 Ross, 'Improvements to the Grant estates in Strathspey', p. 300.

of improvement, being set in tack to new tenants who undertook to turn the rough pastures over to arable. The scheme was largely a failure, many of the old shieling grounds being too marginal and vulnerable to the vagaries of the climate to support full time agriculture. Tenants were unable to pay their rents due to the interruption in the traditional cattle trade and this affected the Grants' own finances.[156] As a result many new farms were re-converted back to summer pasture by the nineteenth century.

Mentions of the shielings in the regality court records appear only sporadically, with the final acts of court governing the shielings appearing in 1721. In comparison the baron court records from the 1660s show that there was a steady flow of court work relating to shielings during this period, with the dates for flitting to, and returning from the shielings being annually set out by the court and recorded in the court books. It is unclear whether this is once again a question of what evidence has survived or rather evidence of changing practices with the estate becoming less interested in the regulation of summer grazing. Study by Winchester of the pastoral economy in the borders and northern England suggests that the repetition of customary regulations in local courts there, such as those governing shieling practices, was an attempt by manors to stem changing practices.[157] A parallel may be found here. The subsequent disappearance of these edicts in the eighteenth century may show that the courts failed to accommodate changing demands and lost their authority to regulate this area. However, given the events of the 1760s it seems more likely to be a question of what records have been passed down to us.

7.4 Conclusion

In Highland Strathspey, where farming focussed on the production of cattle rather than arable produce, there is virtually no evidence of the court being used to promote the improvement of agricultural practices. As we have seen limited examples exist of the court being used to try and improve the lives of farmers such as: taxes to pay for bounties to destroy vermin, and a compensation scheme for the victims of damage done by straying livestock. Yet beyond this the court records are silent. There was no great revolution on the Grant estates until 1762 when James Grant of Grant initiated his controversial improvement schemes for Strathspey.

156 Ibid, p. 306.

157 Winchester, *The Harvest of the Hills*, pp. 150–1.

Instead, during the period 1690–1748 only woodlands evidence a transformation. The forests of Strathspey came to be regarded as the regality's greatest economic asset. To realise this economic potential and protect the forests, there was a greater resort to the regality court as a means of control and deterrent. However, the Grants were clearly unwilling to implement the wholesale changes to local life needed to make the best advantage of their forests. Thus, the traditional rights of the local tenantry were forced to coexist with attempted commercial extraction by enterprises such as the York Building Company. Transgressions of the acts of court for the protection of the woodlands were common, and regard for the authority of the court in this sphere was severely tested. Banishments and corporal punishments handed down by the court for the worst offences appeared to do little to deter the tenantry from molesting the woods.

The contrast between traditional methods and the new commercial experience gradually began to make an impact upon life and litigation in the regality. Court actions over sequestrations and contracts appeared, sitting side by side with the tenants being questioned over their use of the woods and poaching at judicial rentals in age-old fashion. These cases suggest that the regality court was capable of adapting to a changing society which placed less emphasis on feudalism and clanship and more on commerce. Unfortunately, the records left by the court are fragmentary after this point preventing a fuller analysis of these developments; however, the continuing importance of the baronial courts in Strathspey following 1748 seems to offer further evidence that the franchise courts were capable of adaptation and retained a degree of relevancy until the pace of social change finally rendered them obsolete.

CHAPTER 8

Land Tenure

Barony and regality courts were integral to the administration of the system of landholding. The tenants of the laird of Grant were tied to the laird by their tenure of the land. In turn sub-tenants were tied to their tacksman, and thus to the laird of Grant also. One of the court's core functions was the regulation of the relationships between these parties. New tenancies were recorded, and the entry of the new tenants overseen; in turn, the court might also be called upon to help remove these tenants at the end of their tenancies. Boundaries might be scrutinised, plots divided, while feudal duties and services were enforced.

8.1 Tacks and Tenure

The most essential function of the regality court in relation to tenancies was the production of judicial rentals. A rental was a list or register of the rents due by tenants to the proprietor taken before a judge. Tacksmen, tenants and sub-tenants presented themselves before the bailie for a roll call where, if they had one, they produced their written tack for examination or gave oral evidence of their land holding. They were expected to give up a list of any sub-tenants they had along with evidence of their last rent payments. Tenants would pay to have a duplicate of the tack produced by the clerk, one for the estate records, the other for them to keep.[1]

Whilst wadset lands were usually excluded from estate rentals, sir James Grant of Grant used the regality court to undertake several judicial rentals of the wadset lands in the regality at the beginning of his time as laird. These rentals taken in 1719 and 1720 form the most complete judicial rentals surviving from the Grant estates in the early years of the eighteenth century. They give a detailed picture of the subtenants living on the wadset lands, how much land they held and what they paid to the wadsetter. Only lands which paid rent directly to the lairds of Grant were usually the subject of such scrutiny, making these rentals unusual. Their purpose was to investigate the feasibility of redeeming the large tracts of land wadset by James' predecessors. The rentals confirmed that significant amounts of rent were being lost each year thanks to

1 NRS, Notes from Lorimer to James Grant of Grant, GD248/24/2, fo. 1.

 | DOI:10.1163/9789004472549_009

the extensive wadsetting, £6400 from the yearly rents. However, it would have cost £73233,6,8 in 1720 to redeem the twenty two davochs which were wadset at that point.[2] Many of the pages detailing the rentals undertaken by James Grant have been removed from the court books and reside in different parts of the Seafield muniments, evidence that the rentals taken by the court were actively used by the estate in its day to day workings and were appropriated from the main court book for this end. The undertaking of judicial rentals was more usually motivated by a desire to raise rentals. This could only be done once current rentals, arrears and tenants' ability to pay had first been assessed.

Tacks were also produced by tenants to be recorded in the court books as a means of preservation: 'The said day Jon Grant in Lettoch getes his tak of Lettoch for 19 years from Wit 1712 and payes two hundreth merkes of grassum at mart 1712'.[3] The tack was then witnessed by people present in court, in this case: William Grant of Delay, bailie; David Cuthbert, bailie substitute; and the chamberlain, Alexander Grant of Lethendrie. The signing, witnessing, and recording of tacks are much more frequent in the court records from the 1650s to the 1670s. For instance, at a court at Boat of Cromdale on 21 April 1659, eighteen five-year tacks were set within the Braes of Castle Grant.[4] At another baron court held in February 1670 at Ballintomb, fifteen five-year tacks were recorded.[5] John Grant's 1712 tack of Lettoch, mentioned above, was recorded along with several others in the back pages of one of the court books and not sequential with the other records there. It would suggest that the practice of setting tacks in the court continued but recording of them was either lax or took place in a separate and dedicated book.

Should an element of a tenant's tack become disputed, the court might scrutinise the details of their tack. For instance, in 1711, the minister of Cromdale was called before the regality court to make payment of outstanding duties owed for the previous two years rent of his lands at Port, and to answer for his intromission with the stipends of the lands there.[6] However, producing his tack from the laird, he was able to prove that he was not liable for the sums claimed.

Other issues litigated in court included boundary disputes between neighbouring tenants or townships. A good example of this is provided by a case in

2 NRS, Estate Rentals of Wadset Lands, GD248/150/5. The wadsets were all eventually redeemed but not until 1783 when Mullochard was finally redeemed.

3 Grant Court Book 3, p. 104.

4 NRS, Baron Court Extracts, GD248/76/2, fo. 92.

5 Ibid, fo. 81.

6 Grant Court Book 3, 27/11/1711, p. 11.

August 1719 when Alaster Grant tacksman of Connage alleged that the people of neighbouring Over Congash had encroached upon his land by erecting a bothy upon it.[7] The building of bothies upon other people's ground must have been a recurring problem as a baron court held at Ballintomb in April 1664 enacted 'no tenent in Abernethie shall build ane bothie beyond the Auldcharne and the gleann of the hill [illeg] and whosoever transgressis the same his bothie sallbe castin downe'.[8] He raised an action before the regality court leading to a cognition of the controverted grounds known as the slack of Connage:

> The said day anent the cogntition of the controverted bounds one the east syd of the slack of Conedge and pastur ther betwix Allaster Grant tenant in Conedge and the people of over Congess and Gregor Grant of Congess ther master as prin[cipa]ll takesmen thereof. The people of over Congess having built ane house nyr the head of the brae for purpois to labor which the said Alistar Grant pleadis sould not be donee being ane intraruption of his pastur.[9]

Seven witnesses gave evidence before the court of what they believed to be the boundary between the two townships' grazings and what they understood to be the grazing rights of each township. The witnesses all had first-hand experience of the land in question either having previously resided in one the townships or from living in neighbouring townships. It is interesting that the estate was unable to say what the boundaries were and thus had to defer to local tradition in the absence of written evidence.[10] Having heard the evidence, the bailie submitted the question of the boundary to an inquest of seven tacksmen and tenants who rented lands neighbouring the disputed lands. These seven included Gregor Grant younger of Connage, the son of the tacksman who first raised the dispute in the court. The court then retired to await the verdict of the inquest. When the court reconvened two days later, the inquest found in favour of Connage by a majority of five to two and settled the boundary as follows:

---

7 Grant Court Book 4, 15/08/1719, p. 13.

8 NRS, Baron Court Extracts, GD248/76/2, Fo. 15.

9 Grant Court Book 4, 15/08/1719, p. 13.

10 Andy Wood has highlighted the significance of boundaries and perambulations in folk-memory. Local custom was of great importance in the process of upholding and defining boundaries in early-modern England. A Wood, *The memory of the people: custom and popular senses of the past in early modern England* (Cambridge, 2013), pp. 223–6.

> It is their oppinione that the burn hes become part [of] the march to keip propertie to Conedge on Conedge syd of the burn and that the possessors of Conedge may keep ther own syd … it is ther opinion that Conedge shall have common pastur with the proprietor of Congess on Congess side of the burn and that the said bothie should be thrown down that ther be no shealling one the controverted bounds by other plea.[11]

The bailie accepted the verdict of the inquest, subject to the laird of Grant or his trustees coming in person to perambulate the ground and direct the parties to act otherwise (yet another instance of the court paying deference to the judgement of the laird in person).[12] Gregor Grant of Congash immediately lodged a counter plea and two more witnesses were questioned about the marches before the case drops from the record. Another important aspect of this case is the locations in which the courts were held. The first court, where witnesses evidence was taken, took pace at Boat of Cromdale, a place often frequented by the court. However, judgement was made in a court held upon the controverted ground itself, demonstrating another aspect of how the court was tailored to local needs.

Another boundary dispute appears in the court records on 22 July 1725. William Mcfinlay Roy, a soldier in Ballindalloch's independent company, was unhappy with a perambulation of the marches between his township and neighbouring Knockanbuie, for which he blamed the partiality of the bailie:

> The which day Wm Mcfinlayroy in Culfoichbeg being charged to this dyet anent the debateable marches twixt Culfoich beg and Knockanbuy and it being answered by the judge of court that the samen marches were already decided and determined by Wm Grant of Delay in relation to the differences twixt the inhabitants of both said towns, the said William Mcfinlayroy answered that tho Delay had the Laird of Grants order allowing him to cognose therein that he was bribed there anent and determined not the marches lawfully. Whereupon Robert Grant of Boginduie after craving leave to speake for Delay in absence protested that the said Mcfinalyroy as reproaching Delay in absence should be obliged to prove his allega[tio]ne or otherwise should be decerend ag[ain]st court to make satisfaction to Delay and unlawed for the aspersion according to law in respect the aspersion was spoken judicially in pre[sen]ce of Alexander

11 Grant Court Book 4, 15/08/1719, p. 18.

12 Ibid, p. 19.

> Grant you[nge]r of Delrachney, Robert Grant in Wester Leathendry, Mr Duncan McIntosh m[iniste]r in Cromdale, James Grant in Delvey and James Blair in Dellifure to which the said judge interpones his a[uthori]ty ordains the said Wm Mcfinlayroy to present himself ag[ain]st next court under cautionary to prove his aspersion or otherwise present his person under cautionary to undergo justice as law will. Whereupon the said Robert Grant asked and took instrument in the hands of the clerk of court that all the witnesses were present and heard him speak the reproach and aspersion.[13]

The case frustratingly drops from the record, suggesting that Mcfinlayroy abandoned his allegations against Delay. Nonetheless it provides an exciting insight into the tensions and dissatisfaction that could arise from boundary disputes. Some tenants were clearly dissatisfied even after the official resolution of the dispute by a representative of the laird and were not afraid to make their dissatisfaction known, though whether they were able to furnish the court with any type of proof is doubtful. Davies argues that most boundary disputes were probably dealt with by birlaw men rather than in baron or regality courts in a more informal and conciliatory manner.[14] Records from Strathspey in the later eighteenth century show that birlaw men were employed to determine disputed boundaries by the Grant estates. This could explain why only two boundary disputes appear in the regality court records.

The resignation and subsequent transfer of tacks was also overseen by the court. In December 1725, David Clay and William Grant sought to have an auchtenpart of land in Belnaglach that they held as joint tenants, transferred to the minister of Abernethy 'in respect they can not have the keeping of the said tack both at once'.[15] The bailie was able to authorise the transfer judicially. Along with tacks the court also oversaw and judicially ratified the resignation of women's liferent rights. It was relatively widespread practice for tacksmen or wadsetters to grant the fee of their tack or wadset to their heir or another tacksman whilst granting a liferent of the lands to their spouse. In such situations it was commonplace for the spouse to resign her liferent right in return for compensation from the incoming tacksman who wished to take possession of the lands unencumbered by a right of liferent. Resignation of liferent required an instrument of resignation followed by the liferenter appearing before the

13 Grant Court Book 5, 22/07/1725, pp. 56–7.

14 Davies, 'Law and Order in Stirlingshire', p. 243.

15 Grant Court Book 5, 08/12/1725, p. 74.

superior's representative in court (in this case the laird of Grant's bailie).[16] Eight transfers are recorded in the regality court books. A typical example can be seen from July 1710 when Dalrachney sought to expand his wadset lands:

> The whilk day compeired Marie Grant spouse to Ronald Macdonald sometyme of Kinveachie and outwith the presence of her husband declared to the said judge that she had asyned and deponed in favour of John Grant of Delrachnie her lyfrent right of the lands of Kinveachie robie and Lenthendrie veall lyand in the said regalitie and that she had received compensatione therfor from the said Johne Grant with ane bond and severtie from him for the years annual rent of three throusand and two hundredth merkes scots being the money wadsettof the saids lands … and the said Ronald her husband entered the court and consented to the said rattiffication.[17]

The court also had the power to declare a tack null and void. Sir James Grant's factor attempted to void a tack at a court held at Ballindalloch in 1726.[18] John Grant of Drumbuie had obtained a tack of several mills in the parish of Urquhart through George Grant of Clury the factor there. However, it was alleged that the tack was obtained through bribery, with it being revealed that Drumbuie was paying £20 each year to Clury in addition to his tack duty. Drumbuie appeared before the court claiming that 'Clury extorted and forced him to give him an obligatione to pay him twenty pounds scots yearly during the continuance of the said tack with obligatione'[19] Unfortunately for Clury he had even kept discharges of the payments, although Clury claimed he was only collecting the extra money on the laird's behalf.[20] After consideration Dalrachney decreed that

> the deponent to pay the said twenty pound of augmentatione more than is contained in the tack for all years and terms bygone and to come that's presently resting to the laird of Grants chamberlain of Urqurt and not to Clury and refers the reduction of the tack to his constituents and ordains the said John Grant deponent to give up what recepts or discharges he has from George Grant of Clury.

16 Stair, *The Institutions of the Law of Scotland*, iii, ii, 8–9, pp. 592–3; ii, ii, 6, p. 529.
17 Grant Court Book 2, 04/07/1710, p. 139.
18 NRS, Grant of Grant v Grant of Drumbuie, GD248/108/12, fo. 17.
19 Ibid.
20 Ibid, fo. 18 and 20.

The case drops from the record, so it is unclear whether the tack was ever reduced. However, the court had the power to do so in practice.

When a tenant's tack reached its end, or an irritancy in the lease was triggered, the tenant was expected to quit their holding voluntarily. Failing this they were evicted judicially by process of removing. The most common way that removal was undertaken was solemnly with warning.[21] It was of utmost importance to the laird to be able to regain possession of the land so that it could be re-let to new tenants. The process was enshrined in statute in 1555 and proceeded in the following way. The chamberlain would give the court officer a precept of warning, to be delivered to the tenant forty days before Whitsunday. The precept intimated that the tenant was to remove himself, his goods, family, and subtenants before the term day. A copy of the precept was attached to both the dwelling house and the kirk door (after proclamation there) and before two witnesses. If the tenant failed to timeously remove after warning the process moved to the regality court. In September 1712 several tenants failed to remove from their holdings at the term day of Whitsun:

> The said day anent the actiones of removeing prsued at the instance of Alexr Grant Chalmerlane of Strathspey in name and behalff of the right hono[urab]ll coll Alexr Grant of Grant and his commissioners against Donald Glass and Johne Makeronbuy in Mukerach of Abernethie and Wm Ross in Dellafure this being the first dyot and some of the def[ende]rs not compearing the said bailie Coll Wm Grant ordains the def[ende]rs to be summoned of new againe to ane court to be holdine at Cromdaile upone two weeks nixt the 16th instant And ordains the prsuers to have the precept of warneing and executions therof prepared ag[ains]t the said day ... The officer is ordained to prepare the exicutiones scripto as law requires.[22]

Two weeks later the court reconvened, with some of the tenants still in possession. Donald Glass, one of the tenants in question, appeared before the court to explain that he had failed to remove from his half-auchten part of land because he had not received legal warning from the court officer and therefore was not obliged to remove:

21 Stair, *The Institutions of the Law of Scotland*, i, xix, 40, p. 390.

22 Grant Court Book 3, 05/09/1712, p. 21.

> The def[ende]r being caled compeared and denyed that he got any warneing the officer being caled to instruct his executione confessed he sent him warneing with his sone to Donald Glass but the copie sent was not in his name but ag[ains]t Duncan Makgregor another tenant but finding the copie was wrongly delyvered he took back the copie and brought it to mr Wm Grant who scored out Duncan Makgregor's name and inscrit Donald Glass name and then sent the copie againe with Donald Farrah who had noe power to charge The bailie finds that noe process can be susteined ag[ains]t the def[ende]r upone the warneing inrespect he is not la[wful]lie warned in the termes of law and that ther is noe execution given in under the officeres hand subscribed be him.[23]

Glass immediately sued for absolvitor, but the bailie sustained his initial decision. At a subsequent court in November 1712, Donald Glass finally agreed to remove from his holding by Whitsun 1713 and to pay damages as determined by the laird, to the new tenant who he had deprived of the peaceable possession of his holding for a year.[24] At the court on 16 September 1712 the bailie was unable to sustain the process of removing against another tenant, the officer again failing to deliver the warning in person instead entrusting the precept to 'twa boyes who wer not officeres'.[25]

These cases are of great significance as they demonstrate how vassals of the laird of Grant were able to use the regality court for their own ends, such as by challenging the validity of a precept of warning to remove issued by the laird's own chamberlain. It is too easy to view the franchise courts as operating for the exclusive benefit of the landed classes. Indeed, all social groups can be seen to have had knowledge of the courts and their procedures and could use this against their social superiors. This meant they were able to recognise when they were the victims of undue procedure and exploit the situation to their advantage. Such knowledge also suggests that they had access to legal advice of some sort before defending the action against them in the regality court. A similar example is to be found in the records of the baron court of Monymusk across the Grampians in Aberdeenshire. In 1735 Sir Archibald Grant of Monymusk's factor wrote to him in the following terms: 'Our tenants are such lawiers that they tell me I dare not poind upon our Baillie's decreet

23 Ibid, 16/09/1712, p. 22.
24 Ibid, 29/11/1712, p. 33.
25 Ibid, 16/09/1712, p. 23.

unless he and clerk are qualified'.[26] Evidently local legal culture found expression in franchise courts across the Highlands.

The records show that tacksmen also raised actions in the court to try and get sitting sub-tenants to remove. John Grant in Burnside raised an action against William Rose in Dellifure, to get him to remove; however, in the end he was content to allow him to keep his house and five hens until the next term day, provided he, John Grant gained possession of the agricultural land.[27]

Whilst the regality court of Grant was predominantly concerned with the tenure of the vassals of the regality it was also required to deal with the tenure of the incumbent lord of the regality. The main surviving evidence for this comes when Sir James Grant of Grant was infeft in the Grant estates, following the death of his elder brother Alexander. The record from the court where this took place reads as follows:

> Court of the Sheriffedomes of Invernes, Elgine and Forres, regalitie of Grant and burgh of Elgine holdine at Grantowne upon the 29th October 1720. Be the discreet Gentlemen James Grant of Elckis, Patrick Grant of Delvey, Wm Grant of Delay and Jon Grant of Delrachnie as sherrifs and bailies in that part nominat and appoyntit be virtue of our sovereine Lords commissione direct for the proving of the right hon James Grant of Grant served and retoured as air in special and in general to the deceist Alexr Grant of Grant his brother Germane in all and hail the lands heretagis and estates upon the said defunct dyed last infeft and sensed as offer at the faith and peace of our sovereign lord conforme to the severall breives reased and execut be the said James Grant of Grant for that effect David Blair notar public and clerk Thomas Grant officer and dempster suites called the court lawfully fenced and affirmed.[28]

Several formalities were required for infeftment to be completed.[29] Thus, the four Grants, as bailies representing of the crown, had to be present at the burgh of the regality in Grantown to give James infeftment in the lands formerly held by his brother. Presumably, such formalities were also undertaken in respect of the infeftment of his predecessors in the Grant lands; however, as with many other aspects of the records of the regality of Grant, they fail to appear in the surviving material.

26 Hamilton, *Selections from the Monymusk Papers*, p. 128.
27 Grant Court Book 3, 28/01/1713, p. 34.
28 Grant Court Book 4, 29/10/1720, p. 38.
29 See Bankton, *An Institute of the Law of Scotland*, p. 549.

8.2 Vassal's Labour Services

A key element of landholding was the inclusion of labour services in tenants' leases. Tacksmen and tenants expected their sub-tenants to perform these services owed to the laird alongside rendering labour services to the tenant as well. Services were a means for superiors to establish authority over their vassals. They also provided a very important source of labour, meaning in some cases tacksmen had no need to employ paid labourers at all.[30] Although widely disliked by those of the lower social orders who were expected to render the services, realistically, in a society where cash was often scarce, labour was an important means of payment. Given the importance of services to 'feudalism', it has been claimed that labour services abound in the records of barony and regality courts.[31] However, there are only nineteen examples in the Grant court books, suggesting that the use of franchise court in relation to these services is overstated.[32] The Grant family converted many labour services to cash payments in the late seventeenth century as they tried to raise extra revenue. All remaining labour services were converted to cash payments on the Strathspey estates around 1730, only for this policy to be reversed following the improvement programme initiated in 1762 which demanded a large source of labour.[33] This policy offers some explanation for the small number of cases appearing in the court records.

Labour services were much more common in lowland arable districts than in upland pastoral economies such as Strathspey.[34] There are several reasons for this. Firstly, arable production was much more labour intensive. Cash was more readily in circulation in pastoral areas because pastoral produce was more easily marketed than arable, placing less emphasis on labour as a form of payment. Additionally, pastoral areas were often at a great distance from the residence of the superior making the performance of services difficult.[35]

30 Taylor, *Wild Black Region*, p. 38.

31 Dodgshon, *Land and Society in Early Scotland*, p. 249. The printed baron court records from Stitchill and Urie do not have many examples of labour services being exacted through the court either.

32 The court books of the Monymusk estates, famous for improvement, show more examples of disputes over labour services which were clearly very unpopular. See for instance; Hamilton, *Selections from the Monymusk*, p. 228, where tenants threatened to renounce their tenancies rather than build a mill dam.

33 Fraser, *Chiefs of Grant*, Vol. 1 pt. 1, p. xcv.

34 Whyte, 'Agriculture in Aberdeenshire in the Seventeenth and Eighteenth Centuries: Continuity and Change', p. 23.

35 Ibid.

In fact, study of the tacks granted in Strathspey in the late seventeenth century reveals no specific mention of services other than to, 'accompany and convey the said Ludovick and his servants personallie in his hostings and huntings'.[36] This labour service was the subject of litigation on 13 February 1696:

> The said day Johne Frazer in Achnahannet unlawed in twentie pounds scotis because he did not send his sone Hugh Frazer south with the Lared of Grant and my ladie at the last journey conforme to the list of men appoyntit for thet effect and charge given thereupone and because the said Hugh being present at court could give noe defence save that his father sent ane other man whilk defence is repelled be the judge because he did not tak hi selff off the lairds hand.[37]

Ludovick Grant travelled with an entourage of clansmen, probably as protection on the road especially when traversing the lawless passes to the south, but undoubtedly also for prestige.[38] This case clearly demonstrates how onerous labour services could be for tenants of the Grant family; undertaking long and time-consuming journeys on behalf of their master. It is easy to appreciate the difficulty the Grants would have had in enforcing these services without the threat of legal action in their court.

The main function of the regality court in relation to labour services was advertisement rather than the punishment of non-performing tenants. The service known locally as the 'bailie darracks', a labour service for the benefit of the bailie or laird, was the exception to this rule and punishment for failing to perform this service features several times in the court records.[39] William Mackintosh of Borlum, a tacksman in the neighbouring regality of Gordon in Badenoch summed up what he felt to be the relationship between estate officials and commoners in the Highlands: 'To the great misfortune of these poor people, they are the property of Bailiffs and Chamberlains ... by grinding the faces of your poor tenants with double the service your noble souls would allow'.[40] This labour service is mentioned in the commission of

36 NRS, Tack of Kylintra 1675, GD248/533/5, fo. 19.

37 Grant Court Book 1, 13/02/1696, p. 65.

38 Burt mentions chieftains being escorted thus several times in his letters. See for instance, *Burt's Letters*, p. 220.

39 "Darg", a day's work, nnown elsewhere as Bailie days or Bailie Work. DSL.

40 W Mackintosh, *An Essay on Ways and Means for Inclosing, Fallowing, Planting, etc. Scotland* (Edinburgh, 1729), p. xi. The preface of this book which as a plea to abolish services is addressed to Scottish members of Parliament. The laird of Grant is specifically named.

bailziary appointing Captain Alexander Grant of Grantsfield as bailie principal of the regality in 1723 as being one of the perquisites of the position of bailie.[41] However, in the commission the laird of Grant reserved to himself 'for my own use and desposal so much of the said bailie darraciks and so manie of the said herezals as I shall judge proper and convenient'. Hence, we can presume that the labour service, or conversion thereof, was shared between the laird and bailies of the regality. The first mention of the service to be found in the court records comes in December 1708:

> befor the right hono[ourab]ll Ludovick Grant of Grant sitting in judgement for ane regalitie court of Grant in respect of the disobedience of some persones within the lo[rdshi]p of Glencharnie to pay their bailie dalreges to his bailie of the said lo[rdshi]p tharfor the said Ludovick Grant hes enacted, statute and ordained that in tyme comeing whosoever shall refuse to pay ther bailie dereges as they shall be lyable yeirlie to pay for ilk sten partis deficiencie fourtie shilling scotis to be exacted yearlie be the said bailie by poynding.[42]

There was obviously resistance to the darracks as a labour service and a cash conversion as the court books record the names of nine people who refused to perform the service.[43] Ludovick Grant may have sat as bailie at this court to ensure that the money owed to him in respect of the darracks was received. This service is a clear example of control and authority being exerted through compulsory labour or taxation. Ludovick Grant was the ultimate embodiment of this authority; in the face of widespread non-performance his appearance was important.

Tenants failing to perform the service were fined £10. In addition, they had to pay the conversion or perform the service at a future date.[44] The bailie darracks were evidently valuable. As a result, the court book records that Colonel William Grant of Ballindalloch awarded the bailie darracks from the parish of Cromdale to Serjeant Alexander Jackson in Milltown in 1713 as consideration for services rendered.[45] The bailie darracks continued to be exacted after the abolition of the regality court and reverted back to being a labour service rather than a cash payment clearly due to the labour demanded by

41 Grant Court Book 5, 11/12/1723, p.3.
42 Grant Court Book 2, 21/12/1708, p. 118.
43 Grant Court Book 5, 30/07/1727, p. 117 and 05/07/1728, p. 149.
44 Grant Court Book 5, 05/07/1728, p.149.
45 Grant Court Book 3, 05/02/1713, p. 37.

improvement. In 1767 Elizabeth Cumming, relict of Donald Geddes in Upper Dellifure, was struggling financially. Her situation was worsened when her three horses strayed making it difficult to work her lands. She petitioned the laird 'as ane act of charity to allow and order for her the ballie darracks of the dauch of Dellaphour to harrow her land when called for'.[46]

Whilst most labour services were converted to cash payments by the eighteenth century in Strathspey, certain duties were indispensable to the Grants and men to fulfil these duties could only be found through compulsory labour service. Examples recorded in the court books include leading peats from the peat banks to the laird's stackyard at Castle Grant; leading timber and slates to repair the kirks at Cromdale and Advie; construction of dykes; and maintaining the mills.[47]

Perhaps the best example of the continuing need for compulsory manpower were the quasi military services of watching, warding, hosting, and hunting which demanded the personal attendance of vassals. There is much evidence of these services being enforced using the Grant family's baron and regality courts. The prestige of a lord in the eighteenth century continued to be linked directly to the number of fencible men he could raise. Large bodies of fencible men could only be levied through the terms of their land tenure. Franchise courts were essential for the advertisement of days when vassals were required to turn out for the host and to compel attendance by the threat of court action. The tinchel provides a good example of this as this method of hunting required hundreds of men. Hunting was a popular pastime of the landed classes providing an ideal opportunity to bring the leading men of the district together and indulge in a display of wealth and power.[48] Often hunts were given in honour of an esteemed guest. The Grant court records reveal that guests included the Duke of Gordon.

The services of watching and warding were also important features of life in Strathspey, to which the court records bear testimony. In the 1660s the Strathspey baron courts were frequently used to advertise, manage, and enforce service on the laird of Grant's watch. Private watches were a relatively common means adopted by land owners and burghs during this period for maintaining control over their locality.[49] The watches were a small armed band, numbering around fifty men in total, to which each davoch contributed

46 NRS, Baron Court Petitions, GD248/371/4, fo. 33.

47 NRS, Baron Court Extracts, GD248/76/2 fo. 51; Grant Court Book 3, 25/04/1711, p. 4; Grant Court Book 4, 02/06/1720, p. 34 and 13/05/1721, p. 56; Grant Court Book 5, 31/07/1729, p. 172.

48 Logan, *The Scottish Gael, or Celtic Manners*, vol. II, at 43.

49 Kennedy, *Governing Gaeldom*, p. 136.

one soldier: 'everie daughe is ordained to put out ane prettie man sufficientlye armed and the same to begin at the weastermost auchtenpart of ilk dauch or pay five pounds in lieu'.[50] These men went out on patrol at the same time that people went to the shielings. They would watch for a week before they were relieved by fresh men from their davochs.[51] Their main function was to protect the people and their stock at the outlying shielings by watching the marches of Strathspey for heirship and other unlawful activities.[52] Tenants were required to loan their best weapons to the watch in addition to paying for and provisioning the soldiers who were watching for their benefit:[53]

> Patrick Grant in Gorton hes obliesht himselff to provyd elevin sufficient soldiers and to watch with them the sheallings of Cromdell and Inverallan and to goe out with thame on Fryday nixt the twantie eight day of this instant Sept[embe]r and to watch for the space of eight weikes for the whilk the gentlemen, tenents of Cromdell and Inverallan are ordained to pay to him and his soldiers half ane boll of meall and eight merks of money, ane firlot of meall and two merks to the captain and two peks of meal and one merk weeklye to ilk soldier … the people of Inverallan are ordained to meit at Ballintomb on Thursday 28 of Sept[embe]r to pay ffyfteen days pay[men]t together, the people beneath the Spey in Cromdell are ordained pay[men]t at Ballachastel … and the people of the baronie of Cromdell are ordained … at the Boatman his house.[54]

Presumably, livestock thieves who were apprehended by the watch were brought before the laird of Grant's court, although there are no examples where the capture of thieves is attributed to the watch. The last year that the watch is mentioned in the court records is 1670;[55] however, the Seafield records reveal that watches were still being organised by the estate's chamberlain in the first decades of the eighteenth century, as in May 1717, Alexander Grant of Lethendrie, chamberlain, wrote to Alexander Grant of Grant in London mentioning to him that it might soon be necessary to send out a watch to guard the

50 NRS, Baron Court Extracts, GD248/76/2, fo. 62.

51 NRS, Baron Court Extracts, GD248/76/2, fo. 40.

52 There was a proposal for a Highland wide network of such watched to curb lawlessness. Kennedy, *Governing Gaeldom* p. 135.

53 NRS, Baron Court Extracts, GD248/76/2, fo. 40.

54 Ibid, fo. 65.

55 Ibid, fo. 72.

frontiers.[56] The court records for most of 1717 do not survive, so it is unknown whether any enactments to this effect were made in the regality court. The existence of this letter is especially interesting as watching was abolished by parliament in 1717 following the 1715 uprising.[57] Whether the watches were still regularly going out at this point is unclear; however, their absence from court records may suggest that cattle thievery was not as great a problem as it had been in half-a-century earlier.

The final time that the regality court is known to have raised the fencible men of the regality for the service of the laird was on 18 January 1700, when an act of court was issued requiring the men of Glenchernick to give service 'anent the credit and honour of the countrey' by serving under a clan commander and to 'remaine and abide with him in all trabell and la[wfu]ll undertakings and not retreat till the comander please to give libertie' when chasing and apprehending cattle thieves.[58] The commander was given the power to poind the best stock of any men who through cowardice or otherwise deserted. This was a much more forceful incentive than the £5 fines which the clan captains of the ordinary watches were empowered to uplift. Much local and clan tradition recalls the perils and glories of the expeditions such as that advertised on 18 January 1700. It is easy to see how such quasi-military duties as enforced by the court could lead to claims that heritable jurisdictions helped to underpin the clan system and Jacobite rebellions in the Highlands. With the Grants being a pro-Hanoverian clan, no light is cast on the validity of these claims; however, we can say that defence and lordly prestige were the main motivations for calling out the fencible men of the regality.

Whilst we have seen examples of soldiers being raised for defence of property and there is also evidence of the court being used to hold wapinschaws,[59] there is only one example of the court being used to raise troops for military service. This entry comes in January 1716, when four men from each davoch in Abernethy were 'outrigged'[60] to Inverness upon 'his majesties service', and provisions were made to cover their absence:

> It is statute enacted by the said bailie that since there is ane man listed out of each twa aughtenparts that dureing ther stay from home that the

56 NRS, Letter from Alexander Grant of Lethendrie to Alexander Grant of Grant, GD248/18/4/41.

57 1 Geo. 1. St. 2. c. 54.

58 Grant Court book 1, 18/01/1700, p. 146.

59 NRS, List of Fencible Tenants, GD248/38/2, 26/04/1705.

60 "Outriging", supplying or fitting out for military service. *DSL*.

> aughten part that does not outrig the man shall uphold the work of the tenant listed out of the other aughten part per vices and day about under the failie of ane shilling stent for ilk dayes deficiency and ilk malender and servant that goes out as listed shall have to pay from the possessors of the 2 aughten partes they go out for two shilling scotis or ane hadish[61] meal ilk day he is from home in this expeditione.[62]

The Grant force raised in this way was sent to help garrison Inverness. The town had just been taken from the Jacobites after the siege of November 1715, in which the Grants also played their part. Perhaps in retaliation for the small role that the clan Grant played in both 1715 and 1745 rebellions inhabitants of the regality suffered depredations at the hands of both rebel and government troops. Regality courts were convened in 1716 and 1747 to hear the complaints of vassals who had suffered due to the actions of soldiers in the area.[63]

8.3 Conclusion

At the heart of the relationship between the inhabitants of the regality and the regality court was the land owned by the Grant family and inhabited by their vassals and dependants. The court was the key institution in the management of this land and all aspects of the tenancies of the men and women residing there. Of particular importance amongst these records are cases which demonstrate the attention paid to proper process and legality by the regality's bailies. These reveal that franchise courts had high procedural standards which may have helped to enhance their legitimacy. Those in the regality who were aware of legal process were adept at manipulating these procedures to their advantage. Examples like the action of removal against Donald Glass in 1712, where failure by a court officer to observe procedure provided Glass with the means to have the case against him dismissed are important in demonstrating that the court was able to work to the advantage of tenants. This turns on its head the perception of regality courts as tools of the landowner to oppress vassals. It is reasonable to assume that when these functions were transferred to the sheriff court in 1748, it was a huge inconvenience to both laird and tenants.

---

61 "Hadish", measure of grain equal to 1/3 or ¼ of a peck, *DSL*.

62 Grant Court Book 3, 19/01/1716, p. 91.

63 NRS, Baron Court of Urquhart, GD248/68/6, 23/01/1747; NRS, Grant Charters, GD248/18/6/22/7, 01/06/1716.

Those residing in the regality were required to render labour services or taxes in lieu to their superiors. Of these, few appear in the pages of the court records. This is in contrast to what has been written about other jurisdictions.[64] However, of those that do appear several are of significance to this study. The services of watching, warding, hosting and hunting appear in the court records before disappearing in the early years of the eighteenth century. These disappearances suggest that life in Strathspey was becoming less militaristic, as conditions in the region became more peaceful and the military aspects of clan life gradually disappeared. On the other hand, fleeting references made to the Grants' armed watch in a letter in 1717 reveal that some practices which were previously the subject of management by the court, continued in practice but ceased to be regulated by the court.[65] The survival of the military aspect of clan life in Strathspey until after the 1715 rebellion must have been an important outlet for both tacksmen and commoners to exercise traditional military functions. It also suggests that criticisms of the heritable jurisdictions as conduits for raising troops were misplaced but not necessarily entirely without foundation.

64 Dodgshon, *Land and Society in Early Scotland*, p.249.

65 NRS, Papers of Alexander Grant of Grant, GD248/18/4/41. 18/05/1717.

CHAPTER 9

Conclusion

In 1794, the reverend John Grant's account of the state of the parish of Abernethy was published in the OSA. He concluded his description of life in his parish with praise for the Heritable Jurisdictions Act,

> To increase our gratitude for the protection afforded by our constitution to the lives and properties of individuals in these countries at present, we will mention the blessings we enjoy by the ["]abolition of the jurisdiction["] act in 1748.[1]

If the stories that the minister of Abernethy had heard were true, he had good reason to be grateful. In his entry in the OSA he relates several stories about the fearsome bailies of the regality. According to him one of these bailies, named James Grant, 'drowned two men in sacks ... and endeavoured to compel a man from Glenmore, in the barony of Kincardine to assist him and the executioners he had with him in the business; which the man refusing to do, the bailie said to him, if you was in my regality, I would teach you better manners than to disobey my commands'.[2] In another tale one of the bailies 'became so odious that the country people drowned him in the Spey'.[3] Not unnaturally after hearing stories such as these, John Grant was certain that the current prosperity of his flock was largely thanks to the freedom from abuses and arbitrary justice afforded by the Heritable Jurisdictions Act.

Unfortunately, like much of what has subsequently been written by historians about heritable justice in Scotland, the reverend John Grant's observations are based upon local lore and assumptions rather than first-hand eyewitness accounts or documentary evidence. It is largely upon claims such as these that the story of Scotland's franchise courts has been written. A modern abhorrence to the notion of heritable justice, one where landowners were motivated to do justice by the fine money ingathered, has made it easier to accept the popular image of Scottish franchise courts. In addition, some historians continue to believe the Whig-propaganda of the eighteenth century that heritable jurisdictions were an important aid to the Jacobite cause in Scotland. However,

1 Sinclair, *The Statistical Account of Scotland*, Vol. XIII, p. 150.

2 Ibid, p. 151.

3 Ibid.

 | DOI:10.1163/9789004472549_010

considering the records left by the regality court of Grant it is possible to dispute these claims. The courts of barony and regality in Strathspey were part of a vibrant local legal culture; these courts were well patronised and part of the fabric of the local community.

9.1 Justice, Society, and Heritable Jurisdictions

Life was hard in Strathspey during the late seventeenth and early eighteenth centuries, a period beset by economic and climatic downturns, not to mention recurrent political turmoil. Such factors severely tested the inhabitants of Strathspey, many of whom were eking out what can at best be termed a subsistence living from the land. The chiefs of Grant appear to have been reasonably beneficent landowners. They evidently aspired to fulfil the role of paternalistic superiors and the provision of justice was integral to this function. On the other hand, the regality and baron courts of the Grant lairds contributed to the difficulties experienced by the peasantry, especially when we think in terms of the degree of control that was exercised by the gentry, kirk and landowners over aspects of these people's lives through mechanisms of social control such as wage controls, compulsory labour services, judicial interrogations and the threat of censure by the kirk sessions. Controls such as these were accepted features of life throughout Scotland. By the eighteenth century strict social controls could have been maintained without heritable jurisdictions, through resort to the sheriff court and J.P.s. However, enforcement would undoubtedly have been more difficult for landowners without jurisdiction.

For those with greater social status, such as the gentry of clan Grant, the regality court was integral to the reinforcement of social stratification. Tacksmen and wadsetters could demonstrate their social standing by obtaining offices in the court, principally that of a bailie. At a lesser level even the act of standing caution for a subtenant was a social statement. Whilst these acts were notionally done for the benefit of the common weal, the regality court was vital for the protection of their own property rights and controlling their own followers; vested interests such as these ensured the provision of justice. Attending court sessions assured gentlemen of the opportunity to participate in the governance of the community, by voting on acts of court on economic regulations and sitting on assizes. In this way the gentry of Strathspey played an active role in a local legal, political, and economic jurisdiction and exerted real influence on the local stage.

The regality and baron courts offered legal protections for all members of rural society. Importantly, this meant that even the peasantry, including unmarried women and landless servants, had access to local justice. Evidence in the court records show that people were adept at making the best advantages of the opportunities presented to them. In practice this meant that vassals of the regality were not only able to seek redress in legal actions against their peers, such as in cases of assault or debt, but also their social superiors such as tacksmen and representatives of the Grant lairds, for instance, by challenging the legality of procedures. Mitchison's assertion that 'There would be no guarantee of good justice so long as the Heritable Jurisdictions survived' is clearly not reflective of the situation in Strathspey.[4] As one of the few means available for protecting their rights, it is perhaps no wonder that people generally appear to have had a much greater familiarity with the legal system than is true when we consider their modern-day counterparts. The continuing patronage of the laird of Grant's baron court after 1748 confirms that the courts were a useful local service offering important legal safeguards.

The findings of this book regarding heritable justice and society have wider European significance. As local heritable justice has traditionally been regarded as being in decline during the seventeenth and eighteenth centuries historians have seen little reason to study it, instead focussing on growth at the centre.[5] The parallels with recent research in France, Germany and Sweden suggest a shared pan-European experience of patrimonial jurisdictions in rural areas across diverse and varied parts of western Europe. Further consideration of local court records in other jurisdictions is needed if we are fully to understand their role in the management of European society.[6] Closer to home there are also important implications for English scholarship, especially concerning popular engagement with the legal system. English historians such as Brooks, Wood, Muldrew and Harrison have also emphasised that there is evidence of greater skill and awareness amongst the lower orders than is often recognised by historians; the Grant records also bear testimony to this.[7] These same English historians also suggest that heritable and other local jurisdictions were

4 Mitchison, 'The Government and the Highlands, 1707 – 1745', p. 44.

5 C Harrison, 'Manor Courts and the Governance of Tudor England', in C W Brooks and M Loban (eds.), *Communities and Courts in Britain, 1150–1900* (London, 1997), p. 45.

6 H Pihlajamak, 'On forgotten jurisdictional complexities: The case of early-modern Sweden' in S P Donlan and D Heirbaut (eds.), *The Laws many bodies: Studies in Legal Hybridity and Jurisdictional Complexity, c. 1600–1900* (Berlin, 2015).

7 C W Brooks, *Law, Politics and Society in Early Modern England* (Cambridge, 2010); C Muldrew, 'Rural Credit, Market Areas and Legal Institutions in the Countryside in England, 1550–1700', in C W Brooks and M Loban (eds.), *Communities and Courts in Britain, 1150–1900* (London, 1997); Harrison, 'Manor Courts and the Governance of Tudor England'; A Wood, *The Politics of Social Conflict: The Peak Country, 1520–1770* (Cambridge, 1999).

cultural, fiscal and social institutions alongside being bodies for administering law and order and that they were thus central to the government of England. The regality of Grant records show the same to be true in the Highlands of Scotland, suggesting that the socio-political role of local jurisdictions should be re-evaluated both north and south of the border.

9.2 Jurisdiction

The jurisdiction of regality courts has often been debated by historians.[8] Indeed, even during the time of the regality courts, lawyers such as Mackenzie and Stair could not agree on the exact extent of the jurisdiction bestowed upon lords of regality.[9] However, it is now possible to say that, in Strathspey, there was little difference between the baron courts held by the Grants in the mid-seventeenth century and the new regality court that the Grants were awarded in 1694. This is especially true when we take into account the commissions of justiciary the Grants received in the seventeenth century. This sense of *plus ça change* is reinforced by there being no mention of the new regality in the Grant muniments until 1700, six years after the charter for the regality was granted by the King. Whilst Ludovick Grant seized the opportunity to change his designation from Grant of Freuchie to Grant of Grant immediately in 1694, there was no mention of the new jurisdiction in letters or estate records, suggesting that prestige may have been more important to him than the enhanced jurisdiction.

The divergence between the theoretical powers bestowed upon the Grants and the practical realities of administering justice is also evident when we consider the geographical extent of the regality of Grant. In practice this proved to be fluid: several of the lands which fell under the jurisdiction of the court in practice, such as the Lordship of Abernethy, were never legally part of the regality as they weren't included in the charter of erection. Similar jurisdictional anomalies must have been common throughout Scotland. With land often changing hands it was impractical for jurisdiction and land holders to seek re-grants of jurisdiction from the crown for every property transaction that took place. Nonetheless, it is indicative of a relaxed or pragmatic attitude to jurisdiction amongst landowners, far removed from the precision we often expect from the legal system, and which the regality court itself displayed in its handling of day to day procedure.

8 Goodare, *The Government of Scotland*, pp. 184–5.

9 Mackenzie, *The Laws and Customs of Scotland*, pp. 402–3; Stair, *Institutions of the Law of Scotland*, ii, iii, 63–65, pp. 386–7 and iv, xxxvii, iv, p. 944.

In many respects the regality of Grant fell short of exercising the jurisdiction of a full regality. In the years following the ratification of the regality in 1696, the court often convened as a baron court rather than a regality court. In fact, initially the designation regality was only used when the court was entertaining serious pleas. Such was the retrenchment in the local community that fifteen years after the erection of the regality the vassals of the laird still called the laird's court the 'baron court' when questioned in precognitions for a case in the justiciary court in Edinburgh.[10] In 1719 the lord of the regality, Brigadier Alexander Grant of Grant himself, referred to his jurisdiction as 'the barony'.[11] Other examples exist, for instance, in the charter of erection the lords of the regality were endowed with the right to chapel and chancellery. However, in practice, whilst the court did retour heirs it did not issue its own brieves from a regality chapel, instead obtaining them from the chapel royal.[12]

Other aspects of the regality's jurisdiction were exercised more fully, and perhaps even more so than traditional histories of the franchise courts would have us believe. An example of this is the right to repledge panels, ordinarily resident within the regality, accused of crimes from other courts where they were being tried. The laird of Grant most famously attempted this in 1700, when he attempted to repledge one of his musicians named Patrick Brown from the Sheriff court in Banff. The Grant estate accounts suggest that attempts at repledging were made as late as 1719.[13] However, these are exceptions and in general the assertion made by Goodare that the jurisdiction of regalities was much restricted in practice and 'in most respects it [the regality court] acted as an ordinary baron court' seems to be true.[14] Nonetheless, it should be emphasised that Grant's baron courts were powerful institutions in their own right, that handed down the death penalty, in contrast to the regality of Falkirk cited by Goodare. From this it might also be possible to say that the theoretical powers of jurisdiction holders mattered less in practice than the local circumstances which shaped procedures in each jurisdiction. We should thus be aware of potential great regional variations in practice when interpreting the records left by the regality court of Grant.

10 NRS, Minutes of the High Court of Justiciary, JC7/5/231.

11 NRS, Letter regarding arbitration between Grant younger and Grant elder, GD248/22/6, fo. 5.

12 Grant Court Book 5, 15/07/1726, p. 98.

13 NRS, Estate Accounts, GD248/113/7, fo. 9.

14 Goodare, *The Government of Scotland*, p. 185.

9.3 Heritable Justice after 1748

Bruce Lenman and Geoffrey Parker asserted in 1980 that 'for half a century before 1747 the feudal courts had been losing their grip. Their records show a steadily decreasing amount of business, and more and more interference by the central courts'.[15] Evidence from the regality of Grant suggests a different picture with an increasing number of court days in the regality court and new types of business appearing before it. Clearly such jurisdictions still had a role to play in isolated rural communities such as Strathspey, which were a day's travel from the nearest sheriff courts and several days travel from the central courts in Edinburgh. The courts of barony and regality were probably as important socially, culturally, and economically as they were for the administration of the law in these places.

The regality court was still well suited to the type of society present in Strathspey throughout most of the eighteenth century: one which had a largely non-transient population, was reliant upon cooperative methods of agriculture and with land ownership concentrated in one individual. For this reason, the Grants continued actively to exercise their right to convene baron courts upon their lands after 23 March 1748. Unfortunately, besides a few isolated pages, no court books from this period survive; however, the numerous petitions and court extracts from the Seafield muniments in the latter half of the eighteenth century show that the newly coined 'Baron Court of Strathspey' was primarily a small claims court used by tenants seeking payment for small debts known as 'sundries'. The court was clearly still well patronised by Strathspey-folk for this purpose. In many of these cases tenants sought restitution as a primary remedy. McIntyre's claim that 'it became increasingly evident, however, that they [heritable jurisdictions] had long outlived their usefulness'[16] is seriously questioned by evidence from Strathspey following 1748.

Several of the cases determined by the baron bailies went beyond the limits of the jurisdictional restrictions placed upon baron courts by the 1747 act. Mostly this meant that the civil pleas entertained by the bailies were worth more than 40 shillings sterling.[17] For instance, at a court held in Grantown on 14 January 1782 Archibald McIntosh in Congash sued James Falconer in Grantown for payment of a debt worth £2,2,11, whilst at a subsequent court held four days later James Grant in Rinrory sued a former subtenant for payment of

15 Lenman and Parker, 'Crime and Control in Scotland', p. 17.

16 McIntyre, 'The Franchise Courts', p. 362.

17 NRS, McIntosh v. Falconer, GD248/372/2, 14/01/1782; NRS, Grant in Rinrory v. Grant in Achvocky, GD248/372/2, 18/01/1782.

a rent arrears worth £2, 5, 5. Such petitions were only just beyond the limit of the court's jurisdiction, but this did not prevent James McAndrew, miller in Tulloch from complaining to the court of session in 1793, when a decree was issued by the baron court requiring him to pay a debt owed to his former tacksman Robert Lawson of Bellimore.[18] He argued that the decree should be deemed void because 'Barron Baillies have no power to pronounce decreets for civil debts'. Whilst the sum sued for by the tacksman was £2, 3, 2., the bailie John Grant of Kinchurdy, restricted the claim awarded to £1, 6, 9., within the jurisdiction of baron courts. The opinion of the lords of session on the matter is unrecorded.

Lawson of Bellimore's case against his former sub-tenant McAndrew was heard at an afternoon sederunt of a baron court held in Grantown by John Grant of Kinchurdy, the baron bailie. Lawson had sought payment of the debt before a justice of the peace court held in Grantown earlier on the same day. Before the justices his claim had failed. Therefore, he decided to try again in the other local jurisdiction available to him, the baron court. That the baron bailie found in his favour whilst the J.P. did not, is especially surprising given that the same man held both offices.[19] This tells us several things about heritable justice in Strathspey after 1748. Firstly, the tacksmen managed to side-step the possible pitfalls of the 1747 act with much of their judicial authority intact by taking commissions as J.P.s. The disappearance of the bailies of the regality also meant that families who had never received commissions from the Grants of Grant now had an opportunity to undertake meaningful judicial work. For the tenants of the barony, particularly those with frequent small claims such as the growing merchant class in the new town of Grantown, there were now more opportunities than ever to take advantage of overlapping jurisdictions in the region, as is made clear by Lawson's success before the baron court.

In many respects the J.P. courts, alongside the baron court, assumed the mantle left by the regality court of Grant. The J.P.s could convene courts wherever they saw fit, meaning that justice continued to go to the people. They even began to receive references, alongside mentions of the baron courts, in tacks set to Grant tenants:

> that you [the tenant] and your forsaids shall furnish a sufficient man when required by the Baillie, the Chamberlain, a Justice of the Peace, or Constable, for watching and guarding the town and assist in keeping

---

18 NRS, The Baron Court of Strathspey, GD248/533/5/2, fo. 54.

19 Kinchurdy's great, great, grandfather was John Grant, 6th Laird of Freuchie. He was married to one of the daughters of Robert Grant of Lurg.

> peace and good order therein, and give suit and presence in my Baron Courts to be holden in said town of Grantown, when and as often as you shall be required thereto, and submit to and obey all acts and regulations made or to be made by the Baillie, or Justices for the good and police of said town.[20]

With all the known baron bailies also being J.P.s the jurisdictions of baron and J.P. were complementary rather than competitive. Thus, the two jurisdictions cooperated over matters such as the prosecution of a wood thief in 1757.[21] Whilst the court which tried the theft in this case was a baron court, the thief was incarcerated in the tolbooth in Elgin.

There is further evidence that people continued to petition the baron court regarding thefts after 1748, although this part of the baron's jurisdiction was restricted to cases warranting fines of less than 20s only.[22] Thus, in 1783 a resident in Grantown petitioned the baron bailie over the theft of stockings from her yard in the town; whilst another petitioner in the same year sought restitution for sheep that he alleged had been stolen by Grant tenants in Derraid.[23] There is no record of how the bailie handled these petitions; nonetheless, that tenants continued to view the baron court as a viable forum for resolution of these disputes is in itself revealing. With the baron bailie also being a J.P., the petition was likely to end up in the correct jurisdiction regardless of which jurisdiction the petition was addressed to. One of the main problems with the provision of J.P. courts in Inverness-shire and Moray following 1748 was the scarcity of J.P.s who were in a fit state to sit. A petition addressed to the Lord Justice Clerk in 1767 from the laird of Grant craving that more J.P.s be appointed in these counties emphasises this issue.[24] As a result the baron court of Strathspey remained important. With most small civil cases going to the baron court pressure was taken off the J.P.s.

Besides small claims, the baron court also regularly heard disputes about poindings, muir burn, poaching, wood cutting, boundaries and grazing. In addition, many pleas which might previously have been heard by the regality court found their way directly to the laird who was expected to dispense a kind of equitable justice. Margaret Grant, a tenant in Uchtogorm, petitioned Sir James Grant of Grant in 1789 complaining of poor neighbourhood in her township.[25]

---

20 NRS, Tack of land in Grantown to James Grant alias McPhater in 1792, GD248/533/1/2.

21 NRS, Court Pages, GD248/24/2, fo. 2.

22 17 Geo II. c.43.

23 NRS, Baron Court Petitions, GD248/372/3.

24 NRS, Tenant Petitions, GD248/371/4, fo. 37.

25 NRS, Baron Court Petitions, GD248/372/6. No fo. numbers.

A dispute with her neighbours had led to her neighbours killing seven of her poultry, the dead birds being left at her door. Margaret closed her petition as follows: 'may it therefore please your honour to direct that an enquiry may be made into this matter and if it is found that there is a just cause of complaint that your petitioner's grievance may be redressed as may be just and equitable'. The provision of justice continued to be perceived as one of the duties of the chief and landlord. Yet the lairds of Grant had long since ceased to be personally associated with their franchise jurisdiction. Margaret Grant's petition is clearly of a type which might formerly have been addressed to the regality. Her neighbour, Donald Grant in Achnarrowbeg, lodged a counter petition with the J.P.s complaining of the actions of Margaret.[26] Clearly the equitable justice of the laird was perceived as running concurrently to the jurisdiction of the J.P.s and baron courts.

The personal justice of the laird stretched beyond settling estate matters and pleas for clemency in rent payments. In 1766 Sir Ludovick Grant of Grant and his son James Grant received a petition from William Grant in Dell of Abernethy alleging that his twelve-year-old daughter had been raped by Alexander Fraser in Ryduack.[27] The petitioner craved that the lairds in their role as J.P.s appoint constables to apprehend and incarcerate Fraser before he was able to take flight. The laird and his son duly ordered constables to be dispatched in search of Fraser. This is a very rare example of a petition being personally addressed to the lairds recognising their role as J.P.s. Ordinarily petitions were addressed to men such as Grant of Tullochgorum or Grant of Ballintomb who regularly presided over J.P. courts. Once again, we find that the personal authority of the laird carried special significance to the tenants and clansmen of Strathspey. Paternalistic expectations of the landowner endured. Landowners' appointments as J.P.s are perhaps best appreciated as an official recognition of this expectation. Although in this case, William Grant the petitioner at least observed the new jurisdictional realities imposed by the Heritable Jurisdictions Act, by ignoring them, the case of Margaret Grant in Uchtubeg is a more significant display of faith in lordly jurisdiction.

Whilst the baron court of Strathspey undoubtedly continued to provide a valuable service to the inhabitants of Strathspey, it is questionable whether a regality court with a higher jurisdiction could have remained relevant for long into the nineteenth century given the changes that rural society in the region was undergoing from the late eighteenth century onwards. The baron court of

26 Ibid.

27 NRS, Tenant Petitions, GD248/371/4, fo. 26.

Strathspey continued to meet until at least the late 1790s when the reverend John Grant, minister of Abernethy was collecting his stories for the OSA. It is unfortunate that he did not realise that the baron court meeting in his parish at that time was essentially the same as the regality court which had been abolished fifty years earlier.

Bibliography

1 Archives and Manuscripts

Highland Archive (HA)

CH2/437, Presbytery of Abernethy Minutes
CH2/983, Kirk Session of Cromdale Minutes
CH2/1054, Kirk Session of Abernethy Minutes

National Records of Scotland (NRS)

GD44 – Gordon Castle Muniments, Duke of Gordon
GD80 – MacPherson of Cluny Papers
GD248 – Seafield Muniments, Earl of Seafield
CC – Commissary Court Records
CS – Court of Session Papers
CS4 – Court of Session, Warrants of the Books of Sederunt.
E70 – Poll tax records
JC7/5 – Minutes of the High Court of Justiciary
JC10/2 – Minutes of the Northern Circuit 1671
JC10/5 – Minutes of the Northern Circuit 1701–2
JC11/1-17 – Minutes of the Northern Circuit of the High Court of Justiciary
PCA – Privy Council Acta
RD – Register of Deeds
RH2/8/96, 'The Knock Notebook'
RH11/27/28-40, Regality Court of Dunfermline
RH11/28/10, Regality Court of Dunkeld
RH11/34/1-5 – Regality Court of Grant
RH11/40/4, Regality Court of Huntly

2 Printed Primary Sources

Anderson P, *The Copie of a Barons Court, newly translated by whats-you-call-him, clerk to the same* (Edinburgh, 1680).

Anon, *An ample disquisition into the nature of Regalities and other Heritable Jurisdictions, in that part of Great Britain called Scotland, As now under the consideration of Parliament* (London, 1747).

Anon, *An enquiry into the causes of the late rebellion and the proper methods for preventing the like misfortune for the future* (London, 1746).

Bankton, A MacDowall Lord, *An Institute of the Laws of Scotland in Civil Rights: with observations upon the agreements or diversity between them and the laws of England* (Stair Society, 1993–5).

Bell R, *A Dictionary of the Law of Scotland* (Edinburgh, 1826).

Barron D R (ed.), *Baron Court Book of Urie* (SHS, 1892).

Black R (ed.), *To the Hebrides; Samuel Johnson's Journey to the Western Islands of Scotland and James Boswell's Journal of a Tour of the Hebrides* (Edinburgh, 2007).

Brown K M et al (eds.), *The Records of the Parliaments of Scotland to 1707* (St Andrews, 2007–2017).

Burton J H et al (eds.), *Register of the Privy Council of Scotland [1545–1691]*', 16 volumes (Edinburgh, 1877–1970).

Cramond W, *The Court Books of the Regality of Grant: A True Statement of their Contents* (Banff, 1897).

Dickinson W C, *Court Book of the Barony of Carnwath* (SHS, 1937).

Erskine J, *An Institute of the Law of Scotland* (Edinburgh 1773).

Gordon J (ed.), *The Second Statistical Account of Scotland*, vol. xiii and vol. xiv (Edinburgh, 1845).

Gunn G (ed.), *Records of the Baron Court of Stitchill* (SHS, 1905).

Hamilton H (ed.), *Selections from the Monymusk Papers, 1713–1755* (SHS, 1945).

Hannay R K (ed.), Acts of the Lords of Council in Public Affairs, 1501–54 (Edinburgh, 1932).

Hindley C (ed.), *Works of John Taylor; the water poet* (London, 1872).

Hunter D M (ed.), *Court Books of the Barony and Regality of Falkirk and Callendar*, 1638–1656 (Edinburgh, 1991).

Littlejohn D (ed.), *Records of the Sheriff Court of Aberdeenshire*, Vol III (Aberdeen, 1841).

The Lords of Session, *Copy of the Report and Certificate Made to his Majesty in his Privy Council, Pursuant to the Act of Parliament ... for taking away and abolishing the Heritable Jurisdictions* (Edinburgh, 1748).

Mackenzie G, *The Institutions of the Law of Scotland* (Edinburgh, 1730).

Mackenzie G, *The Laws and Customs of Scotland: in matters criminal: Wherein is to be seen how the civil law, and the laws and customs of other nations doth agree with, and supply ours* (Edinburgh, 1678).

Mackenzie G, *Observations on the acts of Parliament, made by King James the First, King James the Second, King James the Third, King James the Fourth, King James the Fifth, Queen Mary, King James the Sixth, King Charles the First, King Charles the Second: wherein 1. It is observ'd if they be in desuetude, abrogated, limited, or enlarged, 2. The decisions relating to these acts are mention'd, 3. Some new doubts not yet decided are hinted at, 4. Parallel citations from the civil, canon, feudal and municipal laws, and the laws of other nations are adduc'd for clearing these statute* (Edinburgh, 1686).

Cartwright J J (ed.), *Report on the Manuscripts of his Grace the Duke of Portland*, Vol. V (Historical Manuscripts Commission, 1904).

Logan W, *A View of the Present State of Scotland in Regard to the Tenures and Slavish Dependencies of the Subjects of that Part of North Britain* (London, 1733).

Mackintosh W, *An Essay on Ways and Means for Inclosing, Fallowing, Planting, etc. Scotland* (Edinburgh, 1729).

Malcolm C A(ed.), *Minutes of the Justices of the Peace in the Shire of Lanarkshire 1707–1725* (Edinburgh, 1931).

Pennant T, *A Tour in Scotland, and Voyage to the Hebrides, 1772* (Cambridge 2014).

Romanes C S(ed.), *Selections from the Records of the Regality of Melrose 1605–1661*, Vol I (SHS, 1914); *Selections from the Records of the Regality of Melrose 1662–1676*, Vol II (SHS, 1915); *Selections from the Records of the Regality of Melrose 1547–1706*, Vol III (SHS, 1917).

Scott H (ed.), *Fasti Ecclesiae Scoticanae*, Vol VI (Edinburgh, 1926).

Simmons A (ed.), *Burt's Letters from the North of Scotland* (Edinburgh, 1998).

Sinclair J (ed.), *The Statistical Account of Scotland*, Abernethy and Kinchardine, Inverness, Vol. XIII (Edinburgh, 1794).

Sommerville J P (ed.), *King James VI and I: Political Writings* (Cambridge, 1995).

Stair, J Dalrymple, *The institutions of the law of Scotland: deduced from its originals, and collated with the civil, canon and feudal laws, and with the customs of neighbouring nations in iv books* (Edinburgh, 1693).

Stuart J (ed.), 'Process against the Egyptians at Banff 1700', *Miscellany of the Spalding Club* Vol III (Aberdeen, 1843).

Stuart J (ed.), 'Records of the Regality of Spynie', *Miscellany of the Spalding Club*, Vol. II (Aberdeen, 1842).

Taylor J, *The pennyles pilgrimage or The money-lesse perambulation of John Taylor, alias the Kings Majesties water-poet. How he travailed on foot from London to Edenborough in Scotland not carrying any money to or fro* (London, 1618).

3 Session Cases

Defences and Objections for His Majesties Advocate in behalf of the Crown v. The Claims of Sir Ludovick Grant of Grant.

Dunbar of Westfield v. Grant of that Ilk, (1697) 4 Bro. Sup. 386.

4 Printed Secondary Sources

Bardgett F D, 'The Monifieth Kirk Register', *Records of the Scottish Church History Society*, 23 (1987–9), pp. 174–195.

Barrett J R, *The Making of a Scottish Landscape: Moray's Regular Revolution 1760–1840* (Croydon, 2015).

Blum J, 'The Internal Structure and Polity of the European Village Community, *The Journal of Modern History*, 43 (1971), pp.542–57.

Brooks C W, *Law, Politics and Society in Early Modern England* (Cambridge, 2008).

Brown K M, *Bloodfeud in Scotland: 1573–1625* (Edinburgh, 1986).

Brown K M, *Noble Society in Scotland* (Edinburgh, 2000).

K M Brown, *Noble Power in Scotland from the Reformation to the Revolution* (Edinburgh, 2011).

Cairns J W, 'Historical Introduction', in K G C Reid and R Zimmermann (eds.), *A History of Private Law in Scotland*, Vol 1 (Oxford, 2000).

Cannon J, 'Labourers, Statute of' in, *The Oxford Companion to British History* (Oxford, 2009).

Carmichael E K, 'Jacobitism in the Scottish Commission of the Peace, 1707–1760', *SHR*, 58:1 (1979), pp. 58–69.

Cathcart A, *Kinship and Clientage: Highland Clanship, 1451–1609* (Leiden, 2006).

Chambers R, *History of the Rebellions in Scotland, Under the Viscount of Dundee and the Earl of Mar, in 1689 and 1715* (Edinburgh, 1829).

Cribhaugh A, "Local Justice and Rural Society in the French Revolution." *Journal of Social History* 34 (2000), pp. 327–50.

Cregeen E R, 'The Changing role of the House of Argyll in the Scottish Highlands', in N T Phillipson and R M Mitchison (eds.), *Scotland in the Age of Improvement: essays in Scottish history in the eighteenth century* (Edinburgh, 1970).

Cregeen E R, 'The tacksmen and their successors: a study of tenurial reorganisation in Mull, Morvern and Tiree in the early Eighteenth century', *Scottish Studies*, 13 (1969), pp. 93–144.

Cullen K J, *Famine in Scotland: The Ill Years of the 1690s* (Edinburgh, 2010).

Davidson N, *Discovering the Scottish Revolution 1692–1746* (London, 2003).

Davidson N, 'The Scottish path to capitalist agriculture: From the crisis of feudalism to the origins of agrarian transformation (1688–1746)', *Journal of Agrarian Change*, 4 (2004), pp. 227–268.

Davies S, 'Courts and the Scottish Legal System 1600–1747: the case of Stirlingshire', in V Gatrell, B Lenman and G Parker (eds.) *Crime and the Law: The Social History of Crime in Western Europe since 1500* (London, 1980).

Hart-Davis D, *The Monarchs of the Glen* (London, 1978).

Devine T M, *Clanship to Crofters' War: the social transformation of the Scottish Highlands* (Manchester, 1994).

Devine T M, *The Scottish Clearances. A History of the Dispossessed* (London, 2018).

Devine T M, *Clearance and Improvement: land, power and people in Scotland, 1700–1900* (Edinburgh, 2006).

Dickinson W C, 'The High Court of Justiciary', in *An Introduction to Scottish Legal History, The Stair Society,* 20 (1958), pp. 408–412.

Dickson W K, 'Heritable Jurisdictions', *JR*, 9 (1897), pp.428–444.

Dixon G A, 'Forestry in Strathspey in the 1760s', *Scottish Forestry*, 30:1 (1976), pp. 38–61.

Dixon G A, 'William Lorrmier on Forestry in the Central Highlands in the early 1760s', *Scottish Forestry*, 29:3 (1975), pp. 191–208.

Dodgshon R A, *From Chiefs to Landlords: Social and Economic Change in the Western Highlands and Islands, c. 1493–1820* (Edinburgh, 1998).

Dodgshon R A, *Land and Society in Early Scotland* (Oxford, 1981).

Dodghson R A, *No Stone Unturned: A History of Farming, Landscape and Environment in the Scottish Highlands and Islands* (Edinburgh, 2015)..

Dow F D, *Cromwellian Scotland 1650–1661* (Edinburgh, 1979).

Falconer J R D, *Crime and Community in Reformation Scotland: negotiating power in a burgh society* (London, 2013).

Fraser- Mackintosh C, 'The depopulation of Aberarder in Badenoch', *Celtic Magazine*, 2 (1877), pp. 418–426.

Emerson R L, *An Enlightened Duke; The Life of Archibald Campbell (1682–1761), Earl of Ilay, 3rd Duke of Argyll* (Kilcerran, 2013).

Ewan E, 'Women and Daily Life in Late-Medieval Scotland', in Y G Brown and R Ferguson (eds.), *Twisted Sisters: Women, Crime and Deviance in Scotland Since 1400* (East Linton, 2002).

Finlay J, *Legal Practice in Eighteenth Century Scotland* (Boston, 2015).

Findlay J, *All Manner of People; The History of the Justices of the Peace in Scotland* (Edinburgh, 2000).

Fletcher C, *Drawn from the Past: Voices from Dava Moor* (Grantown-on-Spey, 2021).

Forsyth W, *In the Shadow of Cairngorm* (Aviemore, 1999).

Foster W R, *The Church Before the Covenants; The Church of Scotland 1596–1638* (Edinburgh, 1975).

Fraser W, *The Chiefs of Grant* (Edinburgh, 1883).

Gaffney V, 'Summer Shealings', *SHR*, 38:1 (1959) pp. 20–35.

Garnot B, 'Une réhabilitation? Les justices seigneuriales dans la France du XVIIIe siècle', *Histoire, économie, et société*, 24:2 (2005), pp. 221–32.

Gasparini E, 'Justice seigneuriale et régulation sociale : l'exemple de quelques seigneuries comtoises dans la seconde moitié du xviiie siècle', in François Brizay, Antoine Follain, and Véronique Sarrazin, eds. *Les Justices de village: Administration et justice locales de la fin du Moyen Âge à la Révolution* (Rennes, 2002), pp.259–68.

Gibson A and Smout T C, *Prices, Food and Wages in Scotland, 1550–1780* (Cambridge, 1995).

Gilbert J M, *Hunting and Hunting reserves in Mediaeval Scotland* (Edinburgh, 1979).

Godfrey M, *Civil Justice in Renaissance Scotland: the Origins of a Central Court* (Leiden, 2009).

Goodare J, *The Government of Scotland 1560–1625* (Oxford, 2004).

Goodare J, *State and Society in Early Modern Scotland* (Oxford, 1999).

Gordon A, *Death is for the Living* (Edinburgh, 1984).

Grant A, 'Franchises North of the Border: Baronies and Regalities in Medieval Scotland', in M Prestwich (ed.), *Liberties and Identities in the Medieval British Isles* (Woodbridge, 2008).

Grant E, *Abernethy Forest, its people and its past* (Nethy Bridge, 1994).

Grant I F, *The Clan Grant: the development of a Clan* (Edinburgh, 1955).

Grant J, *Records of the County of Banff 1660–1760, One Hundred Years of County Government* (Aberdeen, 1922).

Hamilton- Grierson P J, 'Fencing the Court', *SHR*, 21:1 (1923), pp. 54–62.

Harrison C, 'Manor Courts and the Governance of Tudor England', in C W Brooks and M Loban (eds.), *Communities and Courts in Britain, 1150–1900* (London, 1997).

Harrison J G, '"Policing" the Stirling area, 1660–1706', *Scottish Archives*, 7 (2001), pp. 16–24.

Hayhoe J, *Enlightened Feudalism: Seigneurial Justice and Village Society in Eighteenth-Century Northern Burgundy* (Rochester, 2008).

Hill A, 'Decline and Survival in Scottish Witch-Hunting, 1701–1727', in J Goodare (ed.) *Scottish Witches and Witch-hunters* (London, 2013).

Hislop A, *The Book of Scottish Anecdote* (Edinburgh, 1874).

Hopkins P, *Glencoe and the end of the Highland War* (Edinburgh, 1998).

Houston R A, *Bride Ales and Penny Weddings: recreations, reciprocity and regions in Britain from the sixteenth to the nineteenth century* (Oxford, 2014).

Jones M B, *I, Richard Waitt, picture drawer: Portraits of a Highland Clan* (Grantown-on-Spey, 2017).

Keillar I, 'Edinkillie Stone Circle', *Discovery and Excavation: Scotland,* (1972), p.30.

Kelly J, '"A most inhuman and barbarous piece of villainy" An Exploration of the Crime of Rape in Eighteenth-Century Ireland', *Eighteenth Century Ireland/Iris an dá chutúr*, 10, (1995), pp. 78–107.

Kennedy A, Earl of Cassilis, *The Rulers of Strathspey: A History of the Lairds of Grant and Earls of Seafield* (Inverness, 1911).

Kennedy A, 'Crime and Punishment in Early Modern Scotland: The Secular Courts of Restoration Argyllshire, 1660–1688', *International Review of Scottish Studies*, 41 (2016) pp. 1–36.

Kennedy A, *Governing Gaeldom: the Scottish Highlands and the Restoration State* (Boston, 2014).

Kennedy A, 'Managing the Early-Modern Periphery: Highland Policy and the Highland Judicial Commission', c. 1692–c. 1705, *SHR*, 96:1 (2017) pp. 32–60.

Kilday A M, 'The Barbarous North? Criminality in Early Modern Scotland', in T M Devine and J Wormald (eds.), *The Oxford Handbook of Modern Scottish History* (Oxford, 2012).

Kilday A M, *Woman and Crime in Enlightenment Scotland* (Woodbridge, 2007).

Knox W W J, 'Homicide in Eighteenth-Century Scotland: Numbers and Theories', *SHR*, 94:1 (2015) pp. 48–73.

Kuzmics H and Axtman R, *Authority, State and National Character: The Civilizing Process in Austria and England 1700–1900* (Aldershot, 2007).

Larner C, Enemies of God: the witch-hunt in Scotland (London, 1981).

Lenman B P and Parker G, 'Crime and control in Scotland, 1500–1800', *History Today*, 30:1 (Jan. 1980), pp. 13–17.

Lenman B P, *The Jacobite Risings in Britain 1689–1746* (London, 1980).

Leneman L, *Living in Atholl: A Social History of the Estates, 1685–1785* (Edinburgh, 1986).

Leneman L, *Promises, Promises: Marriage Litigation in Scotland 1698–1830* (Edinburgh, 2003).

Levack B P, 'The Prosecution of Sexual Crimes in Early Eighteenth-Century Scotland', *SHR*, 89:2 (2010), pp. 172–193.

Livingstone S, *Scottish Customs* (Edinburgh, 1996).

Logan J, *The Scottish Gael; Or, Celtic Manners, as Preserved Among the Highlanders: Being an Historical and Descriptive Account of the Inhabitants, Antiquities, and National Peculiarities of Scotland; More Particularly of the Northern, Or Gaelic Parts of the Country, where the Singular Habits of the Aboriginal Celts are Most Tenaciously Retained*, Volume I (Inverness, 1876).

Lynch M (ed.), *The Early Modern Town in Scotland* (London, 1987).

Macinnes A I, *Clanship, Commerce and the House of Stuart 1603–1788* (East Linton, 1996).

Macinnes A I, 'Repression and Conciliation: The Highland Dimension 1660–1688', *SHR*, 65:2 (1986), pp. 167–195.

Mackenzie W M, *The Scottish Burghs* (Edinburgh, 1949).

McCallum J, *Reforming the Scottish Parish. The Reformation in Fife, 1560–1640* (Farnham, 2010).

McKillop A, *More fruitful than the soil: Army, Empire and the Scottish Highlands, 1715–1815* (East Linton, 2000).

McIntyre P, 'The Franchise Courts', *Introduction to Scottish Legal History, Stair Society*, (1958), pp. 374–383.

McNeill F M, *The Scots Cellar* (Edinburgh, 1973).

Mitchison R M and Leneman L, *Girls in Trouble: Sexuality and Social Control in Rural Scotland 1660–1780* (Edinburgh, 1998).

Mitchison R M and Leneman L, *Sin and the City: Sexuality and Social Control in Urban Scotland 1660–1780* (Edinburgh, 1998).

Mitchison R M, *A History of Scotland* (London, 2002).

Mitchison R M, *Lordship to Patronage: Scotland, 1603 – 1745* (Edinburgh, 1983).

Mitchison R M, *The Old Poor Law in Scotland, The Experience of Poverty, 1574–1845* (Edinburgh, 2008).

Muldrew C, *The Economy of Obligation: the culture of credit and social relations in early modern England* (Basingstoke, 1998).

Muldrew C, 'Rural Credit, Market Areas and Legal Institutions in the Countryside in England, 1550–1700', in C W Brooks and M Loban (eds.), *Communities and Courts in Britain, 1150–1900* (London, 1997).

Murray D, *The York Buildings Company: A chapter in Scotch History* (Glasgow, 1883).

Mutch A, *Religion and National Identity: Governing Scottish Presbyterianism in the Eighteenth Century* (Edinburgh, 2016).

Nairne D, 'Notes on Highland Woods, Ancient and Modern', *Transactions of the Gaelic Society of Inverness*, 17 (1891), pp. 170–221.

Nenadic S, *Lairds and Luxury, The Highland Gentry in Eighteenth-century Scotland* (Edinburgh, 2007).

Palmer R C, *English Law in the Age of the Black Death, 1348–1381: a transformation of governance and law* (North Carolina, 1993).

Parker G, 'The Kirk by Law Established and the Taming of Scotland: St Andrews, 1559–1600' in, G Parker, *Empire, War and Faith in Early Modern Europe* (London, 2003).

Pihlajamak H, 'On forgotten jurisdictional complexities: The case of early-modern Sweden' in S P Donlan and D Heirbaut (eds.), *The Laws many bodies: Studies in Legal Hybridity and Jurisdictional Complexity, c. 1600–1900* (Berlin, 2015).

Pittock M, *The Myth of the Jacobite Clans: The Jacobite Army in 1745* (Edinburgh, 2009).

Poos L R, *A Rural Society after the Black Death: Essex 1350- 1525* (Cambridge, 1991).

Rao A M, 'The Feudal Question in the Kingdom of Naples' in, A Forrest and P H Wilson eds. *The Bee and the Eagle; Napoleonic France and the End of the Holy Roman Empire, 1806* (Basingstoke, 2009).

Raffe A, 'Scottish State Oaths and the Revolution of 1688–1690', in S Adams and J Goodare (eds.), *Scotland in the Age of two Revolutions* (Woodbridge, 2014).

Ross A, 'Improvements to the Grant estates in Strathspey in the later Eighteenth century: Theory, Practice and Failure', in R W Hoyle (ed.), *Custom, improvement and the landscape in early modern Britain* (Farnham, 2011).

Ross A, *Land Assessment and Lordship in Medieval Northern Scotland* (Turnhout, 2015).

Ruff J R, *Violence in Early Modern Europe 1500–1800* (Cambridge, 2001).

Sambrook P, *Country-house brewing in England, 1500–1900* (London, 1996).

Sanderson M H B, *Scottish Rural Society in the Sixteenth Century* (Edinburgh, 1982).

Scheuttinger R L and Butler E F, *Forty Centuries of Wage and Price Controls: How Not to Fight Inflation* (New York, 2009).

Scott D, 'Astronomical Survery of Three Groups of Standing Stones in Strath Spey, Scotland, *Journal of the History of Astronomy*, 15 (1990), pp. 56–58.

Sellar D, 'Birlaw Courts and Birleymen', *Stair Society*, 62, Miscellany vii (2015), pp. 168–178.

Shaw L, *The History of the Province of Moray* (Elgin, 1827).

Simpson P, *The Independent Highland Companies* (Glasgow, 1996).

Smith J S, 'Background to Planned Village Formation', in J S Smith and D Stevenson (eds.), *Fermfolk and Fisherfolk: Rural Life in Northern Scotland in the Eighteenth and Nineteenth Centuries* (Aberdeen, 1989).

Smith L M, 'Sackcloth for the sinner or Punishment for the crime? Church and Secular Courts in Cromwellian Scotland', in J Dwyer, R A Mason and A Murdoch (eds.), *New Perspectives on the Politics and Culture of Early Modern Scotland* (Edinburgh, 1982).

Smout T C, *A History of the Scottish People, 1560–1830* (London, 1972).

Smout T C, *A History of the Native Woodlands of Scotland 1500–1920* (Cambridge, 1995).

Spence C, *Women, Credit and Debt in Early Modern Scotland* (Manchester, 2016).

Stevenson D, *Alasdair MacColla and the Highland Problem in the Seventeenth Century* (Edinburgh, 1980).

Taylor D, *The Wild Black Region: Badenoch 1750–1800* (Edinburgh, 2016).

Thompson E P, *Whigs and Hunters: The Origin of the Black Act* (Harmondsworth, 1977).

Todd M, *The Culture of Protestantism in Early Modern Scotland* (London, 2002).

Tommaso A, *The Continuity of Feudal Power; The Caracciolo Di Brienza in Spanish Naples* (Cambridge, 1991).

Tyson R E, 'The Rise and Fall of Manufacturing in Rural Aberdeenshire' in J S Smith and D Stevenson (eds.), *Fermfolk and Fisherfolk: Rural Life in Northern Scotland in the Eighteenth and Nineteenth Centuries* (Aberdeen, 1989).

Watt D, ' "The laberinth of thir difficulties": the Influence of Debt on the Highland Elite, c. 1550–1700', *SHR*, 85:1 (2006), 28–51.

Whatley C, *Scottish Society 1707–1830: beyond Jacobitism towards industrialisation* (Manchester, 2000).

Whetstone A, *Scottish County Government in the Eighteenth and Nineteenth Centuries* (Edinburgh, 1981).

Whyte I D and Whyte K A, 'Debt and Credit, Poverty and Prosperity in a Seventeenth Century Scottish Rural Community', in R M Mitchison and P Roebuck (eds.) *Economy and Society in Scotland and Ireland, 1500–1939* (Edinburgh, 1988).

Whyte I D, *Agriculture and Society in Seventeenth Century Scotland* (Edinburgh, 1979).

Whyte I D, "Agriculture in Aberdeenshire in the Seventeenth and Eighteenth Centuries: Continuity and Change", in D Stevenson (ed.), *From Lairds to Louns. Country and Burgh Life in Aberdeen 1600–1800* (Aberdeen, 1986).

Whyte I D, *Scotland before the Industrial Revolution: An Economic and Social History, c.1050–c.1750* (Harlow, 1995).

Winchester A J L, *The Harvest of the Hills: Rural Life in Northern England and the Scottish Borders, 1400–1700* (Edinburgh, 2000.

Withers C W J, *Gaelic Scotland: The Transformation of a Culture Region* (London, 1988).
Wood A, *The memory of the people: custom and popular sense of the past in early modern England* (Cambridge, 2013).
Wood A, *The Politics of Social Conflict: The Peak Country, 1520–1770* (Cambridge, 1999).
Wormald J, *Lords and Men: Bonds of Manrent in Scotland, 1442–1603* (Edinburgh, 1985).

5 Unpublished Sources

Ph.D. Theses

Carmichael E K, 'The Scottish Commission of the Peace, 1707–1760' (University of Glasgow, 1977).
Cornell H J, 'Gender, Sex and Social Control: East Lothian, 1610–1640' (University of Edinburgh, 2010).
Davies S, 'Law and Order in Stirlingshire 1637–1747' (University of St Andrews, 1984).
Ewan L, 'Debt and Credit in Early Modern Scotland: The Grandtully Estates 1650–1765' (University of Edinburgh, 1988).
Fredericks R S, 'Death Practices and Burial Rites in Scotland from the later Medieval Period to 1780: with Particular Reference to the Influence of Theology', (University of Edinburgh, 1967).
Jewell B F, 'The Legislation Relating to Scotland After the Forty-Five' (University of North Carolina at Chapel Hill, 1975.).
Kilday A M, 'Women and Crime in South – West Scotland: The Study of the Justiciary Court Records, 1750–1815 (University of Strathclyde, 1998).
Leneman L, 'A Social History of the Atholl Estates 1685–1785' (University of Edinburgh, 1982).
Livingstone L H, 'Shieling, transhumance and changes in land use in the Scottish Highlands' (University of Edinburgh, 1973).
MacKillop A, 'Military Recruiting in the Scottish Highlands 1739 – 1815: The Political, Social and Economic Context' (University of Glasgow, 1995).
Moir S, 'Some Godlie, Wyse and Vertious Gentilmen: Communities, State Formation and the Justices of the Peace in Scotland, 1587 – 1660' (University of Guelph, 2002).
O'Grady O, 'The Setting and Practice of Open Air Judicial Assemblies in Medieval Scotland: a Multidisciplinary Study' (University of Glasgow, 2008).
Spence C, "Content and Pay': Women's Economic Roles in Edinburgh, Haddington, and Linlithgow, 1560–1640' (University of Edinburgh, 2010).
Symms P S M, 'Social Control in a Sixteenth Century Burgh: A Study of the Burgh Court Book of Selkirk' (University of Edinburgh, 1986).
Wasser M, 'Violence and the central criminal courts in Scotland', 1603–1638 (Columbia University, 1995).

Websites

www.canmore.org.uk.
www.dsl.ac.uk.
www.historyofparliamentonline.org.
www.nms.ac.uk/explore-our-collections/collection-search-results/?item_id=19627.
www.patrickspeople.scot.
www.rps.ac.uk.
www. scotlandsplaces.gov.uk.
witches.shca.ed.ac.uk.

Index

www.ingramcontent.com/pod-product-compliance
Lightning Source LLC
Chambersburg PA
CBHW071323230926
51849CB00002B/302
* 9 7 8 9 0 0 4 4 7 2 5 1 8 *